The Claim of God

The Claim of God

Karl Barth's Doctrine of Sanctification
in His Earlier Theology

Ethan A. Worthington

Foreword by John Webster

☙PICKWICK *Publications* • Eugene, Oregon

THE CLAIM OF GOD
Karl Barth's Doctrine of Sanctification in His Earlier Theology

Copyright © 2015 Ethan Worthington. All rights reserved. Except for brief quotations in critical publications or reviews, no part of this book may be reproduced in any manner without prior written permission from the publisher. Write: Permissions. Wipf and Stock Publishers, 199 W. 8th Ave., Suite 3, Eugene, OR 97401.

Pickwick Publications
An Imprint of Wipf and Stock Publishers
199 W. 8th Ave., Suite 3
Eugene, OR 97401

www.wipfandstock.com

ISBN 13: 978-1-4982-0028-8

Cataloguing-in-Publication Data

Worthington, Ethan A.

The claim of God : Karl Barth's doctrine of sanctification in his earlier theology / Ethan A. Worthington ; foreword by John Webster.

xxii + 244 p. ; 23 cm. Includes bibliographical references.

ISBN 13: 978-1-4982-0028-8

1. Barth, Karl, 1886–1968. 2. Sanctification—Christianity—History of doctrines. 3. Sanctification—Christianity—History of doctrines—20th century. I. Webster, J. B. (John Bainbridge), 1955–. II. Title.

BT765 .W68 2015

Manufactured in the U.S.A.   07/01/2015

Dedicated to my wife, Juliane, for the journey we took together

Contents

Foreword by John Webster | ix
Acknowledgments | xi
Introduction | xiii
Abbreviations | xxi

1　The Divine-Human Encounter | 1
2　The Calvin Lectures | 36
3　"The Theology of the Reformed Confessions" | 61
4　The Resurrection of the Dead | 94
5　Göttingen Dogmatics and "Rechtfertigung und Heiligung" | 121
　 Conclusion | 231

Bibliography | 237

Foreword

That Barth's theology is, amongst other things, a moral theology is beyond contest. Earlier readings of Barth, both friendly and hostile, often failed to notice his interest in human life and action, their attention drawn to other features of his theology considered more characteristic—his christological concentration, his teaching about revelation, or his theology of grace. A quarter-century of (largely English-language) Barth scholarship has steadily built up a rather different picture, in which Barth's theology is understood to have, not an exclusive concern for divine priority, but a double theme: God's being and acts and the being and acts of the creatures whom he summons to active fellowship with himself. That the two objects of this double theme—the works of God and the works of God's creatures—are to be understood and expounded in an irreversible order, with creaturely action wholly derivative from divine action, indicates, not the redundancy of creaturely moral life, but rather its proper setting and shape.

The cogency of this presentation of Barth derives, in part, from its capacity to make sense of features of the *Church Dogmatics* which might otherwise be neglected: the ubiquity of the concept of covenant, or the long tracts of writing devoted to depiction of human life caught up in the realm of divine grace. There is, however, another formative factor in the reappraisal of Barth as moral theologian: the availability in the Barth *Gesamtausgabe* of a much extended body of material from the period around the middle of World War I to 1930. Some of this material is rescued from the obscurity of its first publication, but much of it is made up of Barth's early university lectures from Göttingen and Münster, in print for the first time. The effect of this material on the interpretation of the period of Barth's work before he embarked on the *Church Dogmatics* has been to revise a common picture of his earlier theology's dominance by an oppositional account of God and creaturely nature, accomplished by a segregated doctrine of God and an inflamed eschatology. The Barth who emerges from the lectures in his first two professorships is already one who has found in some of the definitive texts of the early Reformed tradition a concern for life in the world as the necessary correlate of Christian teaching about God and salvation.

These two interests—Barth's deep interest in ethics, and the significance of his early work for the shaping of his lifelong theological commitments—come together in the following study of Barth's theology of sanctification, which gives the first sustained treatment of the topic in Barth's earlier theological writings, and demonstrates with some skill that what Barth has to say about sanctification indicates much about his fundamental convictions. It possesses the qualities of good interpretation of Barth: wide acquaintance with his *oeuvre*, an eye for both the large design and the details of what Barth has to say, readiness to follow Barth and to be surprised by what his texts contain. It is an exemplary interpretation of a neglected topic in a critical phase of Barth's theological and spiritual development.

—John Webster

University of St. Andrews

Acknowledgments

THIS WORK WAS CHURNED out in its original form in the process of my doctoral endeavors a few years ago. I am so grateful for my time in Scotland and the way I was challenged and encouraged by my colleagues in the Department of Divinity and Religious Studies at King's College, University of Aberdeen. I am especially thankful for the relationships made and sustained along the way—Alfred Yuen, Dave Nelson and Tim Yoder in particular have been great friends and conversation partners in theology and life. They have left their marks within these pages.

Professors Donald Wood and David Clough offered me fantastically careful reading, and pointed me in fruitful directions of thought as I was finishing my work in Aberdeen.

And to my doctoral supervisor, John Webster, whose patience, calm encouragement, and theological insights back in Aberdeen and beyond have shaped my life and ministry—thank you. This work would not have been possible without your help.

Introduction

THIS BOOK CAME ABOUT in response to the call by many recent interpreters of Barth's theology for a more detailed and careful reading of Barth's texts. Concerning the divine-human relationship that is the focus of this book, John Webster has written that the

> conventional treatment of Barth often revolved around an anxiety that the sheer abundance of Barth's depiction of the saving work of God in Christ tends to identify real action with divine action, and leave little room for lengthy exploration of human moral thought and activity.... More recent accounts have been much more sympathetic, seeking to unearth what Barth is about in his ethical work rather than castigating him for failing to do what he did not set out to achieve. Yet a great deal of work remains to be done. What is required more than anything else is detailed study of Barth's writings which, by close reading, tries to display the structure and logic of his concerns without moving prematurely into making judgments or pressing too early the usefulness (or lack of it) of Barth's work for contemporary moral theology.[1]

Webster appeals for a form of reading which displaces thematic and interpretive schemes with close readings of specific texts in order to clarify and even trace Barth's thoughts as put together over single pieces of writing. The overall strategy, he writes in *Barth's Earlier Theology*, "is to read Barth through particular texts rather than across them, and to restrict as much as possible the use of general categories which do not emerge

---

1. Webster, *Barth's Moral Theology*, 1. In another work, Webster suggests that the "study of Barth should develop in some new directions, and return to some tasks which have been prematurely laid aside.... Despite the immense literature which surrounds him, reception of Barth is in certain respects still in its infancy, and will remain hampered until more and better work is done on what he wrote" (*Barth's Earlier Theology*, 13).

from textual analysis."[2] In this manner, the attempt is made to ascertain a clearer picture of Barth's theology through careful and thoughtful reading that resists as much as possible pressing Barth's thoughts into abstract schemes. This book attempts such an interpretation and aims to clarify and analyze Barth's teaching concerning sanctification in his earlier theology based upon tight readings of significant Barth texts.[3]

Webster's words echo the general shift in Barth interpretation and the increasing interest in Barth's moral theology over the past few decades.[4] Accounts which have sought to debunk earlier interpretations of Barth which portrayed him as either an enemy of human temporal existence because of an over emphasis on divine transcendence, or, in the other extreme, incapable of positing a true sense of human freedom and participation in relationship to the grace of God because of an overbearing divine immanence.[5] The result of these new works, notes Paul Nimmo, has been "a recognition that while the theological ontology of Barth yields a very particular concept of the context of ethical agency, it is a context in which there is nonetheless created a clearly defined space for meaningful theological ethics and being in action."[6] At the centre of these works is not simply a concern to distinguish the importance of human existence and action over and against God, but to carefully and properly give an account of Barth's theological anthropology, that is, to rightly understand the way in which Barth portrays the divine-human relationship.

As such, this book broadly stands alongside other works that have sought to offer close, fresh readings of Barth's texts concerning the divine-human relationship, especially those works that have focused at least in part on this earlier period. Such works include Webster's *Barth's Moral Theology: Human Action in Barth's Thought*, and *Barth's Earlier Theology*, Archie Spencer's *Clearing a Space for Human Action: Ethical Ontology in the Theology of Karl Barth*, Mark Husband's *Barth's Ethics of Prayer: A Study in Moral Ontology and Action*, and David Clough's *Ethics*

---

2. Webster, *Barth's Earlier Theology*, 6.

3. This "earlier" period is defined roughly in relationship to Barth's "break" with liberalism and his attempt to begin re-thinking Christian theology in 1915, and the beginning of his *Church Dogmatics* in 1930.

4. See for example Biggar, *The Hastening that Waits*; Clough, *Ethics in Crisis*; Mangina, *Karl Barth on the Christian Life*; Nimmo, *Being in Action*; Matheny, *Dogmatics and Ethics*; and Webster, *Barth's Ethics of Reconciliation*.

5. Mangina, *Barth on the Christian Life*, 2–3.

6. Nimmo, *Being in Action*, 3.

in Crisis: Interpreting Barth's Ethics.[7] Each of these works offers close textual analyses of various lectures, addresses, and sermons from Barth's earlier theology. Taken together, they amount to a serious reassessment of Barth's theological anthropology, a reassessment in which Barth's view of the divine-human relationship is seen to be much more positive than has been acknowledged in the past.

Additionally, though, this work seeks to fill a specific void in Barth scholarship by extensively engaging Barth's pre-*Church Dogmatic* material in relationship to his doctrine of sanctification. Barth's doctrine of sanctification, as set forth in his later *Church Dogmatics,* has been seriously, if somewhat sporadically, studied in the last two decades.[8] In 2002, for example, a series of articles in the *Zeitschrift für Dialektische Theologie* was dedicated to various aspects of Barth's doctrine of sanctification. Bruce McCormack emphasised in his closing summary and analysis of these articles that, though divergent in presentation, each paper in its own way challenged the age-old problem of the nature of the divine-human relationship.[9] In this sense, these works share a common theme with what is offered here.

There has, however, been no major exposition of Barth's doctrine of sanctification pre-*Church Dogmatics* in over seventy years, and even then, the lone exposition was not geared toward specifically pre-*Dogmatics* material.[10] H. W. Tribble's 1937 doctoral thesis, *The Doctrine of*

---

7. Specifically chapters two and three of Webster's *Moral Theology*; Spencer, *Clearing a Space for Human Action*; Husbands, *Barth's Ethics of Prayer*; and Clough, *Ethics in Crisis*.

8. See, for example, most recently Neder, "A Differentiated Fellowship of Action"; the January 2002 issue of the issue of *Zeitschrift für Dialektische Theologie,* which featured the following articles on Barth's doctrine of sanctification: Migliore, "*Participatio Christi,*" 286–307; Sonderegger, "Sanctification as Impartation in the Doctrine of Karl Barth," 308–15; Hunsinger, "A Tale of Two Simultaneities," 316–38; Anderson, "The Problem of Psychologism in Karl Barth's Doctrine of Sanctification," 339–52; Neven, "'Just a Little," 353–63; and McCormack's "Afterword," a short summary and responses to these papers, 364–78. See also Stubbs, "Sanctification as Participation in Christ"; J. S. Rhee, "Secularization and Sanctification"; Tribble, "The Doctrine of Sanctification in the Theology of Karl Barth"; Lombard, "*Die Leer van die Heiligmaking* by Karl Barth"; Otterness, "The Doctrine of Sanctification in the Theology of Karl Barth"; and den Dulk, "Als Twee Die Spreken: Een manier om de heiligingsleer van Karl Barth te lezen".

9. McCormack, "Afterword," 378.

10. Rhee "Secularization and Sanctification," spends about fifty pages highlighting some of the most significant themes and texts for Barth's doctrine of sanctification between 1909 and 1952 as background for his exposition of sanctification in Barth's

Sanctification in the Theology of Karl Barth, was an attempt to present an up-to-date systematic account of Barth's doctrine of sanctification. Tribble systematically traced Barth's doctrine of sanctification through the material available to him at the time, limited by comparison with what is available to scholars today, but which included many of Barth's exegetical texts, such as Ephesians and the Gospel of John, Barth's *Credo*, and even *Church Dogmatics I*.[11] Arguably the most important source for Tribble's thesis though was Barth's 1927 *Zwischen den Zeiten* article "Rechtfertigung und Heiligung," which also features prominently in this work as well. It was, however, also his earliest source. Despite its material impact on Tribble's thesis as a whole then, its later date allows significant room for treatment of Barth's texts written around and before the "Rechtfertigung und Heiligung" article. Between the continued work of the monumental *Gesamtausgabe* and various important works also translated into English, including many of Barth's Göttingen and Münster lectures from the 1920's, the amount of primary texts that have become available since Tribble's thesis was written is considerable. While there is pertinent material overlap, then, the point is that Tribble's use of later texts, along with the abundance of new texts available, presents the need for a new in-depth treatment of Barth's doctrine of sanctification in this earlier period.

While thorough in its reading and analysis of Barth's texts this book is not an attempt to be a comprehensive interpretation of Barth's thoughts during this period though. Its goal is to explore the primary characteristics and insights that drive Barth's doctrine of sanctification from 1916 through 1929, yet even in this sense, it cannot claim to be exhaustive. There are, even with regard to this interpretive focus, important limits, which in part, direct the content and shape of what is presented. For example, Barth's view of scripture and a more precise examination of his ecclesiology would be essential components of a broader study—not least because of the inner-connectedness of his thoughts. Topics such as these have not been explicitly taken up within this analysis, however, because the content surveyed is in part dictated by the amount of attention Barth paid specifically in relating it to his understanding of the divine-human

---

CD. While this material is perhaps good for a quick, broad view of sanctification in Barth's earlier works, and admirable for its attempt to incorporate the material, it is far too brief to be considered a thorough representation.

11. Hereafter, *Church Dogmatics* will be abbreviated in both text and notes as *CD*, followed by volume number.

relationship, of which his doctrine of sanctification is an expression. In relation to this, the specific texts examined have been chosen to cover a range of material—historical theology, exegesis, dogmatics—dispersed more or less evenly throughout this period.[12] Rather than attempting to cover Barth's doctrine of sanctification thematically, and risk imposing certain patterns of thought that might be either unhelpful or misleading, this work focuses on only those concerns which appeared most pressing for Barth in articulating his doctrine of sanctification, or for understanding him more clearly on the issue.

A possible downside to this method is a certain amount of repetitiveness that is bound to occur throughout, seemingly leaving the question open if it would not have been better to organize the material around some type of schematic structure after all—even if such a scheme were to ask Barth questions that he was not willing or prepared to answer. While significant effort has been made to limit undue repetitiveness by focusing on the distinct contributions within the various texts, there is, however, something to be gained by an amount of repetition. Not only does it convey a sense of consistency in Barth's thought which is essential for highlighting portions of his theology that have been missed or dismissed, but along with that it also allows Barth to articulate himself more precisely over several different texts helping to avoid the all too common characterizations of his thoughts by reading certain passages in isolation.

The upside of analyzing Barth's work in this way then, including a certain amount of repetition, is a much more in-depth examination of his theology, which accords more weight to understanding his logic and reasoning than systematic coverage. The benefit is a clearer and more comprehensive portrait of Barth's theology and writings during this period.

As a point of analytical clarification it is important to make an initial distinction here regarding the term "sanctification" in order to demarcate a field of study from the use of the term in Barth's own texts very early on. In a very general sense this work assumes that sanctification pertains

---

12. The only major exceptions to this selection are Barth's Romans commentaries. Over the years, they have assumed most of the attention paid to this earlier phase because of their explosive reception and general importance in Barth's development—particularly the second edition. They have been passed over here largely in order to concentrate more thoroughly on lesser-known works, which have been overshadowed in their aftermath, but also in order to avoid many of the characterizations that have become attached to them which may bring unnecessary prejudices. For an excellent reassessment of Barth's earlier theology that focuses specifically on *Romans* II see Clough, *Ethics in Crisis*.

uniquely to the grace of God in a way that means something specific for the way in which one lives in fellowship with God. This definition is concerned with a description of faithful human life and living within the work of reconciliation which points beyond formal reference to "new creation," or the "new man." Such terms could become confusing in light of Barth's serious concern to address both justification and sanctification as the one work of reconciliation concerning humanity; in this sense, both early and late, Barth's description of justification and sanctification often overlap significantly as they depict the one work of grace from two different angles. While Barth infrequently uses the term "sanctification" in lectures and addresses specifically in the years preceding his time in Göttingen, then, this term will be used to demarcate the impact of the work of grace upon faithful human life and living in relationship to the person and work of God as opposed to merely renewed fellowship with God, or the creation of a new form of human existence.

Each chapter focuses on key primary texts; and at the start of each chapter I begin by briefly locating the works to be discussed in the broader context of Barth's early career, and then summarize the work.

During the period from 1916 to 1922, Barth expressed the content of the Christian life in fellowship with God primarily by disabling false constructions of human piety, by emphasizing that faithful human living is grounded and vividly portrayed in *God's* own righteousness. Chapter 1 explores Barth's use of the notion of *encounter* to affirm that God has in fact drawn close to humanity, yet maintains His uniqueness over against them, and in this way shapes human life. This notion becomes the basis for Barth's early discussion of sanctification, and is explored in three key works: "The Righteousness of God" (1916), "The Christian's Place in Society" (1919), and "The Problem with Ethics Today" (1922). These works give ample evidence that from the beginning Barth viewed sanctification as a specific relationship in which God draws near to people in grace and uniquely transforms them.

Chapter 2 analyzes Barth's 1922 lectures on "The Theology of John Calvin," highlighting the growing Reformed influence on Barth's doctrine of sanctification, specifically Calvin's use of doctrine to positively articulate the divine-human relationship. The first section of the chapter investigates the influence of Calvin and the Reformers on the way Barth articulates his doctrine of sanctification. The bulk of the chapter builds upon this connection by examining the impact of Calvin's positive use of doctrine upon Barth's conception of human life as lived within time.

It does so through the lens of Barth's reflections on *Faith and Obedience, Time and Eternity,* and *The Danger of Moralism.*

Chapter 3 investigates Barth's 1923 lectures "The Theology of the Reformed Confessions" in which the theological principles that underlie Barth's doctrine of sanctification are set forth and analyzed. Succinctly stated, for Barth the doctrine of sanctification is oriented towards and developed around rightly understanding the reality of the divine-human relationship, towards understanding what it means to say that God the Father, in Jesus Christ His son, through the Holy Spirit, transforms human life and living. It will be shown that Barth's account of sanctification is shaped by focusing on *God's* sanctifying activity, and all that this entails for human living, over and against an account of the divine-human relationship which favors moral transformation or a process of gradual perfecting. That sanctification, because it only exists in dynamic relationship with *Christ*, is never without the continual and sustaining work of the Holy Spirit. And finally, because sanctification is localized around this God who sanctifies in Jesus Christ it necessarily addresses its impact upon and relevance to the life and living of individuals as the ones united with Christ through the *Holy Spirit.*

Chapter 4 offers an exposition of Barth's book *The Resurrection of the Dead*, the published version of his 1923 lectures on 1 Corinthians 15, in which the resurrection of Jesus Christ is shown to be of supreme importance for Barth's doctrine of sanctification. In the reality of Jesus' resurrection lay equally the foundation *for* and the possibility *of* human sanctification. The resurrection is also tied to the ideas of struggle and hope, which are examined as key forms of sanctified existence—life rendered as "existence in anticipation." These themes are finally drawn together in the final section under an initial description of Barth's doctrine of sanctification that clearly prioritizes the relational connection and impact of God's claim upon human existence over spiritual and moral development.

And finally, Chapter 5 builds upon the primary themes addressed throughout as Barth's first full-scale dogmatic treatment of sanctification in his 1924/5 *Göttingen Dogmatics* and the corollary article "Rechtfertigung und Heiligung" of 1927 are examined.[13] Thus, this chapter presents a more structured account of Barth's doctrine of sanctification in relationship to these significant texts. Section 1 highlights the relationship

---

13. Various other primary texts, such as *The Holy Spirit and the Christian Life*, will also occasionally be referred to in support of the main analysis.

between sanctification and key doctrines of the corpus of the *Göttingen Dogmatics*, doctrines that produce an explicit impact on the content and structure of Barth's doctrine of sanctification: Revelation, the Holiness of God, Election, and Eschatology. Section 2 offers a preliminary discussion of God's reconciling activity—the specific context in which Barth takes up his description of sanctification; and an exposition of the relationship between justification and sanctification as forms of reconciliation. And Section 3 presents an in-depth analysis of the primary contours of Barth's doctrine of sanctification in these dogmatic works: *The Claim of God*—the uniquely conceptual key around which Barth structures the content of sanctification, *The Sinner Reconciled in Grace*—the purpose and limits of sanctification, and *Grace in Time*—the object and impact of God's sanctifying grace. A brief portion of this final section is devoted to Barth's 1928/9 *Ethics* lectures, in which he links the claim of God more explicitly to the work of grace in time.

Abbreviations

CD *Church Dogmatics*

GD *Göttingen Dogmatics*

RH "Rechtfertigung und Heiligung"

1

The Divine-Human Encounter

Introduction

THE DOCTRINE OF RECONCILIATION, to which Barth devoted over two thousand pages in his thirteen-volume *Church Dogmatics*, is introduced first under the heading "God with Us" as the "most general description of the whole complex of Christian understanding and doctrine."[1] Barth admitted that he was "very conscious of the great responsibility laid on the theologian at this centre of all Christian knowledge. To fail here is to fail everywhere. To be on the right track here makes it impossible to be completely mistaken in the whole."[2] Failure here is failure everywhere because it threatens to erode the central message of the gospel, namely, that there is a specific relationship between God and humanity. Failure here threatens to obscure both the name of God as Emmanuel ("God with Us"), and the implications this has for the existence and actions of human beings. For Barth, the doctrine of sanctification lies at the heart of that discussion of the divine-human relationship because fundamentally, for him, "sanctification" means the intimate relationship between God and humans. It is wholly concerned with the reality and distinctiveness of the divine-human relationship in correlation to the life of individual people.

Eduard Thurneysen, one of Barth's closest friends from his Safenwil pastorate, once wrote that "because his concern was with this [Jesus Christ's] message, . . . Karl Barth's theological thinking was from the beginning directed to the life of man. The existence, the life of man, on the one side, and on the other the Word of God that meets this life, lays hold

---

1. Barth, *Church Dogmatics* IV: I, 4.
2. Ibid., ix.

of it, and transforms it."[3] Even before Barth's break with liberalism, he was a theologian concerned with struggling to get the divine-human relationship correct.[4] It was partially his keen observation that the majority of his theological mentors must have misunderstood this relationship when they aligned themselves with Wilhelm II that caused him to search elsewhere for a secure theological foundation. It was also Barth's desire to understand correctly the relationship between the Kingdom of God and the corresponding actions of humanity that caused him to distance himself from certain forms of the socialist movement. Barth sensed deep-seated deficiencies both dogmatically and ethically in the theology of his day.

In constructing a new theological foundation, Barth felt that he needed to say something new, something different from what had already been said, something "wholly other."[5] The pale theology dominating modern discussions, relegating God to passive activity in a thriving human culture was now exposed as a fraud in Barth's eyes. In 1915, several years of struggle, discontent and development came to a head, and as Barth stated the question of the "living God" "came down on me like a ton of bricks."[6] What needed to happen was now clear to Barth. The old idols needed to be knocked down; modern theology had to be stripped of its lifeless content and Protestant Theology set back on the right path: God must be God and humanity must be humanity. Only then could anything real and true be said.

> Was it the discovery that the theme of the Bible—contrary to the critical and orthodox exegesis, in which we had been brought up—definitely could not possibly be man's religion and religious ethics—could not possibly be his own secret godliness, but—this was the *rocher de bronze* on which we first struck—the

---

3. Barth and Thurneysen, *Revolutionary Theology in the Making*, 13–14.

4. That Barth was concerned with man's ethical response in relationship to God can hardly be ignored considering his great interest and enthusiasm in studying with both Adolph von Harnack and Wilhelm Hermann. Although at this stage in Barth's life he was focused on the "role and response of man to God, rather than to the action of God towards man . . . which also assumed a given *relationality* between the human and the divine" (Willis, *The Ethics of Karl Barth*, 7).

5. "'My child, what are we now to speak?' These well-known words from *The Magic Flute* continue: 'The truth, the truth, lest she also be complicit'. But that was easier said than done. It was Thurneysen who once whispered the key phrase to me, half aloud, when we were alone together: what we needed . . . was a 'wholly other' theological foundation" (Barth, *The Theology of Schleiermacher*, 264).

6. Busch, *Karl Barth*, 91.

Godness of God, precisely God's Godness, God's own peculiar nature over against not only the natural, but also the spiritual cosmos, God's absolutely unique existence, power and initiative above all in His relationship to man? We felt that it was in this way, and only in this way, that we could understand the Voice of the Old and New Testaments, and that it was from here, and only from here, that we could from now on be theologians and particularly preachers, *ministri Verbi Divini*.[7]

Barth's earlier writings are extremely significant because they emerge from the fast-paced period when he had set himself to the task of clearing away what was being said in modern theology and restating what needed to be said in its place. As John Webster rightly noted this was a period of reinvention for Barth. It was a time when he began to rebuild "Christian theology from the ground up. . . . The process of reinvention involved Barth in a two-fold task of ground clearing and construction . . . Barth found himself having to say 'no' in order to create a space for the affirmations which he wished to make."[8] Barth's lectures and writings from this early period are a tremendous force that catapulted him into the forefront of a theological coup. It was during this time that Barth began to drastically reshape the theological landscape of the world, changing the face of the Christian church's dialogue.

During the period from 1916 through 1922, just before and slightly overlapping his appointment as Professor of Reformed Theology in Göttingen, Barth expressed the content of the Christian life in fellowship with God primarily by disabling false constructions of human piety or self-righteousness by emphasizing righteous human living grounded in and vividly portrayed in *God's* own righteousness. This notion, which drastically shaped Barth's doctrine of sanctification, was one of the key theological components for upholding and describing the divine-human relationship for Barth in which the gospel message was seen as the power that affirmed both God's love and redemption of humankind, and humanity's faithful life response. This chapter explores the notion of *encounter* in which Barth affirms that God has in fact drawn close to humanity in distinction over and against them, and in this way transforms their existence in freedom. This conception becomes the basis for Barth's discussion of sanctification early on, and is explored in three important works: "The Righteousness of God" (1916), "The Christian's Place in Society" (1919),

7. Torrance, *Karl Barth*, 39.
8. Webster, *Barth*, 20–21.

and "The Problem of Ethics Today" (1922). As this chapter will show, Barth's doctrine of sanctification was not only shaped by an intimate portrayal of the divine-human relationship, but was also inherently linked to his fundamental concerns at the time.

Several comments are required up front concerning Barth's work during this period. First, these writings should not be treated as if they are pieces of systematic or dogmatic theology proper. There is a real danger in overly systematizing these earlier writings because of the congruencies that are noticeable with his later dogmatic works. Barth had been in the pastorate since 1909 and it was not until the fall of 1921 when he was appointed to the University of Göttingen that he began a somewhat more developed approach to his theological task. Therefore, these earlier writings are marked more by pastoral thrust and tone rather than dogmatic nuances. They are to be sure infused throughout with deep instinct and great passion, but anyone seeking tidy exposition of Christian doctrine will perhaps come away frustrated.

For example, in the years directly following Barth's 'break' with Protestant liberalism he did not often refer distinctly to the term 'sanctification,' or 'justification' for that matter, to describe the impact of the work of reconciliation within human life. Rather, Barth frequently seems to press in on the reality of the encounter between God and humanity and the meaning this has for human life and living to describe that actuality. The point in this first chapter then is not to argue for a direct equivalency of terms, i.e. righteousness or encounter equals sanctification as such, but to explore themes related to the way in which Barth describes the relationship between the grace of God and the 'living' of the object of God's attention, and thereby gaining insight into the way in which Barth discussed the divine-human relationship from the beginning. While many of his earlier writings might not expressly detail Barth's use of the term 'sanctification' they do in fact lay down a framework or pattern of discussion which characterizes Barth's concern about the life of those encountered by God beyond the mere forgiveness of sins.

Second, because these are not systematic pieces one must continually be on guard not to import later developments back into them. In many ways these earlier writings offer great insight into later developments and the theological instincts which Barth possessed from the beginning, but when the informal-pastoral distinction is not maintained there is a danger of casting a light upon these writings which might not be fair or helpful: either making the early writings say too much, or seeing a complete discontinuity between the early and later works.

Thirdly, and closely related to the previous two, is the inevitable danger of perceiving this younger Barth as an entirely negative thinker; believing that he was more concerned with overturning idols than re-establishing any positive theological agenda, and, therefore, taking him as a merely de-constructive theologian. It should be noted from the beginning, then, that the strokes from Barth's theological brush which clear the canvass do in fact also at the same time lay down crucial foundations for a content rich doctrine of sanctification that carry through the entirety of his work.

An Encounter with Grace

Many of Barth's early theological manoeuvrings were related in particular to the modern Protestant theological establishment. What seemed to frustrate Barth the most about modern theology was its confusion about the relationship between God and humanity.

> With all due respect to the genius shown in his work, I *cannot* consider Schleiermacher a good teacher in the realm of theology because, so far as I can see, he is disastrously dim-sighted in regard to the fact that man as man is not only in *need* but beyond all hope of saving himself; that the whole of so-called religion, and not least the Christian religion, *shares* in this need; and that one *cannot* speak of God simply by speaking of man in a loud voice. There are those to whom Schleiermacher's peculiar excellence lies in his having discovered a conception of religion by which he overcame Luther's so-called dualism and connected earth and heaven by a much needed bridge, upon which we may reverently cross. . . . The very names Kierkegaard, Luther, Calvin, Paul, and Jeremiah suggest what Schleiermacher never possessed, a clear and direct apprehension of the truth that man is made to serve *God* and not God to serve man.[9]

Barth felt that both liberal theology and the Religious Socialist movement, both of which had strongly influenced him, seemed to confuse this relationship to the point of inverting it. Modern theology, he felt, was essentially "anthropocentric theology." This meant that talk about God was really talk about humanity, that theological language was primarily and essentially

9. Barth, "The Word of God and the Task of the Ministry," 196.

anthropocentric language. As a result, sanctification was perceived by liberalism as stages of psychological development, or as cultural advancement by the socialist movement (notions of sanctification expressed wholly inward or entirely outward); both of which seriously lacked any sense of a critical divine objectivity.[10] Their views were not critical in the sense that they did not regard "God as a Reality which is complete and whole in itself apart from and prior to the knowing activity of human individuals."[11] Their views were not objective in the sense that, "where nineteenth-century theology originated in a 'turn to the subject,' Barth's course now clearly gave evidence of a 'turn to theological objectivism.'"[12] Barth proposed that without a critical objectivity descriptions of the Christian life are merely descriptions of "the preliminary but not the final, the derived but not the original, the complex but not the simple. It sees what is human but not what is divine."[13] Any account of the divine-human relationship that lacks the specifically objective component derived from the reality of God is incomplete and, therefore, entirely misleading. In the end, it binds rather than looses people for freedom in God.

One of the first issues that Barth sought to correct in light of this confusion was the re-establishment of a proper understanding of the divine-human relationship—God must be God and humanity must be humanity. That is, Barth sought to re-establish "a relation in which the two members stand over against each other with no possibility of a synthesis into a higher form of being."[14] This idea is specifically taken up in the theme of *encounter* which, significantly, was also one of the key themes Barth utilized to express the precision of the divine-human relationship in his final writings as well. He wrote at the end of his career, "God and man do in fact confront one another: two partners of different kinds, acting differently, so that they cannot be exchanged or equated."[15] The idea of *encounter*, which

---

10. Barth himself wrote in his article "Moderne Theologie und Reichsgottesarbeit" (1909) that "all questions can be answered only by [man] himself and there is neither any universally applicable *ordo salutis* nor any generally valid *Offenbarungsquelle* [source of revelation]." Barth's early conception of religion was highly individualistic and inwardly focused (yet highly ethical). See Barth, "Moderne Theologie und Reichgottesarbeit," 342f.; quoted in Rhee, *Secularization and Sanctification*, 54.

11. McCormack, *Karl Barth's Critically Realistic Dialectical Theology*, 129.

12. Ibid., 130.

13. Barth, "The Righteousness of God," 9.

14. McCormack, *Barth's Critically Realistic Dialectical Theology*, 129.

15. This is a theme fundamental to all of Barth's work throughout his life and is captured succinctly in this quote from his final work, *The Christian Life*. Unfortunately

critically differentiates God and humans, was Barth's basis for discussing the impact of the grace of God within human life in any meaningful way even early on, because fundamentally what he recognized even here was that the doctrine of sanctification is the exposition of a specific relationship. Within these earlier texts, Barth is largely concerned with stating that as God approaches humans in grace a transformation occurs, the form and content of this transformation are not always entirely clear. What is clear, however, is that for Barth any theological account that confuses or disregards the critically realistic priority within which the divine-human relationship exists has already failed.

"The Righteousness of God"

This relational concept was forcefully stated in Barth's 1916 lecture "The Righteousness of God." In this address given at the Town Church in Aarau, Barth declared that, because human righteousness had been taken for the righteousness of God, humanity was continually condemned to and preoccupied with self-delusion, forever entangled in their own web of deceit. Humanity's intense focus on self-piety and human righteousness effectively silences the "conscience," a term which, as David Stubbs indicates, "is used [here] by Barth not so much to refer to a human capacity, but rather becomes a kind of conceptual placeholder for the event of the in-breaking of God's will in the human realm,"[16] and its proclamation of the righteousness of God and any true good.[17] This address, which flows like a sermon rebuking and encouraging, is split

---

all too often many readers simply focus upon the clearing aspect of this encounter and see Barth as attempting to disable the human agent altogether, instead of simply "making space" to speak rightly about both God and Man. John Webster examines the theme of "encounter" in *The Christian Life* which Barth uses to depict the relationship in which the divine commanding and human willing exist. See Webster, "The Christian in Revolt," 123.

16. Stubbs, "Sanctification as Participation in Christ," 82. A similar notion of conscience as described by Stubbs is taken up again in Barth's 1928/9 *Ethics* lectures in much greater detail as a way of understanding in part how the grace of sanctification effects man concretely within his life.

17. Barth wrote in the foreword to *The Word of God and the Word of Man*, which contains the lecture "The Righteousness of God," that "as the reader takes his way between the first and last of these addresses he will find the landscape changing . . . (Naturally I would no longer speak of 'the voice of him that crieth in the wilderness', as I have done here on the first page, as "the voice of conscience)."

into three main sections. Section 1 sets out the fundamental issue: God is the truly righteous one. Here Barth posed what he saw as the seminal question in light of the righteousness of God: How should human beings respond to God's righteousness; or put differently, how should people live in light of the reality of the in-breaking presence of God?[18] Section 2 addresses the fundamental problem: Humanity, upon feeling the call of God's righteousness, lapses too quickly, gives up, and accepts their own self-righteousness instead of God's. "Now comes a remarkable turn in our relation with the righteousness of God," writes Barth, "we stand here before the really tragic, the most fundamental, error of mankind. We long for the righteousness of God, and yet we do not let it enter our lives and our world"[19] And the third section deals with the confrontation between human self-righteousness and God's own righteous will. In the end Barth states that it is only when the question of God's righteousness is truly posed to humanity by God that false piety may be demolished. "We make a veritable uproar with our morality and culture and religion. But we may presently be brought to silence, and with that will begin our true redemption."[20] Only in confrontation with the "Wholly Other" then can real human righteousness exist as lived righteousness.

What is striking in this lecture is Barth's desire to affirm true righteousness in both God and humanity. But the *way* he does this is not by building up human beings along side of God as a partners, co-operators with God living within the world, but by emphasizing that God and human beings truly are different subjects *encountering* each other, one establishing yet limiting the other. It is only in differentiation, Barth's argument follows, that human righteousness, in relationship with and dependent upon the righteous God, garners any concrete significance.

In Barth's estimation, modern theology had confused this encounter, blurring the lines of action so that the identities of each subject were either exchanged or equated, essentially stripping humanity of any "real" basis for righteousness.[21] He writes, "The righteousness of God which we have looked upon . . . changes under our awkward touch into all kinds

18. Barth, "Righteousness of God," 9.
19. Ibid., 14–15.
20. Ibid., 23–24.
21. "The 'real' for Barth was not the world known empirically. The truly 'real is the wholly otherness of the *Self*-revealing God in comparison with whom the empirical world is mere shadow and appearance" (McCormack, *Barth's Critically Realistic Dialectical Theology*, 130).

of human righteousness."[22] This, Barth saw, was the fundamental error of the modern conception of the divine-human relationship, that when human righteousness is taken for God's righteousness those things that have the possibility of becoming good within the world are destroyed. And this was the problem that Barth tried to highlight and rectify by re-establishing the critically realistic character of the divine-human relationship, by affirming true human righteousness within God's self-righteousness. By rightly stating who God and humans are in relationship the foundation was laid for a meaningful account of human life lived in fellowship with God.

What follows is a brief exposition of the primary matters concerning the divine-human encounter set forth in "The Righteousness of God."

Humans Are Needy

Throughout this essay, Barth emphasises that humanity exists in utter need. They are unrighteous, unholy, and above all seek their own self-will. Though at times they may glimpse their deepest and most profound inner need, may perhaps even call out for divine aid, they cannot help turning even this need into a perversion:

> As a drowning man grasps at a straw, all that is within us reaches out for the certainty which the conscience gives. If only we might stand in the shining presence of the other will (God's will), not doubtfully but with assurance! If only, instead of merely guessing at it as men who can only hope and wish, we might contemplate it quietly and take enjoyment in it! If only we might approach it, come to know it, and have it for our own! The deepest longing in us is born of the deepest need: oh that Thou wouldest come down! Oppressed and afflicted by his own unrighteousness and the unrighteousness of others, man—every man—lifts up from the depths of his nature the cry for righteousness, the righteousness of God. Whoever understands him at this point, understands him wholly. . . . In what haste we are to soothe within us the stormy desire for the righteousness of God! And to soothe means, unfortunately, to cover up, to bring to silence.[23]

In this sense humanity's deepest need, the need for God's righteous will and ways to be expressed *within individual lives*, is not simply a

22. Barth, "Righteousness of God," 17.
23. Ibid., 13.

matter of knowing what one ought to do and therefore doing it.[24] Neither individual morality nor social justice embodies this "other will," the will of God. In actuality, the need signals something completely lacking in human nature. Which is precisely why even though humans may recognize their deep inner need, that which they long for, they still turn away and take up their own self-sanctification—the attempt to justify their way of living. Barth writes, "We are inwardly resentful that the righteousness we pant after is God's and can come to us only from God. We should like to take the right thing into our own hands and under our own management, as we have done with so many other things."[25] Humanity, though, cannot supply that which they desperately desire by turning to themselves. Simply stated, Barth says, humans cannot make themselves righteous.

In emphasizing this deficiency within humanity Barth in one stroke attacked the modern idea of moral and spiritual autonomy, and at the same time began a perceptive discourse concerning the divine-human relationship, which placed high value upon the notion of human dependence on God, rather than despising it.

God Is Holy

For Barth then, righteous human living, as an expression of the will and ways of God breaking forth within one's life, is only ever derived from *God's* gracious activity. God's righteousness is the "surest fact of life," the "final," the "original," the "simple"—it is that from which all other righteousness derives. In other words, humanity must seek beyond themselves to satisfy their needs, and ultimately this "beyond" is not an extra *human* quality, but God Himself:

> God himself, the real, the living God, and his love which comes in glory! These provide the solution. . . . We have prayed, Thy will be done! And meant by it, Thy will be done not just now! We have believed in an eternal life, but what we took for eternal life and satisfied ourselves upon was really only temporary. And for this reason we have remained as we are. . . . When we let conscience speak to the end, it tells us not only that there is something else, a righteousness above unrighteousness, but

---

24. Stubbs, "Sanctification as Participation," 95.
25. Barth, "Righteousness of God," 15.

also—and more important—that this something else for which we long and which we need is God.[26]

For Barth, righteous human living, rightly stated, comes from above; it is that which is beyond and greater than all human self-righteousness. And yet it is not found in searching for that which is beyond, for an "other" type of righteousness than our own. Humanity has continually reaped the fruitless benefit of pursuing righteousness for its own sake because, as Barth stated, "we have been much too eager to do something ourselves."[27] Like praying "Thy will be done," but meaning "Thy will be done not just now." The force of this critically realistic approach comes through as Barth states simply, "And then God works in us."[28] Thus righteous human living can come only by encountering "God himself, the real, the living God." God himself is holy, and He graciously transforms those with whom He *lives* in fellowship with.

Emphasizing God's holiness, that which is above all else—the most appropriate form of God's own will, was perhaps the clearest way in which Barth was able to affirm real goodness within the world. Only in God's holiness can a positive answer be given to the question posed to Religion, the State, our Morality, and Duty: *Cui bono?* Apart from God's righteousness, such things become oppressors and false gods, but when God takes up His work those human things may now be transformed, though never apart from God's present action, into something good.

God and Humanity Encounter Each Other

Finally, Barth writes, within this divine-human encounter, God is the active One. Humans, for their part, must simply listen:

> He is right and not we! His righteousness is an eternal righteousness! This is difficult for us to hear. We must take the trouble to go far enough off to hear it again. We make a veritable uproar with our morality and culture and religion. But we may presently be brought to silence, and with that will begin our true redemption. It will then be, above all, a matter of our recognizing God once more as God.[29]

26. Ibid., 23.
27. Ibid.
28. Ibid., 25.
29. Ibid., 23–24.

The whole address converges on this final idea that *something real happens*, indeed "the only real thing which can happen," when God takes up His work. God acts and humans receive. God is the primary and humanity the derived. This derivation is no negative quality, although it lacks the doctrinal specificity that will come later on. Within the divine-human relationship, "life receives its meaning again—your own life and life as a whole. Lights of God rise in the darkness, and powers of God become real in weakness."[30] Something new begins to flourish within humans who are, in humility and joy, which here Barth calls faith, overcoming their own unrighteousness. In faith, "Real love, real sincerity, real progress become possible; morality and culture, state and nation, even religion and the church now become possible—now for the first time!"[31] Righteous human living, then, says Barth, is not simply a divinely "corrected continuation" of our own will, a positive human spirit set back on the right track. It is the "re-creation and re-growth" given in the encounter between the Holy, Living, Righteous God, and the humble, joyful human. In this sense human righteousness is the aspect of the fellowship between God and man in which human existence and action is affirmed in God's own self-righteousness. This, Barth believed, was the correct expression of the divine-human relationship, which neither pandered to an abstract anthropology or a divine fatalism. Neither God nor humanity can truly be known or understood if this critically realistic relationship is confused or exaggerated. When human endeavour becomes a central subject of interest, the divine-human relationship becomes deceptive and misleading; for ultimately individual morality cannot help but to shut oneself off from and forsakes one's neighbours, the state eventually crushes with one hand what it frees with the other, and religion above all else manipulates and gives a false sense of security.[32] Only in confrontation with the holiness of God does true righteous *living* occur. This means, first and foremost, that God must be recognized as God and humanity as humanity.

Implications

At first glance, "The Righteousness of God" appears to lack the theological specificity to actually set this critically realistic distinction between

30. Ibid., 26.
31. Ibid.
32. Ibid., 17–20.

God and man apart from the modern theological account. For example: it becomes clear by the end of the article that there is no distinct Christology or pneumatology present. Barth does briefly discuss the "simple way of faith," which is the way of Christ that "wherein one simply believes that the Father's will is truth and must be done."[33] But even this is found only in the last paragraph. There is no explicit discussion of reconciliation, although the notion is implied throughout, or of Christ's sacrifice, or resurrection. Nor is there any mention of the Holy Spirit, particularly as the bond between God's righteousness and human participation. Barth does affirm that "we ought to apply ourselves with all our strength to expect more from God, to let grow within us that which he will in fact cause to grow, to accept what indeed he constantly offers us, watching and praying that we may respond to his originative touch."[34] Yet he never explicitly describes how these benefits are accomplished, except to say that God gives and humans receive. At this point, one wonders if Barth has gone far enough to distinguish his idea of the objective encounter with "this God" from modern theology's anthropocentric account.

However, two things must be remembered. First, Barth is only at the beginning of his theological revolution. Many of his ideas here are truly vibrant and full of content. For example, Barth writes that people should expect "a joy that God is so much greater than we thought. Joy that his righteousness has far more depth and meaning than we had allowed ourselves to dream. Joy that from God much more is to be expected for our poor, perplexed, and burdened life."[35] Barth wants to convey a real fullness, one that goes beyond a mere abstract existentialism, about the reality of the divine-human encounter. Much of the time, however, he simply lacks the framework to develop certain specific theological arguments (i.e., the formal distinction between justification and sanctification as the single work of reconciliation). In the following years though as Barth pursues this critically realistic description of the divine-human relationship further many of these ideas gain tremendous clarity, and Barth will go to great lengths to specifically, and positively, articulate who God and humanity are in relationship.

Secondly, Barth's specific purpose must be kept in mind. Barth was in the midst of rebuilding Protestant theology from the bottom up, a process

---

33. Ibid., 26.
34. Ibid., 25.
35. Ibid., 24–25.

that included both construction and *ground clearing*. While Barth's goal of methodologically dismantling modern theology's "anthropocentric theology" would have benefited tremendously from a more constructive Christological and pneumatological account here, nevertheless, the importance of his ground-clearing efforts should not be overlooked. Statements such as: "As with a blare of trumpets from another world it [God's righteousness] interrupts one's reflections concerning himself and his life, concerning his duties to family, calling, and country. It interrupts even the cultivation of his religious thoughts and feelings!"[36] fly in the face of core modern theological accounts of religion. Barth himself recognized that much more would need to be said to effectively deal with modern theology, and it would take time to do so.[37] In the end, though, it is these seemingly incidental clearing-statements scattered throughout this work that differentiate it from the type of modern accounts he despised.

By focusing on the reality in which God and humanity truly encounter each other within "The Righteousness of God" Barth's ideas about Christian life in fellowship with God, based upon his later comments on Christian doctrine in *CD* 4:1, were "on the right track" even early on. The idea of *encounter*, which critically differentiated God and human beings, was the basis upon which Barth began discussing concrete human existence and living in a meaningful way.

New Life "In Christ"

Between "The Righteousness of God" address given in January of 1916 and the Tambach lecture given in September of 1919 at the Conference on Religion and Social Relations, one can discern an increasing maturity in Barth's thought, as well as a greater facility in articulating that thought. Several of the implicit theological foundations found in Barth's earlier work are now made more explicit. Where he once spoke of "the will to which the conscience points is . . . the perfect will of God, . . . won only in fierce inner personal conflict,"[38] he now speaks of "how unapproachably

---

36. Ibid., 10.

37. In a letter to Thurneysen in January of 1916, Barth remarked after reading Ritschl's history of pietism that "when the time comes to strike the great blow against the theologians, these ideas, too, will have to be considered and digested very thoroughly" (*Karl Barth-Eduard Thurneysen Briefwechsel*, 2:121).

38. Barth, "Righteousness of God," 24.

the Divine, when it is really the Divine, veils itself from the human, to which today we would so gladly unite!"[39] His concern is the same—the right ordering of the divine-human relationship as it pertained to the life of man, the untangling of what humans "so gladly unite." However, now, Barth's language becomes even more precise as he gives expression to the objective reality of Jesus Christ and his eschatological power. These articulations are extremely significant for Barth's understanding of the doctrine of sanctification, because they become the critical basis upon which Barth begins to positively discuss renewed human existence *and* action. As far as Barth saw it, "The church has too long directed its efforts to the consideration of types of godliness," to form instead of content.[40] The new life lived in fellowship with God "revealed in Jesus Christ is not a new form of godliness," but the movement of God, "which penetrates and even passes through all our forms of worship and our experiences; it is the world of God breaking through from its self-contained holiness. . . . It is the bodily resurrection of Christ from the dead. To participate in its meaning and power is to discover a new motivation."[41] In Barth's estimation, modern theology had gotten this relationship backwards.[42] It is precisely here in this fellowship between God and human beings that the power of the gospel truly captures God's love for and reconciliation of them as human righteousness is affirmed in the *futurum resurrectionis*.

"The Christian's Place in Society"

For the 1919 Tambach lecture, Barth was given the task of discussing the Christian's place *in society*. He surprised his listeners by emphasizing instead the *Christian's* place in society. The ideas generated in "The Righteousness of God" were carried forward in this work, but from a slightly different point of view. Barth was still concerned with God and "the movement originating in God, the motion which *he* lends us. . . .

---

39. Barth, "The Christian's Place in Society," 278.
40. Ibid., 285.
41. Ibid., 286–87.

42. "And that is the reason why the synoptic accounts of Jesus can be really understood only with Bengel's insight: *spirant resurrectionem*. The Catholic Middle Ages and the Reformation understood this in some measure. It remained for pietism, Schleiermacher, and modern Christianity to read the New Testament Gospel backwards. We must win again the mighty sense in which . . . Christ is the absolutely *new from above*... in whom humanity becomes aware of its *immediacy* to God" (ibid., 286).

Hallowed be *thy* name. *Thy* kingdom come. *Thy* will be done."[43] But he further developed the relational concept of the Christian life by incorporating the theologically specific reality of existence "in Christ." This thought was largely developed while Barth worked through the first edition of *The Epistle to the Romans*, but was brought out just as significantly in relationship to this ethically concentrated piece.

The lecture is divided into five main sections: Section One addresses what it means to discuss *the Christian's* place in society, referring first and foremost to the person and work of Jesus Christ in society, and only secondarily to the impact of those "in Christ." Barth then asks what this means in relationship to the Christian's place *in society*.[44] In Section Two, he focuses on the general nature of the ethical movement in discussion. But, he says, this is the tricky part of the topic, since it is actually God himself who is the movement in history, and any attempt to describe God and "the motion which *he* lends us" directly inevitably fails. "The so-called 'religious experience' is a wholly derived, secondary, fragmentary form of the divine. Even in its highest and purest examples, it is form and not content."[45] It is just at this most crucial point, when pointing towards the work of God within society, that Barth laments that he cannot give what is needed "except a miracle should happen. . . . There is nothing to do but to paraphrase actuality in dead words."[46] Section three moves into a particular discussion of the relationship between God and the world. The Christian's main task is to view life in such a way that he acknowledges the good in the world, specifically God's YES-that which God calls good, because he sees that he himself is a part of the kingdom of God, and, therefore, the kingdom of God exists in the world (thesis). Life can be praised because there are, in this world, parables of the Kingdom of God. In Section Four, Barth states that the encouragement of the human Yes must summarily be followed by the admonishment of the human No (antithesis). While there may indeed be real value in this world, it too comes under divine judgment along with everything else. Importantly, however, Barth explains that neither the human affirmation of life nor

---

43. Barth, "The Christian's Place in Society," 285,

44. "So this is what I find in our theme: on the one hand a great promise, a light from above which is shed upon our situation, but on the other hand an unhappy separation, a thorough-going opposition between two dissimilar magnitudes" (Barth, "The Christian's Place," 281–82).

45. Ibid., 285.

46. Ibid.

the denial of it should become themes in their own right, as they typically do, because above all human judgment is God's judgment, His YES and NO. In Section Five, Barth carries over the thrust of that message: "The synthesis we seek is in God alone, and in God alone can we find it. If we do not find it in God, we do not find it at all."[47] The human Yes and No will only ever find real significance in God's YES and NO because the human word carries "limitation in itself." Yet, just as Barth had argued in "The Righteousness of God," human limitation and dependence ought not to be construed in such a way as to demean human existence and action; but instead in critically realistic fashion affirm what it really means to be human.

"The Christian's Place in Society" is fundamentally an attempt to discuss what happens to human life when it is encountered by God; to understand the effects of the gospel on people as they live amongst other people. This is for Barth the entryway into discussing the notion of sanctification. Barth knew as he began this address that what those in attendance really expected to hear from him was how they could "use the thought-forms of Jesus as the law for every economic, racial, national, and international order!"[48] What they expected to hear were ethical theories and plans for how *they* could transform or sanctify society around them. Instead, what they received was a sketching of a series of contrasting positions, human action taken up by, and given meaning in the action of God. The import of this argument is that for Barth the life lived in fellowship with God, the place where dogmatics directly and expressly becomes ethics, can only ever be described in the same way, by sketching the contrasting images of the movement of God in the lives of humans. As a result, any serious description of sanctification, which is really the "movement from above . . . which transcends and yet penetrates all these movements,"[49] is only comparable to the momentary view of a bird in flight. The attempt to capture the motion of God's sanctifying activity in human understanding and words can only be expressed in momentary images of "the real, the flying, bird" which results in "the painted picture-puzzle."[50] "Aside from the movement it [the painted picture] is absolutely meaningless, incomprehensible, and impossible. . . . I mean the move-

---

47. Ibid., 322.
48. Ibid., 279.
49. Ibid., 283.
50. Ibid., 285.

ment of God . . . whose power and import are revealed in the resurrection of Jesus Christ from the dead."[51] Modern theological conceptions of ethics and the Christian life, Barth felt, had proceeded with the theoretical and left the movement from "above" behind. Because Barth recognized the extreme danger of focusing on the theoretical, which he thought "almost unavoidably . . . ends in the ridiculous attempt to draw the bird flying," his account of the Christian life lived in fellowship with God, frustratingly to many, began to take shape explicitly around the divine movement, recognizable, but only in faith. The objective reality of Jesus Christ, and his eschatological power, became the basis for all of Barth's discussions concerned with renewed human existence and action.

Thus Barth began his Tambach lecture with a concept that ran completely contrary to modern theology's anthropocentrism. What is the hope for society with all of its social changes and revolutions? It is *the Christian*. But, as Barth quickly emphasised, *the Christian* is none other than Jesus Christ—the Saviour!

> Here is a new element in the midst of the old, a truth in the midst of error and lies a formative life-energy within all our weak, tottering movements of thought, a unity in a time which is out of joint. The Christian: we must be agreed that we do not mean the Christians, not the multitude of the baptized, nor the chosen few who are concerned with Religion and Social Relations, nor even the cream of the noblest and most devoted Christians we might think of: the Christian is the Christ.[52]

What this means effectively is that *Christ* is the focal point for any discussion of what it means to be a Christian. It is Christ, the "image of the invisible God," the "firstborn of every creature" in us (Col 1:15) who "indicates a goal and a future."[53] Christ is the reality by which the new human disposition is formed and sustained. "The Christian is that within us which is not you yourself but Christ in us. 'Christ in us' understood in its whole Pauline depth is not a psychic condition, an affection of the mind, a mental lapse, or anything of the sort, but is a presupposition of life. 'Over us,' 'behind us,' and 'beyond us' are included in the meaning of 'in us.'"[54]

---

51. Ibid., 283.
52. Ibid., 273.
53. Ibid., 275.
54. Ibid., 273–74.

Discussion of renewed human existence and action, therefore, can never venture from what it means to speak about being encountered by Christ, about being "in Christ." The Christian life happens importantly and primarily in Christ; "Christ is the absolutely *new from above*; the way, the truth, and the life of *God* among men; the Son of Man, in whom humanity becomes aware of its *immediacy* to God."[55] Through the grace of God, "There is in us, over us, behind us, and beyond us a consciousness of the meaning of life, a memory of our own origin, a turning to the Lord of the universe, a critical No and a creative Yes in regard to all the content of our thought, a facing away from the old and toward the new age—whose sign and fulfilment is the cross."[56] This is the movement of God—'the real, the flying, bird" that surrounds and permeates the question: What happens to us?

It is this "in Christ-ness," Barth maintains, that guards Christians from attempting to do what they cannot do: that is, renew their own existence and action in relationship to God and the world. The objective nature of being "in Christ" guards descriptions of the Christian life, as Barth stated in the first edition to *The Epistle to the Romans*, from throwing people "back and forth" between two extremes, "exultant and depressed, believing and unbelieving, proud righteousness and absurd error, a feeling of being saved and a feeling of being abandoned or even damned!"[57] The new life of Jesus Christ is, rightly stated, the centre of all renewed human existence and action.

Equally as significant is the eschatological power of that relationship. In fact, the two cannot be separated. The eschatological power of Christ's resurrection is the power by which humans may now truly *live* "in Christ." It is the eschatological power that makes that which is impossible, the bridging of the gap between God and faithful human existence and action, possible.

> If then we appeal to this Highest Court (God), how can we help coming eventually to an understanding of ourselves in spite of all possibilities to the contrary; how can we help understanding that we *live* by the power of the resurrection, in spite of the inadequacy of our perception of it and our response to it. . . . As a matter of fact we *do* share in the resurrection movement: with or without the accompaniment of religious feelings we

---

55. Ibid., 286.
56. Ibid., 274.
57. Barth, *Der Römerbrief* (1919), 277.

are actuated by it.... We are not unofficial observers. We *are* moved by God.[58]

It is the force of Barth's argument that, "the relation between God and the world is so thoroughly affected by the resurrection, and the place we have taken in Christ over against life," that adds such a unique element to his description of the Christian life. In spite of everything that seems to point to the contrary, human beings are given the promise of, and power for living the future life of the resurrection here and now. Not only are humans forgiven as they are cast upon the judgment of the divine No, but they are given new life in Christ through God's creative Yes. Not that they might build themselves up in holiness and piety through their renewed nature, or transform society by opening up the "sluices" and letting Christ pour forth. "The *resurrection* of Jesus Christ from the dead is the power which moves both the world and us, *because* it is the appearance in our corporeality of a *totaliter aliter* constituted corporeality." Again, renewed human existence and action is not the continuation of a divinely corrected human will. It is the appearance of a totally alien holiness, one that transforms the unrighteousness of humanity from beyond and above, in and through Jesus Christ. What makes Barth's description of human existence and action unique here is his emphasis upon its eschatological nature. The reality of the *futurum resurrectionis* is the reality by which all other being and action is characterized, which means that renewed human existence and action is a reality already accomplished in Jesus Christ and known, therefore, only in faith.

Barth's eschatological characterization of reality allowed him to maintain the distinction between the divine and human and yet truly affirm renewed human existence and action despite all appearances to the contrary and devoid of any subjective misconstrual. Despite how humanity may think or act, whether they accept or reject this promise, they are "in Christ" new beings.

Barth's use of concepts such as the reality of being "in Christ" and the power of his resurrection show a definite growth in terms of theological articulation. This invariably has to do with his increasing affinity for the Reformed theologians, particularly Calvin, the "doctor of sanctification," which will be looked at in more detail in the next chapter. From Calvin Barth no doubt rediscovered the power and promise of the *futurae vitae*— the eschatological objectivity, as well as the import of concepts

---

58. Barth, "The Christian's Place," 296.

such as mortification and vivification, which he in turn, in this piece, applied to the ethical relations of Christians in society. Interestingly both the critical and optimistic attitudes towards society—the human yes and no—which Barth details in this work, could be viewed as abstractions of those concepts.

One of the pitfalls of adhering to an extremely objective framework of soteriology though, as Barth seems to utilize here, is the slippery slope that often allows theological content to be construed in a very static way. That is to say, the objective reality of the divine accomplishment or decree becomes lifeless; it loses its relational character. Emphasis is placed so one-sidedly upon the critically realistic divine action that all relational aspects between God and humanity become wooden and immobile. This in turn usually leads towards a tendency to fatalism, and an overwhelming emphasis on God's raw power. In the doctrine of sanctification, this type of divine one-sidedness often results in an exaggerated preoccupation with human mortification and self-denial to the exclusion of any real concept of the new life or vivification.[59]

Barth's heavy emphasis upon the objective reality of being "in Christ" and his insistence on the primacy of the eschatological reality quickly call to mind those same dangers. In the end, one must ask whether Barth's resolve to maintain a critically realistic stance engenders a type of fatalism, which in terms of the Christian life focuses upon the denial of everything human? Barth himself, perhaps in anticipation of such thoughts, asks a very similar question, "Will the creation of this new life, in which God makes us believe, consist in the last end simply in the annulment of the creaturehood in which, in contrast to the life of God, we live our life on earth?"[60] His answer, while perhaps unexpected, is significant for understanding some of the intricacies of his doctrine of sanctification.

Barth cheerfully and willingly admits that in the end the creation of the new life means *precisely* the negation of unredeemed creaturehood. He is eager to affirm the difference between the eschatological reality of Jesus Christ and present temporal human life because he sees the negation not as an attempt to limit humanity negatively, but rather to fulfil it. Continually drawing on the reality in which God and humans

---

59. Interestingly Barth notes in *CD* 4:2 that this was sometimes an issue for both Calvin and Kohlbrügge who tended to miss the point that mortification did not function for its own purposes but was of one accord with and for vivification. See Barth, *CD* 4:II, 577.

60. Barth, "The Christian's Place in Society," 288.

encounter each other Barth utilizes the objective reality of Christ not to crush people but to lift them up. The objective aspect of this relationship, instead of losing its relational quality, becomes the means by which God draws ever nearer to humanity. Far from becoming wooden or immobile, Barth's enthusiastic "annulment of creaturehood" actually allows faithful human existence and action because the "annulment of creaturehood" is at the same time a grounding and maintaining of creaturehood in God's own person and work—the existence of *new* life. If anything, there is an overwhelming emphasis upon human vivification in this piece as Barth once again guards human righteousness in God's own self-righteousness.

In the end Barth's resolve to emphasise the asymmetry of the divine-human encounter in this piece does not lead to a type of fatalism—a mere resignation to what has already taken place; rather, it functions more like a catalyst in which the eschatological power of Christ's resurrection brings about a great human flourishing. While Barth's view of renewed human existence and action importantly emphasises the divine judgment, God's NO, which indeed leads to nothing else accept total destruction, it does so along with the equally real and important divine YES, the creation of new life.

> The last word concerning the world of men is not Dust thou art and unto dust shalt thou return! but, Because I live, ye shall live also. . . . The unholy equilibrium of a constant relation between God and man is overcome. Our life wins depth and perspective. . . . We live amidst transition—a transition from death to life, from the unrighteousness of men to the righteousness of God, from the old to the new creation.[61]

New Life as Freedom

Barth was entirely convinced that modern theology, for all of its emphases on the dignity and glory of humankind and the ability to rightly discern human righteousness, had in reality done nothing more than indicate the human fall from God.

> There was a time when with Kant or, let us say, with the cheerful Fichte, people took the ethical problem to be the expression and witness of the peculiar greatness and dignity of man. They were not disturbed and embarrassed but felt an exaltation and

---

61. Ibid., 297.

delight when their thought led them from things as they are to things as they ought to be, from facts to norms, from nature to history. Here was the absolute distinction between man and the animals, not to say between civilized man and the savages. Here they even thought themselves to have found the *pou sto* from which any godless, despairing, materialistic view of life might be lifted from its foundations.[62]

In considering humanity as above, or at least as set objectively over against, the moral situation, Barth stated that modern theology had found a place to lift up human achievement apart from God. The possibility of renewed or righteous human conduct was not actually a question; it was an obvious fact of life and culture. This was most clearly seen in modern theology's view of ethics. Ethics, the question of human existence and action, was not a dilemma for them, but a joy because it demonstrated the freedom of humanity. Barth writes, "people considered dogmatics a difficult and ethics a relatively easy undertaking. They regarded the Epistle to the Romans as weighted down and obscured . . . while the Sermon on the Mount seemed lucid as daylight."[63] In this sense, Barth felt that Christianity was reduced to a religious ethic, which meant that the gospel was, "reduced to a few religious and moral categories like trust in God and brotherly love."[64] As a religious ethic, the gospel message was stripped of any thought of the eschatological power of the risen Christ, which led to a complete misunderstanding of Scripture's imperative claim, and thus a misunderstanding of the divine-human relationship.

In one sense, modern theology could be likened to the builders of the tower of Babel, for whom the glory of humanity was measured by their own progress, not in and with the work of God, but in competition and opposition to him. Concerning modern theology Barth wrote, "here was yet a human culture building itself up in orderly fashion in politics, economics, and science . . . progressing steadily along its whole front, interpreted and ennobled by art, and through its morality and religion reaching well beyond itself toward yet better days."[65] And in light of the world situation in the early twentieth century, in which "the ways of European man are now proved impossible in relation to the *ethic* of

---

62. Barth, "The Problem of Ethics Today," 146.
63. Ibid., 147.
64. Ibid.
65. Ibid., 145.

Christianity,"[66] Barth could clearly state, "that over against man's confidence and belief in himself, there has been written, in huge proportions and with utmost clearness, a *mene, mene, tekel*."[67] God has weighed the human kingdom in the balance and found it wanting.

Once again, Barth continued the task of expounding the reality of the divine-human encounter. Like a modern theologian, he too *was concerned* with human existence and action, but recognized that these concepts had been turned on their heads. For modern theology, in Barth's eyes, talk of human existence and action was a way of describing human self-renewal in which the "infinitely imperfect but infinitely perfectible culture" simply carried on in dignity. Barth's concern, however, was that this was not a true portrayal of reality. "We are reminded by the third chapter of Genesis that man's ability to distinguish between good and evil and his consequent greatness and dignity may indicate his fall from God as well as his ascendancy over nature."[68] Human beings deceive themselves, merely playing at being human, when they believe that their actions are truly free. Barth responded to these ideas by demonstrating that true human freedom was upheld and established only in God's own freedom and sovereignty. It was God's freedom that freed human beings from their own limitations and established them as a faithful covenant partners. The objective encounter that occurs "in Christ" frees them from that which they cannot do themselves; the eschatological power of the resurrection frees people to live in faithful obedience to God and, therefore, in loving fellowship with others.

"The Problem of Ethics Today"

In September of 1922, Barth delivered "The Problem of Ethics Today" to a gathering of ministers in Wiesbaden, Germany. Approximately two months before that lecture, Barth's long time friend Eduard Thurneysen responded to him in a letter:

> In this sense, to be sure, the handling of the ethical problem is most urgent and also it is opened up in a basic way by Romans 12 ff. Action or conduct is set in a meaningful relation of

---

66. Ibid., 147.

67. These words refer to the writing on the wall in Daniel 5, in which God pronounces judgment upon Belshazzar and his kingdom. See ibid., 149.

68. Ibid., 147.

a positive kind to the action of *God*. Ethics is no longer regarded
... as something that really ought not to exist ... that awkwardly
continues to exist as long as the *Parousia* is delayed, or ... as
long as the proper eschatological tension has not yet come into
being.... I cannot imagine that your stronger emphasis upon
the ethical problem in connection with Reformed theology is
anything other than an attempt to clarify *these* relationships....
I would not be surprised if, alongside the first report that Karl
Barth has "suddenly" now begun to take *ethics* seriously again,
a second and yet more remarkable report would arrive shortly:
Karl Barth is turning again even to *psychology* (until now the
undisputed and depreciated hunting ground of the "experience"
people): the "personality" becomes an interesting subject.[69]

As Thurneysen alludes in this letter the majority of attention paid to Barth focused on his formula, "God Himself, God alone."[70] What seemed to be overshadowed in the public eye was Barth's deep theological concern for rightly explicating the effects of the divine-human relationship in which the uniqueness of each partner was emphasised not to avoid speaking of human agency, but to speak of it faithfully. This essay, which is quite similar in style to "The Christian's Place In Society," is primarily concerned with not only the possibility of, but also the demand for, true human moral agency. This theme is taken up as Barth explores the problem of ethics, which he states, "is concerned with man's conduct, that is, his whole temporal existence."[71] For Barth, the movement of human life, meaning true human action and existence, is wholly taken up within the discussion of the divine-human relationship.

At first glance, the title and theme of this address can be quite misleading. A literal assessment conjures images of an objective appraisal of modern ethics, and while that is partly true, the lecture is much more than that. Those in attendance most likely expected Barth to theorize about the poor state of ethics in their day, maybe to offer new ethical schemes, perhaps based upon his rousing "dialectical" approach. Once again, however, Barth would not allow himself to be bound by making movements within society themes in their own right, of ridiculously attempting to "paint the bird in flight" as he had called it derisively in "The Christian's Place in Society"; and so he forced his listeners to grapple with

---

69. Barth, *Karl Barth-Eduard Thurneysen Briefwechsel*, 2:82–83.
70. Barth, *The Epistle to the Romans*, 2nd ed., 110.
71. Barth, "The Problem of Ethics Today," 136.

the ultimate question of their own existence.[72] The problem of ethics, he writes, is not the problem *posed to ethics* by us, but rather the problem which *ethics poses* to us. It is the problem of humanity's "whole temporal existence." As people search for the inner truth and meaning of their own conduct, they become aware that they are responsible beings, that there is a *good* that is superior to, and even overshadows, the "highest dignity and worth" of things as they are. This realization creates a *crisis* of existence, for there is a "must," an "ought to," which lays claim to the whole of human life. "Nothing can come of our facing the ethical question from the viewpoint of spectators—as if the question did not arise out of the very fact that we *cannot* find complete satisfaction in playing the part of spectators in matters of life and conduct, and that we are compelled to conceive ourselves as living doers."[73] However, when the question "What ought we to do?" is asked, it reveals to us that life lies under the ultimate judgment of *God's* holiness and perfection, and of our own unfaithfulness. To be asked the ethical question is, then, to be exposed to death. "For by the question, he [man] proves his peculiar connection with the One who regards him from the viewpoint of *eternity*, and so he bids an unavoidable farewell to all viewpoints peculiarly his own. . . . The problem of ethics contains the secret that man as we know him in this life is an impossibility. *This* man, in God's sight, can only perish."[74] But this "all-inclusive critical negation under which we and our world exist" is the very reality that drives people to God.

As the address begins the broad criticisms that had since been waged against Barth, that his too critical concern with God actually devalues the human situation, appear to be valid to some degree. The problem of ethics he writes, after all, becomes the "unbearable human situation," the question of humanity's annihilation. It is at this very point though, when the divine-human tension reaches its peak, when the doom of human reality seems insurmountable, that Barth gently pulls back the veil to reveal a fuller meaning of this relationship. "It is this [the negation of man] that proves that the problem of ethics, when it becomes our own, is

---

72. "Why is the topic assigned us, 'The Problem of Ethics Today?' . . . We are faced not with *a* problem but with *the* problem. When we speak of the problem of ethics *today*, we mean as far as possible to eliminate any time element which might separate us from and cause us to be spectators of the problem in its reality" (ibid., 142).

73. Ibid., 137.

74. Ibid., 140.

the bond that relates us to God."⁷⁵ This crisis, this boundary, which marks humans as the created ones and not God, which most certainly means destruction, is also at its very darkest point the place where a new ray of light shines in. At this place where a person must fully give himself over to the judgment of God, there *is* forgiveness and new life. And as Barth triumphantly states: "Since there is such a thing as forgiveness (which is always forgiveness of *sin*!), there is such a thing as human conduct which is justified."⁷⁶ Where a person is thrust upon the judgment of God, the boundary that distinguishes him *from* God, human existence and action also find forgiveness and new life. There the impossibility of the faithful partner becomes possible; there renewed life in fellowship with God brings freedom for participation in the divine order.

The heart of what this address captures is that God is the truly free one. "He *is* and he *remains free*: else he were not God."⁷⁷ Yet God's freedom is His ability to bring judgment *and* life, in his judgment he is free to give grace and forgiveness even to those whom are infinitely separated from him. God's freedom is freedom *for* humanity. His freedom, therefore, gives motion to all other movements, His holiness may make holy that which is not holy, and it is in this way that Barth is able to speak of actual human freedom and obedience. Essentially then, Barth states, modern theology appears to simply be a symptom of the fact that, "We are (all) tempted in Fichtean insolence to grasp for ourselves what does not belong to us."⁷⁸ In reality, autonomous human existence and action are a *fata morgana*, a mirage, and ultimately a sign of human separateness from God. But taken up within God's own freedom and holiness, and never apart from this, human existence and action are renewed, given new life—they are sanctified. In this sense, individuals are freed from the burden of fulfilling the demands of the divine-human relationship in their own strength and they are able to participate obediently in newness of life.

---

75. Ibid., 168.
76. Ibid., 172.
77. Ibid., 178.
78. Ibid., 177.

Freedom in Co-relation

In developing these points, Barth continued in both ground-clearing and rebuilding. In order for him to comfortably speak of positive human action, he needed to chasten the *pou sto* upon which modern theology had built its understanding of the human moral agent, that human action is gloriously free action in its own strength. Barth's critical emphasis should not be taken as mere theological and philosophical dialectic, though, "which not only allows but calls for its opposite—that this negation, which *removes* from human conduct false value, may *restore* to it new value, may return to it its original value."[79] This type of thinking also places humans in an objective relationship over against the ethical question. What Barth was after, beyond a mere feign of dialectic, was reality. "I simply ask whether the process actually corresponds with *reality*. Who can transform the No of the ethical problem in which we find ourselves today into a Yes? Who is bold enough and omniscient enough to resolve our difficulty from a height above the Yes and the No?"[80] Barth was after a more explicit account of the divine-human encounter, one that called for serious human responsibility, yet also acknowledged the reality of human *sinfulness*, and, therefore, of divine judgment.

> We must still be clear upon one fact: we have no choice as to whether or not *we* will take up the ethical problem, as to whether we will accept or reject the crisis that accompanies all our choices, or as to whether we will approve or disregard our underlying relationship with God. The ethical problem does not wait upon any ethical theorizing we may indulge in, nor the crisis upon our becoming critical—nor our relationship to God upon our so-called religious experiences.[81]

Humanity's relationship with God is fundamental, *a priori*, and the responsibility that this entails is determinative of that relationship. There is an "ought to" that exists for human existence and action in relationship to God's own person and work. But for people autonomous faithful responsibility is an impossibility, and so, the "problem of ethics (which is really the outworking of the divine-human relationship) is not only the

---

79. Ibid., 151. For an insightful discussion of the importance of "dialectic" in Barth's thought, which remains an important feature throughout the entirety of his career, see Clough, *Ethics in Crisis*.

80. Barth, "The Problem of Ethics Today," 151.

81. Ibid., 140–41.

sickness of man but is a sickness unto *death*."[82] Barth is not explicit in this article as to whether this sickness unto death is the result of a fall from a type of original faithfulness, or, rather, the fall is the cumulative effect of all human being and doing, which is simply incapable of answering the ethical question. Either way, Barth *is* explicit that humanity does not exist in autonomous freedom.

> Although in a real sense we may have an *idea* of this freedom, we have not the slightest *knowledge* of it, for we know no motive in our own wills or any imaginable will which could seriously be thought of as free or making for freedom.... The only man we can *know* is one who proves by his desires that he is not a personality grounded in the world of freedom.... Does not the good person represent the annulment of all predicates which man, as we know him, can possess? Is not *his* conduct a negation of all *real* action in history?... What can its ultimate presupposition be but a recognition of the *bondage* which prevents the human will from achieving the good—the *servum arbitrium*?[83]

Simply stated no person can even begin to fulfil the eternal good that is required of him. "He can only continue to recognize that he is wholly incapable of commanding an answer."[84] His only possible love is *Eros*, and the only possible righteousness is *"justitia civilis."* Barth consistently emphasises that "there is nothing in the whole range of human possibilities, from popular indifference to mystical absorption in the All, which is capable of realizing the moral objective, the goal of all history."[85] Humanity is completely incapable of fulfilling what is required of them. This is a sign of the "impassable frontier of death, the unbridgeable chasm before which we are called to a halt, [it] is the boundary that separates and must separate God from the world, Creator from creation, the Holy One from sinners."[86] It is at this point, however—where independent human freedom is recognized as powerless—that real freedom may begin.

> But this insight, this all-inclusive critical negation under which we and our world exist ... is the narrow way and the strait gate that lead to truth, to the real, to the redeeming answer. The first demand is that we stand firm to the negative insight, face it

82. Ibid., 150.
83. Ibid., 155–56.
84. Ibid., 166.
85. Ibid.
86. Ibid., 168.

squarely, and avoid it, *not* by . . . giving ourselves any illusion . . . as to our own ability to escape. . . . It is through the unescapable severity of this doom that we come upon the reality of God. . . . The meaning of our situation is that God does not leave us and that we cannot leave God. It is because God *himself* and God *alone* lends our life its possibility that it becomes possible for us to live. . . . *Through* our doom we see therefore what is beyond our doom, God's love; *through* our awareness of sin, forgiveness; *through* death and the end of all things, the beginning of a new and primary life.[87]

This new and primary life, the life in which humanity is completely shaped by this "annihilating crisis", means participation in the promises of God. In the judgment of God, humanity finds the freedom of God, his mercy, grace, and the giving of new life in Jesus Christ. "The meaning of our situation is that God does not leave us and that we cannot leave God."[88] In this paradox, whereby the No of God is also his Yes, the impossibility of human faithfulness becomes possible. It is "God *himself* and God *alone*" that "lends our life its possibility."[89] The "new creation of man, the renewal of the unrenewable old man" in the eschatological reality of Jesus Christ is his sanctification.[90] Sanctification is freedom for faithful human participation in the divine-human relationship. "Since there is such a thing as forgiveness . . . (t)here is an *obedience unto salvation*. . . . In brief, there is such a thing as the *possibility*—and possibility here means *necessity*—of saying Yes to both the ethical question and to its *answers*—and in a way not sicklied o'er with doubt and pessimism."[91] This freedom offers people the possibility, which in relationship to God and the ethical question is not an option but a demand, of responding faithfully to the ethical question. Human freedom and obedience become certain because of, and only in, salvation; and "salvation is certain because the new man is present from above, bringing the new heaven and the new earth, the kingdom of God."[92] The new man is Jesus Christ, and the way of freedom is from God to humanity.

87. Ibid., 167–69.
88. Ibid., 169.
89. Ibid.
90. Ibid., 170.
91. Ibid., 173.
92. Ibid., 180.

In response to the notion that sanctification was merely the continuation of the human will set back on track, or even the idea of human cooperation in establishing one's righteousness, found within modern theology, Barth refocused his attention on the *way* in which it is accomplished, or more specifically with *whom* it is properly concerned. Barth began to articulate that sanctification, just like the Reformation understanding of justification, is distinctly and primarily God's work. "The only way between God and man is that which leads *from* God *to* man." Barth's unwavering dedication to this reality had nothing to do with a latent hostility to all things human though.

While sanctification is importantly and distinctly God's work it is not God's work alone. Even though "man's will is and remains unfree," because, "he lives and will live to the end of his days under the annihilating effect of the fall," God's will is *not* bound to deal out only death and judgment.[93] This is the point where Barth continually sought to make the corrective to modern theology's understanding of sanctification. Human freedom in and of itself will always remain bound in sin and unrighteousness, but in God's freedom, through the eschatological power of the resurrection, a person is not only forgiven, but set free from the burden of fulfilling the divine will under his own power. Jesus Christ frees people from upholding the eternal demands in their own strength. In this very rich eschatological reality, humanity is liberated to *participate* as witness and reflection of God's own holiness and faithfulness within the world. This freedom arises both because of, and in spite of, humanity's own inability to respond faithfully; it is found only in correlation with the freedom of God. For, once again, human righteousness is grounded in, and vividly portrayed in God's own righteousness. Barth's emphasis on human freedom in sanctification was one of the key theological components for upholding and describing the divine-human relationship in which the gospel "is *not* the crowning keystone in the arch of *our* thinking," but the power that affirmed both God's love and redemption of humanity and the faithful human response.

Implications

Building upon the notion that renewed human existence and action occurs in the encounter between God and humanity, thus freeing humans

---

93. Ibid.

to respond faithfully, Barth began to flesh out what Christian life in fellowship with God looks like concretely. The idea that sanctification is essentially freedom enabled him to speak not only of *possibility*, but also of *necessity*. Freedom in Christ not only allows for faithful human obedience, it demands it. In other words, the objective includes, surrounds, and even requires the subjective. This is extremely significant for Barth's understanding of the doctrine of sanctification, for two reasons.

First, this language of freedom and obedience shows that Barth recognized that sanctification brought about a definite change in human life and living. Although he was quite clear in emphasizing that the "old man" of sin still exists on this side of death, and that he "will live to the end of his days under the annihilating effect of the fall," nevertheless Barth also joyfully spoke of a new creation.[94] The new creation, or "new man", is the invisible reality of the resurrected Jesus Christ who transcends time, giving both the knowledge and power to live triumphantly. It is a transhistorical, or spiritual, reality and so there exists a paradox whereby the "old man" of sin exists, but is defeated, and the "new man" of righteousness is not seen *per se,* but is determinative of his existence. There is, no doubt, a great tension here between what is experienced and what Barth calls the impossible possibility. But the freedom that comes with sanctification is the freedom *from* human possibility and the freedom *to receive* from God what seems contradictory.

Secondly, Barth's portrayal of the objective and subjective demonstrates that he truly was concerned with the bond between God and human beings, that he was genuinely taken up with the question of human existence and action in a most positive way. While Barth surely did emphasise what happened *to* individuals as they encountered God—the objective, he was even more concerned to demonstrate the fact that something was indeed happening between God and human beings—both the objective and subjective. The heart of what Barth was after was not mere monism, but precisely the reality of the divine-human relationship in its fullness.

Summary

In 1916, Barth began to argue that, because human righteousness had been taken as the righteousness of God, humanity would inevitably be

---

94. Ibid.

self-deluded; the intense focus on self-piety effectively silenced the proclamation of the righteousness of God and any true good in relationship to human existence and action. Concerning Christian life in fellowship with God, Barth argued that when human righteousness is mistaken for God's righteousness, things that might have become good within human life are destroyed. This is precisely what Barth saw happening in modern theology, and he highlighted it throughout his career.

Modern theology had exchanged talk of God for talk of human beings, confusing the original with the derivative. Theological language became entirely anthropocentric; and one result in particular was that the doctrine of sanctification was reduced to discussions of psychological development and cultural advancement. As Barth responded to these ideas, his own thoughts began to converge around the notion that something *real happens*, indeed "the only real thing which can happen," when God takes up His work. God acts and humans receive; they are summoned to faithful obedience. Renewed human existence and action is not, therefore, simply a divinely "corrected continuation" of our own will, a positive human spirit set back on the right path. It is the "re-creation and re-growth" found in the encounter between the Holy God and the unrighteous human. It is divine affirmation of righteous human existence and action within God's own self-righteousness. By focusing on the distinction between God and humanity, Barth's understanding of the doctrine of sanctification would gain a unique sense of objectivity.

As Barth continued to revise and rebuild Protestant theology, he gave increasing expression to the objective reality *of Jesus Christ and his eschatological power*. This idea is extremely significant for Barth's understanding of the doctrine of sanctification, because it becomes the basis for all of his talk of renewed human existence and action. In the 1919 lecture "The Christian's Place in Society," Barth expounded the idea that it is Jesus Christ and the movement of God that substantiate and relativize all other reality. The power of the gospel is demonstrated in the Christian life as God's love and redemption of people affirms their righteousness in the *futurum resurrectionis*. In spite of everything that seems to point to the contrary, human beings are given the promise of, and power for, living the future life of the resurrection here and now. Barth's eschatological characterization of reality allowed him to maintain the distinction between the divine and human, yet truly affirm what he called sanctified human existence and action.

In Barth's view, a proper understanding of the divine-human relationship has overwhelming implications for the human moral agent. In exploring the realm of the ethical, Barth focused on the huge impact of the divine-human encounter in the concrete living of individuals. In the 1922 lecture "The Problem of Ethics Today," Barth showed how God's righteousness actually frees man from the latter's unrighteousness. The objective aspect of the divine-human relationship, which occurs in the eschatological power of Jesus Christ, liberates people from the burden of doing what they cannot do—sanctify themselves. Moreover, the objective reality of Jesus Christ not only frees people *from* the bondage of sinfulness and unrighteousness, it also frees them *for* faithful obedience.

In his introduction to Barth's early work, T. F. Torrance comments: "From first to last Barth's main theme has been the turning of God in utter grace in incredible condescension to man to be man's God, so that what we are concerned with in the Gospel is the sovereign togetherness of God with man and the exaltation of man to share in the divine life and love."[95] From the earliest days of his ministry and theological service, Barth was drawn towards this understanding of the divine-human relationship and its implications in this world. Despite the frequent—and negative—portrayal of Barth as a completely theocentric thinker, particularly in his earlier works, it should not come as a shock to see the fundamental concepts of the doctrine of sanctification dealt with so often in many of Barth's earliest works. Perhaps one might even say that it was precisely because of his strong theocentric thinking that he was so concerned with rightly expounding the reality of renewed human existence and action. For Barth articulated the content of the Christian life in fellowship with God by disabling false constructions of human self-righteousness, and emphasizing human righteousness as grounded, and vividly portrayed, in *God's* own righteousness. In this way sanctification became one of the key theological components in Barth's description of the unique relationship between God and humanity.

For Barth, the period from 1916 through 1922 was a time of theological revolution and re-examination of everything important to him. As he began the process of ground- clearing and rebuilding, his depiction of renewed human existence and action demonstrated Barth's deep theological commitment to rightly expressing the reality of the divine-human relationship, in which the gospel message was seen as *the* power

---

95. Torrance, *Barth*, 23.

that affirmed both God's love for and redemption of humanity, and the christian's faithful life response, in a way perhaps more potent than any other concept in his work.

2

The Calvin Lectures

Introduction and Significance of Text

BARTH'S RETHINKING OF THE Christian faith was founded upon intense wrestling with Scripture, particularly as articulated in his 1919 commentary on Romans, which garnered him quite a reputation in Switzerland and Germany. It was not long before he started receiving invitations for new employment; and in 1921, he accepted the position of Professor of Reformed Theology in Göttingen. Thus began a new portion of his life, one that set him upon a course of rigorous theological clarification and joyful service to the world beyond the hills of Aargau.

In the summer of 1922, after Barth's second semester at his new post, he began his third lecture cycle with *The Theology of John Calvin*, following courses on the *Exposition of the Heidelberg Catechism* and an *Exposition of Ephesians*. For Barth these first few years of lecturing evoked a very strong sense of passion, partly because of his drive to familiarize himself with Reformed doctrine—"no one will be surprised to hear that at first I found it a novel experience to be addressed . . . as a Reformed theologian"[1]—but also because, as he worked through material such as Calvin's theology, and Protestant thought in general, he became thoroughly captivated by it and surprisingly aware of many points of agreement with his own thought. In a letter to Thurneysen, written during the summer of the Calvin Lectures, Barth confesses that

> the little bit of 'Reformed theology' that I teach is really nothing in comparison to the trumpet blast which needs to be blown in our sick time. . . . Calvin is a cataract, a primeval forest, a demonic power, something directly down from the Himalaya. . . .

1. Busch, *Barth*, 123.

I lack completely the means, the suction cups, even to assimilate this phenomenon, not to speak of presenting it adequately.... I could gladly and profitably set myself down and spend the rest of my life just with Calvin.[2]

One can sense in this quote, Barth's complete enthusiasm and eagerness for his task as Professor of Reformed Theology, as well as the force of his encounter with the thoughts and ideas of John Calvin.

Since his arrival in Göttingen, Barth was continually working at breakneck speed. He was often "burning the midnight oil" not only to familiarize himself with "the mysteries of specifically Reformed theology," but often simply to produce the next morning's lecture.[3] He often lamented that the Calvin Lectures were giving him trouble; towards the end of the semester he sighed that the lectures were "not anywhere near finished" and "have turned into 'a fair *monstrosity*: biography, theology, history of the time, illumination *sub specie aeternitatis*.'"[4] For all of Barth's apprehensions and misgivings about the shape of this course, it becomes apparent upon reading the lectures that they not only offer a perceptive exposition of the historical landscape and theological situation of the magisterial Reformers, but they also provide excellent insights into Barth's own theological concepts at this point in his career. The Calvin Lectures provide a valuable resource for examining certain aspects of the issues surrounding Barth's doctrine of sanctification, which help to form the structure he builds upon.

The lecture is divided into two main parts. Part 1 takes up the basic presuppositions revolving around the life and theology of Calvin. Within this part, there are two subsections: one dealing with the connection, contrast, and common features between the Reformation and the Middle Ages, the second comparing and contrasting Calvin, Luther, and Zwingli. Part 2 is devoted to the life and theology of Calvin, but is peppered throughout with further comparisons with the other two Reformers. Within this part, there are three major subsections, each of which takes up Calvin's thought and theology within the framework of a detailed biography of his life and early works. What is of greater interest

---

2. Barth, *Karl Barth-Eduard Thurneysen Briefwechsel*, 2:80. Not to completely overstate his infatuation with Calvin, Barth also admitted in the same letter that the situation is typical for him at each point in history.

3. Busch, *Barth*, 129.

4. Barth, *Karl Barth-Eduard Thurneysen Briefwechsel*, 2:86. The original manuscript was handwritten on both sides of 235 pages!

than the mere structure of these lectures, though, is the focus of Barth's analysis of Calvin.

From the beginning, Barth is captivated by the Reformation insight, which finds its clearest expression in Calvin, of what it means to say that theology is about *God*. "The secret was simply this, that it [the Reformation] took this theme seriously in all its distinctiveness, that it names God God, that it lets God be God, the one object that by no bold human grasping or inquiry or approach can be simply one object among many others. God *is*."[5] But in saying afresh that God "is the point of the whole enterprise," the Reformers were also able to be remarkably clear about the possibility of genuine human righteousness and work, of the importance of not only justification, but sanctification as well. To speak about true human existence and action, one must speak about God, but in speaking about God, one will, or rather must, also speak about the human. Barth excitedly remarked that this emphasis on God alone is no preaching of despair; the theology of the cross is a theology of hope! "Who is the God hidden in the passion with his strange work, and what does he desire? . . . The gap in the horizontal line, the disaster of our own striving, is the point at which God's vertical line intersects our lives, where God wills to be gracious. Here where our finitude is recognized is true contact with infinity."[6] Here, where God is God, sinners *are* righteous and the dead *do* live. Here sinners are justified *and* sanctified. It is this theme—that the person and work of God truly impact the life of man—that fascinated Barth and that stands out in the Calvin Lectures.

As John Webster rightly notes of these lectures, "there is something permanently significant here. The lectures constitute very early testimony to Barth's lifelong conviction that theology in the Reformed tradition is concerned with dogmatics *and* ethics, divine *and* human action."[7] Much of what Barth had only been able to hint at in previous years, or had only intuitively laid the groundwork for, would now begin to take on a more explicit form. Moreover, within these early lectures, Barth became increasingly clear about *his own* connection with the Reformers.

This chapter is essentially an elaboration of that notion. As Barth became more fluent within the thoughts of Calvin and the other Reformers, it became increasingly clear to him that he had in fact found

---

5. Barth, *The Theology of John Calvin*, 39.
6. Ibid., 46.
7. Webster, *Barth*, 34.

a baseline within Reformed theology from which he could confidently work. Overall, therefore, this chapter is concerned with the impact of Calvin's Reformed theology upon Barth's doctrine of sanctification—specifically Calvin's use of doctrine to positively articulate the divine-human relationship. The first section investigates the general importance of Calvin and the Reformers for the way Barth articulates his doctrine of sanctification. The rest of the chapter builds upon those connections by examining the implications and relationships of *faith and obedience*, *time and eternity*, and of *the danger of moralism* as they emerge in Barth's work.

Turn to the Reformed Tradition

> Only now were my eyes properly open to the Reformers and their message of the justification and the sanctification of the sinner, of faith, of repentance and works, of the nature and the limits of the church, and so on. I had a great many things to learn from them.[8]

In Göttingen, Barth found himself overwhelmed with the task of teaching Reformed theology, mostly because he was unfamiliar with it. In a characteristic moment, he reflected that "at the time I didn't even have a copy of the Reformed confessions, and I certainly hadn't read them."[9] This is not to say, however, that the Reformers were completely foreign to him. Barth had studied Luther and Calvin in Safenwil. "But," he says, "because I did so through the lenses of spectacles to which I had become accustomed over my years of study, that was not the time and place when I first sought and . . . found access to them."[10] As an assistant pastor just out of school, Barth had even had the opportunity to preach in Calvin's pulpit in Geneva, an experience about which he wryly remarked that "Calvin would hardly have been very pleased at the sermons which I preached in his pulpit."[11] But now in Göttingen Barth found in the Reformers a wellspring of thought with which to interact and struggle. His task as professor allowed him to utilize his time studying these men afresh, not only in preparation for weekly lectures, but also as a means for theological reflection upon his own foundations. Barth began to feel as if his previous

8. Busch, *Barth*, 143.
9. Ibid., 129.
10. Ibid., 143.
11. Ibid., 53–54.

views existed "somehow in a corner, along with nominalism, Augustinianism, mysticism, Wycliffe, etc.," that they were indeed not "the Reformation, but nevertheless the Reformation later sprang out of" them.[12] There may be many reasons why Barth felt that his previous views belonged to a region of theological thought not quite fully developed. The important point is that Barth now felt that his eyes were opened to the Reformers in a way that forcefully brought home their message about the justification *and* sanctification of the sinner, of faith, of repentance *and* works.

To Barth, it seemed as if his own voice of reformation, although still finding its way and working itself out, had stumbled upon a resource that could provide him with the means to express his own message more fully. What Barth found in the Reformation, in relationship to the doctrine of sanctification, was a truth akin to what he had himself been trying to articulate for many years: that to speak truly of human existence and holiness, one must begin by speaking of God's own holiness and work. What Barth found in the Reformation was a return to the *original*, a beginning again. Regardless of the traces of both medieval and modern thought that Barth found in Reformation thinking, the latter was also something completely new. Speaking of Luther in a lecture one year after the Calvin Lectures, Barth reaffirmed what he took to be the basic insight of the Reformation:

> Like a bolt of lightning, this original intuition strikes between the ages as something that neither the old nor the new man . . . [could] grasp: the sinful person made just before God through grace in faith. Neither the earlier typical medieval nor the later typical modern had counted on the immediate actuality of God's relationship with humanity, although there are certainly lines leading both backward and forward from this knowledge. Both sides begin with the human person, with nature, with reason in its best sense and build further on this safe and broad foundation, with the help of revelation. . . . The Reformation . . . does not begin with human interests . . . in God; rather it begins with God's interest in the human person.[13]

This insight, that theological language, though it importantly entails language about humanity, must begin with God, had been the simple foundation upon which Barth had continually attempted to begin again. Now, in Göttingen, as he gained access to the Reformers in a new and

---

12. Ibid., 143.
13. Barth, *The Theology of the "Reformed Confessions,"* 207–8.

fresh way, the faithfulness of their message inspired in him a life-long solidarity with them. At the beginning of the Calvin Lectures in 1922, Barth told his class: "If it is of concern to us as Protestant theologians to be clear where we come from and where we are going as such, then we have every reason to turn again and again to the question of how far what we are and think and say does truly . . . correspond to what the founders of Protestant theology were and to what they thought and said about God and the world and humanity."[14]

Over the course of those few years in Göttingen, as Barth turned to question how far his own thought truly corresponded with Protestant thought, he discovered that his theology was specifically Reformed in nature.

In the Reformed tradition growing out of Geneva, Barth found, over and against Lutheranism, what he perceived as the mature outworking of what beginning with God's interest in the human person means, the full radical nature of the horizontal line of human life being intersected by the divine vertical.[15]

> As we read, there seem to hover before our eyes reminders that call everything into question, the reminders that good works have value only for Christ's sake, and when done in faith. This is no real dishonour to Luther. The dialectic with which he made play so brilliantly is the dialectic of the matter itself. . . . But however that may be, it is a historical fact that Luther's heart concern was with the basis of works and not the will for them, with fighting *against* papist works and not for fighting *for* works of the Spirit and love. . . . To see what it looks like when a theologian really stresses and unites both parts, when the fight *for* works of the Spirit is also self-evident and a heart's concern, we may turn in comparison to the beginning of Calvin's Geneva Catechism. In the closest connection we find here the question of the chief end of human life and the knowledge of God as this end. For God created us and put us in the world in order to be glorified by us. Since he is the origin of life, it is right that we should place this life in the service of his glory.[16]

---

14. Barth, *Calvin*, 13–14.

15. Although Barth critically aligns himself with Reformed theology, he does not simply discard Lutheran thought. Barth is quite complimentary specifically of Luther's work and in these lectures often cites the latter's theological instincts as healthy correctives to the at times wayward notions of Reformed ethics.

16. Barth, *Calvin*, 76.

Luther's remarkable insight of the theology of the cross is completed in Calvin's emphasis on the impact of this insight on human life and work. Barth saw in Calvin a vivid portrayal of his own basic thought that the problem of dogmatics is also the problem of ethics, that as God draws near one must speak of faith *and* obedience, justification *and* sanctification. True knowledge of God is found when "we come to an awareness of the honour we owe him."[17] And, as Barth states, this inextricable link between the divine vertical and the human horizontal means that "nothing worse can happen to us than not living our lives for God."[18] With these concerns and many others in mind, we see in Barth a very strong and committed turn to the Reformed tradition, which directly affects his doctrine of sanctification.

It must also be noted that Barth was by no means uncritical of Reformed theology. His commitment to Reformed theology and its principles was first and foremost a commitment to the Word of God; he was not interested in simple reiteration. As Paul Metzger affirms, Barth's interaction with Reformed theology was certainly constructive, but it was in no way conservative.[19] Barth articulated two main reasons for moving beyond simple repetition. First, he did not think that returning to Reformed principles meant returning to a pre-modern way of thinking; he did not believe that one could simply go behind or merely skip over the parts of history and theology that one did not agree with. Barth recognized that he was a child of his age and that his entire worldview was shaped to some degree by his culture and heritage, including enlightenment and romantic influences. This is nowhere more evident than in Barth's lifelong engagement with Schleiermacher. In the foreword to his lectures on Schleiermacher in the winter of 1923, Barth warned his students that "we *study* Paul and the Reformers, but we *see* with the eyes of Schleiermacher and think along the same lines as he did. This is true even when we criticize or reject the most important of his *theologoumena* or even all of them."[20] Though Barth consistently fought against what he perceived to be the wayward offspring of Schleiermacher's thought, he was always cognizant of the impact that Schleiermacher had even upon his own thought and theology.

---

17. Ibid., 77.
18. Ibid., 76.
19. Metzger, *The Word of Christ and the World of Culture*, 42.
20. Barth, *The Theology of Schleiermacher*, xiii.

Second, true learning involves dialogue, not duplication. Barth explained to his students in the Calvin Lectures that, "we do not have teaching by repeating Calvin's words as our own or making his views ours. . . . Those who simply echo Calvin are not good Calvinists, that is, they are not really taught by Calvin. Being taught by Calvin means entering into dialogue with him, with Calvin as the teacher and ourselves as the students . . . and then—this is the crux of the matter—making our own response to what he says."[21]

Barth was ever the student of those who had gone before him, wrestling and struggling not simply to repeat, but to learn and speak boldly.[22] Barth's renewed encounter with Reformed theology proved a valuable source and sounding board for his own theology; this encounter had a direct impact on his expression of the doctrine of sanctification.

Faith and Obedience

> The Middle Ages died with Luther's discovery, but their problem, the problem of the active life, of ethics in the broadest sense, did not die with them. Nor can it be put to death. . . . Here, however, in the matter of establishing the positive relation between the vertical and horizontal lines—the cross has to be left open in Luther—we find the point at which the second turn in the Reformation, the Reformed theology of Zwingli and Calvin, had to enter and did in fact do so.[23]

Among the many ways that Barth's acceptance of Reformed theology affected his own work, one of the most important was his use of the doctrines of faith and obedience. One can see that even while Barth was for the most part simply analyzing and interpreting Calvin's work in his lectures, he was also laying the foundations for his own first full-scale dogmatics, which would be formally worked out two years later. Not surprisingly Barth's focus within the Calvin Lectures foreshadows much of his own forthcoming work. Within these Calvin Lectures one can see the way in which Barth favourably elucidates the doctrines he calls

21. Barth, *Calvin*, 4.

22. This is nowhere more provocative and powerful than in Barth's reshaping of the Reformed doctrines of election and double predestination even in this Göttingen period.

23. Barth, *Calvin*, 49.

"distinctive," "natural," and "original" in the second turn of the Reformation, and underlines their importance in relation to the grace of God and human existence and action, i.e., sanctification. The doctrines of faith and obedience find themselves virtually surrounded by and engulfed in Calvin's doctrines of justification and sanctification. Therefore, the way Barth responds to Calvin's doctrines of faith and obedience will heavily influence the parameters and distinctions he requires for his own doctrine of sanctification.

The individual conceptions of obedience and faith are not uncommon in Barth's earlier works; a simple skim through either of his Romans commentaries is convincing enough.[24] The difference found emerging in Göttingen, however, in comparison to earlier works, is the necessary and formal place now given to these doctrines—the *positive* relation of the vertical to the horizontal. This is in no way meant to indicate that Barth's previous focus lacked an important concern for faithful human existence and action. What it does indicate is that Barth's concern for faithful human existence action in relationship to the action of God was finding a more coherent form of expression. "What the Calvin lecture cycle enabled Barth to develop," writes John Webster, "was at least the beginning of a theological ethics in which human action would not simply be rather precariously incorporated within a dominant eschatological structure, but seen to be *doctrinally* important, though in a way fundamentally at variance from liberal Protestant dogmatics."[25] In previous works, Barth had largely been responding on some level to the ideas in modern theology, and even to forms of pietism, which begin with human action as a natural form of religious expression. Barth believed that, for them, what they called sanctification was an entirely anthropological matter, although perhaps discussed within the framework of an account of divine grace. In attempting to override this trend in contemporary theology, Barth's initial battle cry revolved more around the *Krisis* in which faith and obedience could exist; and so while there is plenty of discussion of faith and obedience scattered throughout these pre-Göttingen works,

---

24. See for example *Romans* I:3, 21–26; Die Offenbarung; 5. Kapitel: Der Tag; 6, 15–23 Ostern; 7. Kapitel: Die Freiheit; 14. u. 15. Kapitel Die Bewegung (*Der Römerbrief* (1919), first edition, Barth: Gesamtausgabe. Abt. 2: Akademische Werke 1919.; and also *Romans* II:III. 27–30. By Faith Only; III.31–IV.8. Faith is Miracle; IV.9–12. Faith is Beginning; IV.13–17a. Faith is Creation; VI.12–23. The Power of Obedience; XII.I, 2. The Problem of Ethics. (*The Epistle to the Romans*, 2nd ed.)

25. Webster, *Barth's Moral Theology*, 34.

at times they come across as slightly more vague and less descriptive than seen even here in these initial Calvin lectures. However, as Barth became increasingly more consistent and comfortable in positively describing the actuality of human faith and obedience, his doctrine of sanctification also became more distinct and nuanced.

> [We] turn to the horizontal line of human thought and action in time that is so sharply broken by the vertical line of the knowledge of God in Christ. The problem of human life and striving as the Middle Ages unbrokenly pursued it cannot be simply cut off by being put under the shadow of its finitude, that is, in the light of its origin. What does the attack of the vertical mean for what takes place horizontally? What becomes of all that we will and work here below on the line of death? What becomes of all this when we confront the absolute beyond that meets the present world in a way that crushes it but is also full of promise, when we arrive at the sharp edges of despair, humility, and fear of God which, as we saw yesterday, still have their positive side, when we face God the Judge who all the same is none other than the merciful God?[26]

The doctrines of faith and obedience revolve around the knowledge of God and the human hearer; they concern the human "perception and reception"[27] of God's Word—the subjective side of revelation. As Barth poses the question here, "What does the attack of the vertical mean for what takes place horizontally?" The Reformed tradition states that in its essence, knowledge of God (the vertical) is not simply a particular message about God—the gospel message of the forgiveness of sins, for example—but is an encounter with God himself, his will and his glory. "And if because truly God, then God in his Word, God as the authority over all human conceits, obedience not caprice!"[28] As Barth repeatedly points out in these lectures, for Calvin knowledge of God is more than a faith "which is pure and fixed on God alone"[29]; knowledge of God is an encounter with God and therefore requires faith *and* action. In Barth's words: "For [Calvin] faith means putting one's hand to the plough and not looking back (Luke 9:62)."[30] Calvin consistently asserts that knowl-

26. Barth, *Calvin*, 49.
27. Barth, *The Göttingen Dogmatics, Vol. I*, 191.
28. Barth, *Calvin*, 150.
29. Ibid., 77.
30. Ibid., 151.

edge of God means that faith must be lived, because knowledge of God entails faith and obedience, forgiveness of sins and faithful living—not one over against the other, but both in unity and distinction.

> [Calvin] is the man who, appropriating the knowledge of the God of judgment and mercy, at once feels the need to express and confirm this knowledge as wakeful expectation, as will and action; who at once fears the very worst, the loss of this knowledge, if there is a pause, a religious siesta, between . . . justification and sanctification, between faith and life. The peace of the conscience that is comforted by forgiveness is the peace of the living and not for a single second anything else.[31]

What Barth sees in Calvin, as this quote illustrates, is a positive way in which the knowledge of God—the infinite— can be related to human life even in the midst of the shadow of its finitude, by focusing on the light of its origin. The question about what becomes of human willing and action must be asked not in spite of "the sharp edges of despair," but precisely because of them. According to Calvin, the vertical line of the knowledge of God breaking into human existence does not entail simple faith in mercy, nor annihilation in judgment; rather it demands faith and *obedience*—Christian trust and Christian living simultaneously. God's one Word to humanity *is* Jesus Christ, and, therefore, is both mercy and judgment—justification and sanctification. In light of this, talk about faithful human action and living in relationship to knowledge of God cannot simply fall away but is as necessary as faith in that knowledge. The preacher's and theologian's message need not be one of hopelessness and quietism precisely because, as Barth interpreted Calvin, the absolute beyond that meets the present world, even though in a way that crushes it, is also full of promise. The sharp edges of despair, humility, and fear of God still have their positive side, because God the judge is none other than the merciful God. What this implies for Barth's doctrine of sanctification is that dogmatically it will occupy an equally as important place within his conception of the divine-human relationship as the doctrines of justification and faith.

With those insights in mind, it seems as if Barth's doctrine of sanctification could become the expression of an extremely tangible occurrence, possibly filled with programs and even "a system of directions."

---

31. Ibid., 153.

However, at this crucial point, as Barth examines Calvin's emphasis on faith and obedience in his 1536 *Institutes,* we find an important twist:

> Finally, we have to remember how much the predisposition and thrust of Calvin's whole theology lead us to expect that he would have to give a plain, down-to-earth statement here. Did he not attempt a synthesis of divine and human knowledge? Did he not aim to supplement the Lutheran systole with the Reformed diastole? Did he not insist firmly on justification by faith and yet as an ethicist keep both feet solidly on the ground and thus seek to apply the Reformation insight (as a crisis) to the horizontal problem of the Middle Ages and our own time? Why, then . . . are there not at least precise and unambiguous indications of Calvin's view of the way in which Christians should approach the problem of society? Why does he not at any rate pacify us with an attempt to derive from the gospel a way of fashioning life and the world that is in keeping with the gospel, and thus lead us to the goal to which with some impatience we want to be led when someone undertakes to give us instruction in the Christian religion? Is it not the age-long weakness of theology and theologians that the moment we expect them finally to redeem the promise they have long since given and say to us: "Do this and do not do that for such and such reasons," they leave us in the lurch again on fresh dialectical pretexts?... I myself would, of course, say that it is the venture of Reformation and Protestant theology, which distinguishes it from medieval and modern theologies, that it neither can nor will do anything but leave us in this predicament, or, rather, make it fully plain to us that the final word: "Do this and do not do that," must of course, be spoken . . . but that it can be spoken only by God himself as his own Word.[32]

Barth asks in rhetorical surprise how, after all that has gone before this, Calvin can fail to offer a thoroughly robust Christian agenda for life and society. Calvin's distinct contribution to the Reformation was his dual emphasis on faith and obedience. Now, at the moment when one would expect to see this worked out in sequence as a large-scale production, or at least the possibility of doing something pleasing before God—the synthesis of heaven and earth, so to speak—there is nothing except antithesis—the "age-long weakness of theology and theologians," bared to the dread of his readers. Barth describes how instead of marching forward

---

32. Ibid., 204–5.

in triumphant Christian victory, Calvin simply points back to the cross. And yet this is, he explains, the very foundation and essence of faithful human action and living.

> Calvin felt this antithesis, or at least expressed and emphasized it, much more sharply than Luther, and he thus worked out much more sharply . . . the thesis that God is our God, the God of real people living in the real world, that there can be no fleeing from his presence to another world . . . that precisely in *this* world we stand under the *command* of God. Yet under the command of *God*.[33]

To say, "Do this and do not do that" must be spoken because Christian faith demands Christian living. Because there is justification of the sinner by God there is also sanctification, which entails something meaningful and specific.

> Human willing and striving, even when obedient to God, and especially then, has to have specific content. We cannot obey God without willing and seeking something, this or that. But what we human individuals will and strive after, even though it be ever so important and significant, even though it be a whole city of God, always stands as such under the shadow of the relativity of all things human. It neither can nor should become a theme in instruction in the Christian religion if it is not to have the force of a new enslaving of conscience.[34]

This is an extremely important feature that thoroughly reinforces one aspect that has already been at the core of Barth's previous conceptions of the doctrine of sanctification: all things human are relative and should never become themes in and of themselves. When that happens, one ceases to speak *theo*-logically. As Barth frequently described it, this is like attempting to paint a bird in flight. As Barth states it: "This instruction, if it is to remain pure and true, can provide only the basis for the *possibility* of what can and must happen on the human side in obedience to God; . . . it cannot provide a basis for the *reality*."[35] Barth's worry is the same as it has been for many years, that once *possibility* becomes the basis for *reality* faithful human existence and action turn into human possessions—natural capacities for the relating of all things divine and human.

33. Ibid., 205.
34. Ibid., 206–7.
35. Ibid., 207.

What Barth takes from Calvin here are the appropriate and necessary parameters to give shape to the doctrine of sanctification without turning it into a human possession. Sanctification can be discussed theologically only so far before it runs the risk of becoming nothing more than a psychological description of religion. Calvin's doctrines of faith and obedience demonstrated to Barth how he could speak naturally and clearly of the necessity of human action and obedience, and yet maintain the relativity of the human situation hedged in between the knowledge of God and one's own finitude. Or, to use Barth's often repeated illustration: "Pilgrim man stands between Scylla and Charybdis, between two truths that make each other, and man as a third thing between them, impossible." To speak as a Reformed theologian is to tread this narrow path without synchronization.

Two further important conclusions can be drawn from the insights gained by Barth from Calvin's doctrines of faith and obedience. First, because Barth is convinced that the doctrines of faith *and* obedience are critical to the subjective description of the knowledge of God, and are therefore to be maintained in unity and distinction, his doctrine of sanctification will be unapologetically Reformed in nature. The result is that it will critically distinguish his account of sanctification from Lutheran, Roman Catholic, and modern conceptions. While similar at some levels, in fact Barth gleans as much from Luther as he does from Calvin, his description of sanctification will differ from Lutheran accounts in that it will emphasise the centrality and primacy of sanctification along with justification in the event of salvation, yet distinctly separate from it. Although Barth is careful to emphasise that Luther was no quietist, that he too struggled with issues of life and obedience, his point here is that for Luther these concerns were neither "natural" nor "intrinsic." "The whole relation between the vertical line and the horizontal, or rather the working out of this relation, was for him, strongly though he emphasised it, of secondary and not primary importance. . . . We also detect at this point a deficiency."[36] Because Barth views the subjective hearing of God's Word as faith *and* obedience, his account of sanctification will see the Christian life as one of action, if only the action of pointing back to the cross of Christ.

Barth's account will likewise be different from the Roman Catholic perspective in that the latter, along with the Lutherans, emphasise the unity of justification and sanctification over and against their distinction.

---

36. Ibid., 75.

But perhaps even more importantly, Catholic theology places sacramental reception above faith and obedience as the subjective appropriation of revelation, making the issues of justification and sanctification secondary to participation in the sacraments. For Barth, sacraments will indeed play a vital role in relationship to sanctification, but only as confirmation and not initiation. Justification and sanctification articulate the primary subjective encounter between God and man.

Finally, because Barth insists that faith and obedience are not natural human capacities, his view of sanctification, in opposition to the modern and pietistic grasping and possessing, will in every moment remain a work of grace. This means that he will not discuss sanctification as part of anthropology *per se*, but as an area of reconciliation instead.

The second conclusion is really a repetition of the last distinction between Barth and modern and pietistic theology. But it is also extremely important in a much broader aspect as well. Barth is ardently against any type of infused righteousness that would make obedience a kind of divine-human cooperation or synergism—a means of discussing a realm of ethical and spiritual autonomy. Barth's conviction is reinforced in these lectures by the Reformation insight that "Christ does not simply bring grace as a second thing, so that we can then go on without him, . . . but he is himself grace, the proper work of God . . . which threatens our works at their very root."[37] Christ is the proper work of God and, therefore, the proper work of faithful human action and obedience—sanctification. This is where the issues of possibility and possession enter in. They provide the boundaries for what *must* be said and what *cannot* be said without leaving the theological forum. For Barth, then, there will be an essential relationship between the continual working of the grace of God at every moment and human existence and action.

Time and Eternity

> His discoveries in Safenwil and his new appreciation of the Reformers were combined during this period to form a characteristic theology in which the earlier insights were given a different emphasis by having a new foundation, while at the same time Reformation theology was put in a distinctive light.[38]

---

37. Ibid., 47.
38. Busch, *Barth*, 143.

The relationship between time and eternity in Barth's theology, particularly in these early years, was both a rallying point for some (most notably Gogarten, Brunner, and Bultmann) and a source of criticism for others (especially many pastors such as W. Hützen and G. F. Nagel within the Pietistic circles).[39] The essence of the time-eternity relationship was a matter of the correct relation between God and humanity. In the second edition to his explosive Romans commentary, Barth wrote, "The Gospel is not a religious message to inform mankind of their divinity or to tell them how they may become divine. The Gospel message proclaims a God utterly distinct from men. Salvation comes to them from Him, because they are, as men, incapable of knowing Him, and because they have no right to claim anything from Him."[40] The unpacking of this relationship sparked the use of such well-known "Barthian" catch phrases as "infinite qualitative distinction," "*Krisis*-theology" and "dialectical."[41] For Barth's critics, his emphasis on the distinction between time and eternity and the antithesis between God and humanity made it difficult for them to believe that at best he afforded anything more than a formal place for human action in time, and at worst that human action is completely annihilated.[42]

The doctrine of sanctification is directly and inescapably linked to the relationship between time and eternity, because sanctification is the place where faithful human existence and action is taken up in light of God's person and work. The extent to which time and eternity interact will determine the extent to which one can, or must, speak of any continuity between God and humanity, and further, what that continuity might look like. It would be fair to say that Barth's theology, at least from the time of his "break" with liberalism, was thoroughly focused on rightly distinguishing between time and eternity even though his articulation of this relationship was more or less in transition.[43]

39. Robinson, ed., *The Beginnings of Dialectical Theology*; Busch, *Barth*, 154–61.

40. Barth, *The Epistle to the Romans*, 2nd ed., 28.

41. See *The Preface to the Second Edition* of Barth's Romans II for an example of his use of these words, 8, 10. Barth, *The Epistle to the Romans*, 2nd ed.

42. See Webster's "Life from the Third Dimension: Human Action in Barth's Early Ethics," in *Barth's Moral Theology*, 11–39.

43. Bruce McCormack's summary of Barth's thought on this topic from 1915 on helps us to see the centrality of the time-eternity issue amidst the varied expressions of it—even if the reality of its development may be less crisp than McCormack indicates. "What emerged," from 1915 on, "was a form of dialectical theology whose fundamental shape . . . preserved a tension between present realization and future fulfillment in

As H. W. Tribble points out, for Barth the dangerous and inappropriate mixing of the time-eternity relationship led to an "assumption that the relationship between man the sinful creature and God the Holy Creator is continuous, or can be made continuous, which means that man in some measure can cease to be man and become as God."[44] And so Barth, early on, attempting to faithfully preserve the doctrine of God on the one hand and guard the essence of true humanity on the other, went to great lengths to emphasise their distinction. Unfortunately, because of those distinctions Barth was often, perhaps unfairly, tagged as a purely negative theologian. It would be more appropriate in light of his task of reorienting modern theological thinking, of attempting to clear out the "centuries old swamp," to say that Barth's distinctions were a way of marking off the boundaries within which he could speak faithfully of God and, therefore, humanity. As Barth took up his teaching post in Göttingen his task shifted, or perhaps it would be better to say that he proceeded more thoroughly with his original task. While Barth continued to point out the boundaries of theological thought throughout his career, in Göttingen he began to orient himself towards filling in the positive content of his theology:

> All at once we were in the front rank. We had to take on responsibilities which we had not known about while we were simply in opposition. Suddenly we had been given an opportunity to say what we really thought in theology, and to show the church our real intention and ability. . . . It was not just a matter of building on and reinforcing positions which we had already taken up. We had only begun on a course which each one had to follow laboriously in his own sphere.[45]

Earlier insights were given a different emphasis by having a new foundation.

---

its conception of the Kingdom of God." However, "Barth's conception of the Kingdom was . . . altered in early 1920." It was now shaped by a "thoroughgoing eschatology which allowed for very little present realization." And once again Barth's expression of the time-eternity relationship developed further, so that in 1924 as he adopted an anhypostatic-enhypostatic Christology he was able "to conceptualize how revelation can be fully present *in* history without becoming a predicate *of* history" (McCormack, *Barth's Critically Realistic Dialectical Theology*, 21).

44. Tribble, "Doctrine of Sanctification," 10.

45. Busch, *Barth*, 126.

One can see that in the Calvin Lectures Barth was beginning to catch glimpses of how one might think through the antithesis of God and humanity—the relationship between time and eternity—consistently and positively with the help of doctrine.

> If we now turn to what Calvin thinks about Christ when speaking of him expressly, we see at once that we have here the seat and origin of these and all the other tensions and antitheses that characterize his theology. The first thing he has to say in 1536 is that Christ, one with the Father, assumed our flesh and thus concluded the covenant with us, drawing us very close to God, from whom our sins had greatly estranged us (I, 30). He has been made righteousness, sanctification, and redemption for us (1 Cor 1:30). . . . But always Christ is in reality both the one who justified us *without* us and the one who dwells and works and initiates *within* us as the giver of the new life in us. The two can never be separated. . . . Always in Christ we are those who are afar off, sinners, poor, ungodly, referred only to grace. Yet in Christ we are always close, God's children, hoping and already attaining, inseparably related to God.[46]

Barth pored over Calvin's description of the divine-human relationship, and in doing so he discovered that Calvin was able to address the divine-human relationship in wonderfully warm language while maintaining the complete distinction between them. The person of Christ becomes the link or correspondence, which drives the divine-human relationship. Christ, who is one with the Father, has assumed human flesh, thus reuniting sinful humanity with holy God, so that in Christ the distance between time and eternity is overcome. Through participation in Christ, those on earth in time are joined together with the Father in heaven in such a way that they are "inseparably related."[47] The point to be made here is that in these lectures Barth began to see how the use of doctrine was a substantially better way of handling the time–eternity relationship than his previous strictly dialectical conceptions had been.

> Synthesis is something original and creative. It precedes all detailed discussion. It is not itself discussion but the subject in every discussion. It is an ability and desire to see antithesis together, no matter whether we are thinking of spirit and nature, the inward and outward, eternity and time . . . revelation

---

46. Barth, *Calvin*, 166–67.
47. Ibid., 167.

> and history . . . or whatever. . . . Some have a religious bent like Luther. Others have a one-sidedly intellectual or moral . . . bent like the great majority of the Middle Ages and today. . . . They can only confront one another as strangers. . . . But a third group . . . have a powerful urge to present a total view, to set forth the whole. All that they do presses toward this whole . . . they are the great warriors and at the same time the great peacemakers of history. . . . Calvin was a systematician in this sense.[48]

Barth's description of Calvin here leaves the distinct impression that Calvin's insights spoke more clearly and truly of the relationship between God and humanity than any others of his time. Barth prizes Calvin's theological "system" above all the rest not because he is able to so one-sidedly indicate the antithesis, to separate all vestiges of eternity from time, but because Calvin is able to think through the relationship to its conclusion. Calvin's theology presents the total view in which time and eternity must be brought together (not mixed), but rightly distinguished. "The point of this movement is always the same, namely, to think together the divine and human or the vertical and horizontal side, . . . to see God from our side and ourselves from his."[49] Of course there will still be "a constant reference back to a first and original thing." Barth still retains the same radical distinction, the foundational antithesis between God and humanity that significantly remains throughout the entirety of his life and work. The key point here is the emphasis on thinking together the relationship between time and eternity.

> We finally come back to the point we touched on in our general account of Calvin's theological character, to the essentially eschatological orientation of his Christianity, to the sharp and never to be ignored antithesis and connection between time and eternity on which all his thinking rests. . . . In reality the two things go together. The thought of eternity is taken strictly. Eternity is seen as the negation of all time and the position that underlies time, hence not as a second and different thing in a moment of time, but as the primary-finite thing of every moment of time. . . . This concept cannot devalue time or empty it out. . . . It makes time serious and important as the place of training where nothing . . . is eternal, but everything . . . is judged by its relation to the eternal, full of meaning, full of tasks.[50]

48. Ibid., 160.
49. Ibid., 168–69.
50. Ibid., 154–55.

Once again, while Barth is not doctrinally at the place where he can assert that eternity does not simply negate time, but fills it as God enters into it, as he will in the years to come, nevertheless this text points to the fact that Barth is more interested in the positive relation of the antithesis in Calvin's thought than its negation. Barth continually "draws attention [to] the brilliant and consistent way in which Calvin both in theory and practice relates eternity and time without losing either one in the other."[51] This is an important feature for Barth because in Calvin's work he begins to see how one can keep the necessary boundaries of theological thought in view while at the same time building constructively upon that foundation. Barth's appropriation of the doctrines of faith and obedience meant that his doctrine of sanctification needed to be more constructive—even if only expressed as patience and waiting. But that constructive account would necessarily be shaped by the description of the time-eternity dialectic. If Barth never finds a way to speak clearly and consistently of the positive relation between time and eternity then his doctrine of sanctification, his description of faithful human existence and action in light of God's self-revelation, would always be dominated by the negative sign under which it stands. Yet, again, while Barth has not worked out the right doctrinal moves to express himself fully in these lectures he begins to push forward with the simple notion that "the cross really is visible in our life; that time and eternity, God and humans, are not in metaphysical antithesis but indissoluble relation."[52] As Barth's notion of the relationship between time and eternity is expressed more positively his doctrine of sanctification becomes less abstract and more constructive.

The Danger of Moralism

> Its value is that as a converted Renaissance man he felt and saw more sharply than Luther, the liberated monk, the problem of ethics that the problem of God does not eliminate but truly poses for the first time. But this value of Calvin's theology is also a source of danger. Those who emphasise so strongly obedience and working for the glory of God can easily lose sight of the independent weight of the question of God.[53]

---

51. Ibid., Translator's Preface, x.
52. Ibid., 73.
53. Ibid., 82.

We have seen that Barth's analysis of Calvin and the Reformers was centred around the relating of the horizontal to the vertical, the impact of God's self-revelation on human life and obedience in time. "'The just lives by *faith*,' says Luther. 'Yes, indeed,' says Calvin, and he says exactly the same thing, but he makes it a major instead of a minor third, putting the stress at the end in the Latin form: Justus ex fide *viviti* ('The just *lives* by faith')."[54] While throughout these lectures Barth became convinced that Calvin was the climactic figure of the Reformation, the one who arduously attempted to think through Luther's discovery of the cross to its powerful conclusion—the one "who stood with both feet on the earth," he also perceived that in Calvin the Reformation ultimately came to its end.[55] Calvin's great insight that "the content of knowledge, as knowledge of God and ourselves, is in both cases the same," his "bold attempt to overcome the whole distinction of first and second" things was at the same time the central point of his failure.[56] Barth explains:

> In the very first sentence [of the *Institutes*], by speaking about two parts (*duabus partibus*) of wisdom, he betrayed the fact that the unity he had in mind was breaking apart in his hands, so that he could only point urgently to the inseparability and interrelatedness of the two parts, and then the deliberations in book III involve an endless dialectic of the two stand points from which it is clear that Calvin was aware of the original unity, but could assert it only by tirelessly playing off each side against the other and thus expounding the duality that the unity entails.[57]

Ultimately Calvin could not rid his theology of speaking of a here and a there, and because his feet were firmly planted on the earth he could not help but translate the relation between here and there as a moral one. The duality of the vertical and horizontal combined with Calvin's emphasis

---

54. Ibid., 81.

55. Barth writes, "With the posing of this fateful question [the problem of ethics] the second turn in the Reformation came that eventually, by a higher curve in the path, would lead back to the beginning and tragically enough, though in a way that is historically understandable, would lead it back onto a newly repaired stretch of the old horizontal highway, to the Christian secularity from which it had once broken free." Ibid., 67.

56. Ibid., 80-81. Barth is quick to also point out that Calvin's failure to hold fast to this unity is in reality no different from any theologian before or after him. "As we shall see, however, Calvin did not succeed in carrying through the program any more than any other theologians either before or after him" (ibid., 81).

57. Ibid.

on obedience became the entryway for moralism in Reformed theology. Barth, champion against liberal and pietistic moralization of Christianity, was instinctively aware of Calvin's deficiencies. Partway through his lecture cycle he had discovered enough about Calvin's work to aver that, "Calvin became a moralist."[58] He writes: "Certainly Calvin preached God and grace and faith, and did so unambiguously . . . But once his glance leaves this height of knowledge to fall on us—and it is distinctive of the Reformed to look from the height of God directly at us—nothing remains but a *moral* outlook and accusation and demand."[59] It was clear to Barth that it was precisely because of the strengths of Reformed theology—the connectedness of the vertical and horizontal, that it needed to be on guard against "a new righteousness of the scribes and Pharisees."

One might wonder how Barth the combatant of modern theology could remain so calm and forgiving towards Calvin, whose "Genevan system" conjured such words as "tyranny" and "Pharisaism."[60] Yet Barth remained convinced and even optimistic that Calvin's insights, while not without their shortcomings, also offered much to counter any return to the newly repaired "old horizontal highway" of the Middle Ages. The positive notions of Calvin's distinctive Reformation approach—his emphasis on faith and obedience and the consistent relatedness of time and eternity—which were underpinned by the unity of the knowledge of God—were confronted by the seriousness of their own limitations. The weapon with which Calvin tried to repel those shortcomings was "his remarkably sharp understanding precisely of the concept of God."[61] The "insight that It, It, the great It of the kingdom of heaven, of the Holy Spirit, cannot be given or put into effect in any possibility of human action, and that therefore, in practice, it can be seriously seen only in broken form, in the form of the command of God that is appropriate to this world" was the important restraint continually channelled by Calvin.[62] Or, as Barth perceptively pointed out, because Calvin was such an ethicist, he had to be a strong dogmatician.

Barth clearly paints the picture of this narrow bridge that Calvin attempts to walk as he briefly works through Calvin's doctrine of

58. Ibid., 121.
59. Ibid., 121–22.
60. Ibid., 122.
61. Ibid., 82.
62. Ibid., 87.

sanctification (in the latter's Genevan Catechism of 1545). Article 27, which deals with justification, states, "If Christ is really the sum of all the promises, the perpetual object of faith, we can know that what we receive through faith has to be in Christ alone. Stripped of our own righteousness, we are clothed with his. We do not receive anything of this righteousness within ourselves."[63] This is clearly Luther's reformation principle of the relationship between the horizontal and vertical. But, Barth continues to analyze, for Calvin "there is not just a justification by faith but definitely (article 28) a sanctification by faith as well. They are deceiving themselves who think they can boast of their faith in Christ without this second aspect." And further

> There is for Calvin no contradiction between what he had just said and this further point, for in his view justification and sanctification lie from the outset on two different levels, yet they intersect—and this is the important thing—on the line which is Christ from an upward point of view and faith from a downward. . . . To put this in mechanical terms, a hinge has to open here. As the one thing is done for us in heaven, we on earth are put in a position to do the other.[64]

This is Calvin's answer to the problem of ethics, which Barth felt the Middle Ages and the Renaissance had brazenly pursued, namely, the question of good works. The force of distinction here is, as Barth states, that sanctification has to "take place on earth." "But this value of Calvin's theology," as Barth previously stated, "is also a source of danger."[65] Barth did not have the time or space to fully integrate his criticism of Calvin's moralism with Calvin's doctrine of sanctification, but one can see that at this critical theological junction which must take place on earth, the possibility of "observing of the law" becomes a danger for a Pharisaical Christianity if the doctrine of God lies fallow for even a moment.

Because of the very real danger of moralism, this section is also packed with Calvin's insights for combating just such an affront to the graciousness of sanctification. Barth writes: "Especially clear in this article is the way in which Calvin constantly views our human situation dialectically, from a twofold standpoint. There is no doubt . . . that good works which proceed from a clear conscience . . . are pleasing to God. But

---

63. Ibid., 277.
64. Ibid., 87.
65. Ibid., 82.

why and to what extent? Because God recognizes his own righteousness in them."⁶⁶ Good works pleasing to God? Yes, but only through participation in the righteousness of Christ. There is a correspondence between God's righteousness and human works, a reality that is proper to them, but it is an indirect relationship that finds its reality only in Christ, and is, therefore, "broken and indirect." The validation for truly lifting up human works and righteousness exists only insofar as it is a validation of Christ. "Take Christ away, the living relation, the correspondence between heaven and earth, and everything is as it was before, for only in Christ can this inconceivable thing, this paradox, be the truth."⁶⁷ Because the doctrine of sanctification is one of the important dogmatic locations where Calvin works out his unique contribution to the Reformation it uniquely emphasises the earthly, the doing of good works, and the observing of the law. But it is also, precisely because the doctrine of sanctification is the location where Calvin works out the meaning of the earthly etc., the place where Calvin must be extremely clear about the relativity and boundaries of this anthropology of the Christian life. As Barth stresses, precisely because Calvin is addressing the existence and action of human agents, so must he speak about Christ, for "apart from Christ God could not find a single meritorious work in his people."⁶⁸

Despite the perceived proclivity towards moralism in Calvin's theology, Barth remained committed to Calvin's task of developing the positive relationship between the vertical and horizontal. Barth was insistent in these lectures, in his recapitulating style that, while there is a very real danger of running the ship aground in Calvin's theology, that theology also offers its own corrective. The key to avoiding the danger of moralism is to maintain, as far as possible, the unity of the knowledge of God and humanity.⁶⁹ In order not to lose sight of the independent weight of the question of God, one must emphasize

---

66. Ibid., 278.
67. Ibid., 279.
68. Ibid.

69. Barth states, "clearly the aim of all theology is no longer to say first and second but to say the one thing that is the whole." And although Calvin apparently did not succeed "in carrying through the program" he did so no more in Barth's opinion, "than any other theologians before or after him" (Barth, *Calvin*, 81). This duality of the original unity appears to be a foundational struggle of all theology, and as Barth often states later: The one word of God becomes two on our lips.

the connectedness and relativity of faithful human existence and action. This is especially important in the doctrine of sanctification, which has the potential of becoming simply a moral prescription. Barth maintained, therefore, that the key to fighting this all-too-facile drift is to maintain the stringent borders of correspondence between Christ's work and humanity's in the midst of a positive description of real, yet broken human action. As Barth moves toward the Göttingen Dogmatics, these insights remain in the forefront of his thinking.

3

"The Theology of the Reformed Confessions"

In contrast to the historical and psychological account which the "religious man" tended to give of himself at the beginning of the century, the characteristic feature of this theology was "its question about the superior, new element which limits and determines any human self-understanding."[1]

Introduction and Significance of Text

IN THE WINTER SEMESTER of 1922–23, following the Calvin Lectures, Barth resumed his historico-theological and scriptural exegesis lectures, given in tandem at Göttingen, immersing himself in the thoughts of Ulrich Zwingli and the Epistle of James. James proved to be an able "conversation partner" which he presented "as a tough and good outflanking attack on Paulinism."[2] Zwingli, however, did not fare as well. While Barth withheld final judgment on the corpus of Zwingli's theology, he could not help venting his disappointment with the Swiss Reformer, particularly concerning his eucharistic conceptions.[3]

---

1. Busch, *Barth*, 144.

2. Ibid., 142.

3. One night at the beginning of January, Barth experienced a "negative conversion" towards Zwingli in which he began to see in Zwingli's work the very image of modern Protestant theology, "with a few eggshells from the early church thrown in" (ibid., 142). Webster, however, points out that by the end of the semester, Barth's attitude towards Zwingli had "mellowed a little," so that it was only after "straining hard to appreciate the genuine Christian theological force of what Zwingli was attempting" that he remained uneasy with him. See Webster, *Barth's Earlier Theology*, 16, 39.

Following those classes on Zwingli and James, Barth announced lectures on "The Theology of the Reformed Confessions" and an exposition of 1 Corinthians in the summer of 1923. Up to this point Barth had often struggled to overcome his inexperience in the classroom and fought to stave off—under intense scrutiny from himself and others—the mounting pressures of reformulating his own theological foundations. Of the new lecture series, though, he announced with great joy that "the difficulty of preparation has not been that bad," even though in terms of content and structure "The Theology of the Reformed Confessions" and 1 Corinthians were the most complex and sophisticated of his lectures up to that point in time.[4] "The Theology of the Reformed Confessions" in particular offers an excellent summation of Barth's self-positioning in the theological landscape during that period. It is of no little importance that Barth, a product of the "confessionally weak"[5] Swiss church, would take upon himself the challenge of defining his theological identity amidst the churchly confessions. A depth of personal theological understanding and commitment emerges in these lectures that had not been voiced as fully since his Romans commentaries. John Webster wrote: "To read these lecture texts is to observe Barth at a particularly intense stage of his theological development"; for Eberhard Busch the lectures "represented an advance" for Barth.[6]

Later in life Barth commented about his transition to Göttingen that:

> Now it was no longer a question of attacking all kinds of errors and abuses. All at once we were in the front rank. We had to take on responsibilities which we had not known about while we were simply in opposition. Suddenly we had been given an opportunity to say what we really thought in theology, and to show the church our real intention and ability. . . . It was not just a matter of building on and reinforcing positions which had already been taken up. We had only just begun on a course which each one had to follow laboriously in his own sphere.[7]

Because of his commitment to pushing beyond defensive bulwarks and the sheer volume of material, Barth's lectures on the "Reformed Confessions,

---

4. Barth, "Reformed Confessions," viii.
5. Ibid.
6. Webster, *Barth's Earlier Theology*, 57; Barth, "Reformed Confessions," ix.
7. Busch, *Barth*, 126.

offered him a significant opportunity to demonstrate his real intentions and abilities emerging as positive doctrine within the Church.

The characteristic features of the "Reformed Confessions" lectures are *the* foundational boundaries or presuppositions which Barth cites as the framework upon which all constructive theological discussion should be oriented. These presuppositions are also, therefore, the foundational boundaries for discussing his doctrine of sanctification. Alongside Barth's lucid treatment of the "*basic intention*" and "great commonality of Christian thought" gathered around the various Reformed confessions, the theme of sanctification is inherently drawn within. In light of the significance of the nature of the various Reformed confessions for Barth's thought, this chapter will begin with a summary of these lectures with an eye towards highlighting their positive significance as a limited witness— a theme directly applicable to Barth's emerging doctrine of sanctification. Moving on quickly, the majority of this chapter will examine in detail what Barth calls the threefold framework that steers all of Reformed theology as it relates to his doctrine of sanctification. This framework is made up of: (1) a focus upon the initiating and finalizing reality of God, (2) the non-givenness of God in revelation, and (3) the real yet relative human correlate of God's action.

Outline of Text

"The Theology of the Reformed Confessions" is arranged in three chapters, and covers a vast range of material. Each chapter builds upon the previous one, and the whole work culminates in the final chapter, which is subdivided into four important sections. Chapter One, "The Significance of the Confession in the Reformed Church," is a steep jumping off point in which Barth wastes no time setting up the "puzzling and paradoxical picture"[8] of the Reformed confessions. As Barth brings this section to a close, he draws the characteristically absent features of the Reformed confessions, as compared with the Catholic, Lutheran, and modern confessions, together around the remarkable concept of their normative relativity. Writes Barth, "There is *no* standard Reformed resolution for the problem of confessional commitment. . . . Rather, we see a whole series of attempts to resolve the problem, which as a whole can only document the absence of a normative Reformed resolution. They are all

---

8. Barth, "Reformed Confessions," 38.

emergency measures, temporary bridges upon which one can proceed."[9] These "deficiencies" of the Reformed confessions positively attest to the primacy of *God's ways and works* above all else.[10]

In Chapter Two, "The Principle of Scripture and Its Grounds", Barth aligns these characteristically deficient features previously highlighted under their unifying concept—the Scripture principle—the "article upon which the church stands and falls."[11] The Scripture principle states that, "*The church recognizes the rule of its proclamation solely in the Word of God and finds the Word of God solely in Holy Scripture.*"[12] In this section, Barth spends his time teasing out this delicate balance between the church's frail, earthly proclamation dependent upon the Word of God, and the original, "completely other" Word of God proclaimed in Holy Scripture. The Reformed Scripture principle is at once both an assertion and a restriction, something said and not said. "The church's proclamation is to be dependent upon the Word of God, grounded upon it, oriented to it, and indeed to it *alone*" and yet this proclamation "is not the Word of God itself but rather human word ruled by the Word of God, dependent upon it, grounded upon it, oriented to it."[13] As Barth meditates on these statements, he addresses the primary dialectic of the matter: "The knowledge of God is not mediated but is only unmediated, that is, God is known through God himself. . . . *Revelation* is not this and that, not everything and anything, but rather this definitive, incomparable one thing. Therefore, legitimate witness to revelation cannot be any random human word about God but rather this definite human word about God."[14]

Within this paradoxical balance, Barth explains how Reformed theology is able to affirm on one hand God's "superiority, majesty, and freedom,"[15] which limits and shatters every creaturely reality, and yet on the other hand still positively assert the earthly, human possibility and nature of the Reformed confessions in relationship to God's self-giving presence. Affirmations, which at once free humanity *from* the ultimate

---

9. Ibid., 37.
10. Ibid., 39.
11. Ibid., 41.
12. Ibid.
13. Ibid.
14. Ibid., 48–49.
15. Ibid., 48.

responsibility of bearing God's Word, and *for* real, but relative human action and obedience.

In Chapter Three, "Reformed Doctrine as a Whole"—essentially a worked exposition of the first two chapters, Barth begins to question after the basic intentions of the "ocean of Reformed confessions"[16] under four sub-paradigms: 1. *the Debate with the Old Church*, 2. *the Positive Doctrine of Christianity*, 3. *the Controversy with Lutheranism*, and 4. *the Battle against Modern Christianity*. Barth's discussion of these final topics makes up the heart of the lectures.

For Barth, the significance of the Reformed confession consists in its "essential *non*significance, its obvious relativity, humanity, multiplicity, mutability, and transitoriness."[17] The essence of the Reformed confession is characterized by its strikingly unassuming function as a witness. This does not mean, however, that the Reformed confession is finally insignificant; though its worth is derivative, as it points beyond itself, this creates rather than detracts from its import. The Reformed confession, writes Barth, is ultimately "a *fading* bell stroke, a *falling, streaming* cascade, or . . . a *disappearing* shadow."[18] And this, Barth illuminates from the beginning of these lectures, is a supremely *positive* statement. While the bell stroke fades, it also announces fulfilment and calls to action, the falling cascade speaks of the majesty of the heights from which it has come, and the shadow's very disappearance is witness to the light of the rising sun.[19] There is a beautiful sense of dependence and fulfilment within this relationship.

It is no wonder that Barth was drawn so powerfully to the principle of the Reformed confessions. Here the content is always unabashedly oriented towards God's testimony about *Himself*, to the ways and works of *God*, and yet significantly this testimony is witnessed to through *human* words in Scripture forming a distinct relationship. As Barth gleans from Calvin, whatever he may be discussing "he will" at once "always have in view the *totality* of God and the *totality* of the human," for "[n]early the whole of sacred doctrine consists in these two parts: the knowledge of God and of ourselves."[20] The Reformed confession is testimony about

16. Ibid., 66.
17. Ibid., 38.
18. Ibid.
19. Ibid.
20. Ibid., 97.

God, and, therefore also testimony about the relationship between God and humanity forged and sustained in grace. A relationship positively shaped by notions such as limitation, determination, and fulfilment.

Foundational Principles

The summer after Barth's lectures on the "Reformed Confessions," he delivered an address in Emden to the General Assembly of the German Reformed Church on the "The Nature and Purpose of Reformed Doctrine."[21] In this lecture, a by-product of the summer course, Barth pushed his listeners to wrestle with what he had begun to develop constructively as the foundational principles of churchly theological articulation:

> The question of right doctrine introduces us to the vacuum at the *heart* of our (modern) church and inside Christianity. . . . A church does not live on truths, however deep and living these truths might be, but from *the* truth, which man cannot take up *selectively*, choosing between this or that doctrine, theory or conviction. He *must* grasp this truth, because it has *itself first* grasped him. . . . The Reformed Confession lays emphasis not so much upon the idea that man is justified by *faith* and not by *works*, as upon the consideration that it is *God* and not *man* who brings about this justification.[22]

As Barth worked through his lectures at the University of Göttingen and became more explicit about his intentions and capabilities as a constructive theologian, he also became more emphatic dogmatically that theological inquiry does not begin with or generate an independent Christian anthropology, but is continually and thoroughly centred upon the divine-human relationship in a very specific way:

> The Reformation in its original intention begins with revelation, with the Word, and with faith. It is thoroughly unpedagogical. It does not begin with human interests, among which emerges finally, ultimately, and as the highest point, the interest in God; rather, it begins with God's interest in the human person. It does not show the way that the human should seek and follow, but rather, the way that God has already found to him. It is impractical: It demands of humans either too much or too little,

---

21. Busch, *Barth*, 149.

22. Barth, "The Doctrinal Task of the Reformed Churches," *The Word of God and the Word of Man*, 221, 233, 251, 253. Quoted in Busch, *Barth*, 150.

depending on one's view. In terms of its intention, it is very difficult if not impossible for it to integrate itself into what humans otherwise want. With its conception of life it stands there like an erratic block between the splendour of the medieval and the no less splendid modern consciousness. It proclaims that the human is *not* the measure of all things, least of all Christianity, and positions him before the reality *of God.* . . . All Reformed Christianity is to be understood as the attempt to understand the human person, who through the Reformation was placed before the immediate reality of God, as *human*, in the *world*, in *history*, but not at peace with so much as at *war* with the world, and yet in *relationship* to it.[23]

The importance of the doctrine of sanctification in relationship to Barth's conception of the object of, and grounds for theological reflection is not hard to see. For Barth, theology is latent throughout with the nature and meaning of the divine-human relationship because the object of and ground for theological reflection are the same.[24] In this paragraph, centred on the impact of the object-subject relationship within theology, Barth arranges the outline, or floor plan—the description of an uncluttered environment—in which inquiry into the impact of God upon the human creature is not only a possibility but also a necessity. Barth's emphasis here is not simply about a proper starting point for a Christian anthropology though; it is no mere formality, a way of getting more mileage out of the same doctrines. His point is not pedantic at all. The essence of what Barth is getting at is not merely a re-formulation of theological content, but of coming to terms with the fact that *God* has burst in upon humanity like an armed warrior.[25] Doctrinally this is played out in remarks such as: "The decisive thing to be said about faith is not that faith makes just, but that faith is given, awakened, made by God. It is only this faith, or, in other words, it is only God himself who makes just."[26] Sanctification, therefore, is not merely a theme loosely gathered amongst many others in Christian doctrine that maintains its own relative independence—simply a description of the *process* or the way in which one grows in faithful human action and obedience—even if inextricably rooted to God's actions.

23. Barth, "Reformed Confessions," 208–9.

24. "For the human who asks himself why he exists and receives the answer, to the glory of God, cannot and should not only *trust* but also *will*, not only expect something from God but also *do* something for God" (ibid., 99).

25. Ibid., 79.

26. Ibid., 72.

The constant danger facing the doctrine of sanctification is the possibility of its collapsing in on itself, of becoming merely a theme of the human person "in his receiving and having, accomplishing and presenting."[27] Barth's emphasis is not that Christian theology cannot look "at these human matters, including those that take place in the Christian soul," but that "the *soul's* [my emphasis] life with God cannot and may not become a theme."[28] For Barth, the doctrine of sanctification is oriented towards and developed around not merely what it means to say that the *human* creature is sanctified—a sort of self-contained Christian anthropology—but what it means to say that the human creature is sanctified by God the Father in his Son Jesus Christ through the Holy Spirit. Everything that Barth fleshes out concerning the doctrine of sanctification within the "Reformed Confessions" and beyond is shaped by what he articulates in these lectures as the three-fold framework that steers all of Reformed theology: a focus upon the initiating and finalizing reality of God, the non-givenness of God in revelation, and the real yet relative human correlate of God's action.

What this means specifically is that Barth's doctrine of sanctification will be shaped by a focus on *who* sanctifies rather than an anthropological/psychological description of the event of sanctification itself. It means that sanctification, which can only exist in dynamic relationship with *Christ*, remains in need of grace at every moment; it is in no way given to humanity as a special status or grace to be developed or built upon. And finally, it means that because sanctification is localized around this God who sanctifies in Jesus Christ through the *Holy Spirit*, it necessarily addresses its relevance to humanity, to the ones being sanctified, concerning faithful life and obedience in response to God.

Barth's use of Trinitarian themes in these lectures is quite significant, but one must patiently analyse their function—to note their presence, indeed their important presence, yet allow them to speak within their context. Even though Barth bases his conceptualization of sanctification on Trinitarian presuppositions here, he does so almost without noticing that he's doing it, as if its significance had become relatively unremarkable to him because of the frequency of its occurrence in classic Reformed thought. Webster notes:

---

27. Ibid., 144.
28. Ibid., 122.

Barth's identification of these Trinitarian and incarnational themes in the Reformed tradition forms one of his first attempts to explicate the relation of God and creatures, not simply as *via dialectica* or *via paradoxica*, but by putting dogma to work. Barth was only just discovering the power of these doctrines, and was aware of his awkwardness in handling them.... Often, one feels, the doctrines are handled instrumentally rather than descriptively, to solve problems rather than to depict the ways and works of God.[29]

Initiating and Finalizing Reality

From the old Reformed perspective in which to think of "grace" (*gratia*) always meant to think of God, this [moving directly and immediately from the description of divine gift, which contains everything, to the task assigned to man] was the only possible option. At the moment in which the person who has received grace begins to focus his interest on himself, the swift transition had to become problematic.[30]

The polemical thrust of the early Reformed confessions, overtly aimed at the Roman Catholic Church, but nonetheless inherently antagonistic towards the Lutheran church as well, revolved around the theme of Christian doctrine. And just as Barth admonished his listeners in Emden, so the early Reformers passionately declared that "Christendom must be taught anew *because* it must become clear again that the issue in this doctrine is *God.*"[31] Barth notes that the Reformers "are preoccupied not so much with the new formulation of its contents but with the fact that this doctrine deals with *God.*"[32] Rightly dividing this theme, of course, is not new for Barth. He had been heralding a particular understanding of it since his pastorate in Safenwil; and in relationship to sanctification, this theme was certainly at the centre of writings such as "The Righteousness of God." There too it served as a sort of boundary marker between God and humanity. Dogmatically, however, this theme had become pregnant with positive doctrinal meaning. In the "Reformed

---

29. Webster, *Barth's Earlier Theology*, 54.
30. Barth, "Reformed Confessions," 141.
31. Ibid., 79.
32. Ibid.

Confessions," Barth writes that justification and sanctification, faith and obedience, prayer and thanksgiving have several presuppositions. *"One of these presuppositions is, for example, the originalness, the initiating and finalizing reality of God, from which all these relationships either derive or to which they all refer, or both at the same time. Put in the language of Trinitarian dogma, God the Father."*[33] As Barth's thought continued to grow in clarity, this *theme* functioned much more profoundly than simply a right and proper prolegomena. To say "God" directs not only the structure of what one says, but also, significantly, the content as well. The central *theme* of Christian theology that Barth advocates is both the initiating and finalizing reality from which sanctification derives and to which it refers. In Trinitarian dogma, this means that the beginning and end of sanctification is inherently structured around God the Father. Again, for Barth, the doctrine of sanctification is less an account of sanctification *in se* than an explication of what it means to say that it is *God* who sanctifies. The reason for this lies in the unity of the subject-object relationship in theology.

> What was for Luther the question of *salvation* was for them [the Reformed theologians] the question of *truth*. The one question cannot be separated from the other, but it matters greatly whether the one or the other is more acutely pressed. Luther . . . asked the question about salvation, or better, about the truth of *salvation*, and so the anti-Roman banner of his theology was the doctrine of *justification* and *faith*, which says *how* the human is saved in truth. The Reformed [theologians] . . . asked the question about the truth, or better, about the *truth* of salvation, and thus the anti-Catholic thrust of their doctrine was the transcendence of their concept of God, which was the answer to the question of *who* saves the human in truth. . . . The common Reformation knowledge over against the old church was that God and faith "belong together" . . . that in the relationship of God understood in a Christian way the subject and object are one. In Luther, however, the major emphasis in this line of thought is that the object is one with the *subject*, that *faith* and God belong together, that "to have a God is nothing else than to *trust* and *believe* in that one with your whole heart." It is the Reformed concern to emphasise that it is the *object* that in this relationship is one with the subject, that faith and *God* belong

33. Ibid., 161.

together, that all trusting and believing of the human heart must stand on the fact that we have a *God*.[34]

The structure and content of Reformed theology is completely shaped by the *beginning* and the *end* of the question of salvation and truth.[35] That is to say that it emphasises the *object*—God—as the sustaining theme of Christian theology, not because the subject is expendable or unimportant, but because the subject is entirely dependent upon the object. "The *Augustana* asks, How shall I be saved? The *Tetrapolitana* asks, Who saves me?"[36] For Barth, as for the Reformers, the distinction makes all the difference, not only doctrinally, but ethically as well. Righteousness, for example, "because it is imputed by *God*, cannot remain *mere* imputed righteousness. It is to *God* that man flees with his confession and pleading, before *him* man capitulates, to *him* man submits as captive and lost one, and to no one else!"[37] Righteousness imputed by God inherently embraces humanity's response to God. "In Calvin, Luther's problem of the human path to salvation no longer stands in isolation but is worked into the problem of the concept of God. The uniqueness, superiority, and freedom of God and of faith, which Zwingli emphasises in such a radically one-sided way, are set in *relationship* to the life of the human person, to one's distress and hope."[38] For Barth, the doctrine of God unifies faith and obedience, justification and sanctification; it serves to protect sanctification from somehow being characterized as a secondary work, something next in line to justification and faith and riddled with the uncertainty of human emotion. Human righteousness, because it is imputed by God, does not become the foundation for human action and works. Sanctification and obedience have their beginning and end in God just as justification and faith. "Wherever the situation of the sixteenth century reoccurs—necessitating protest against the forgetting of the *theme* of Christian theology and in response to the neglect of this known and yet unknown Christian *presupposition* requiring the reminder that God is not in *our* hand but we are in *his*—there. . . . The claim may be made

---

34. Ibid., 80–81.

35. "There is no further mention in these theses of the *human's way* of salvation. The Reformed confession is interested in the *beginning* and the *end* of this way" (ibid., 75).

36. Ibid., 72.

37. Ibid., 86.

38. Ibid., 78.

that the fathers of Reformed theology have left her a weapon for the task of this struggle that *is* to be used."³⁹

The Theme of Sanctification

One of Barth's primary worries about sanctification was the ease with which this doctrine could become a theme in its own right and quickly swept into an independent Christian anthropology. Subsequently, it was likely to become merely an experiential and psychological account of the human person, if not properly grounded in the doctrine of God. Barth reflects on two particular instances in Reformed theology, in relationship to sanctification, which demonstrate the gravitas that results from shifting the *theme* of Christian theology from God himself to the human person. "In *Beza* . . . and the Westminster Confession," one can see "the broadly drafted attempt to make Reformed theology into anthropology."⁴⁰ Barth asserts that Beza, for all of his intended faithfulness to Calvin's theological agenda, was at once both sawing the branch out from underneath Reformed theology and paving the road that would eventually lead to Pietism and the Enlightenment.⁴¹ "There is less trace in him of outside influences and elements—except for the *one* element that Beza contributed to Calvinist doctrine and by virtue of which his entire system, in spite of all its Calvinism, becomes something very different and very original."⁴² Barth states that Beza projected the entire theme of his theological structure on the inner struggle of the Christian soul. "In Beza, Christianity is in a defensive posture. . . . It is a defence against certain fatal conclusions that could result from his own logic. . . . Beza focused his view on the person, on the Christian as such. . . . He directs his interest toward what

39. Ibid., 81.

40. Ibid., 150–51. It is worth noting that some scholars, such as Richard Muller, particularly in his *After Calvin: Studies in the Development of a Theological Tradition*, have critiqued Barth for relying too heavily upon Heinrich Heppe's nineteenth-century interpretation of the shift from Calvin to later Calvinism, "characterized," says Muller, "by an almost polemical pitting of 'Calvin against the Calvinists'" (63). Muller suggests that Barth and others who followed this interpretation relied upon a too radical reading of the differences between Reformation and post-Reformation thought. While critiques such as this counsel appropriate caution against misreading these post-Reformation works through Barth and others, the important point for this thesis is Barth's use of these works as he perceives them. See Muller, *After Calvin*.

41. Barth, "Reformed Confessions," 151, 123.

42. Ibid., 121.

is going on inside them, their questioning and receiving answers, their unsettledness followed by quiet resolution and then more unsettledness in their souls."[43]

And while Beza, because he is a Reformed Christian, always seemed to find his way back towards the divine subject, Barth laments that to some degree his theology as a whole was characterized by psychological introspection.[44]

Beza's conception of sanctification was threefold:

> He speaks, first, of the *"mortification"* [*mortificatio*] of the old person, the fundamental and effective setting aside of his existence. Then he describes its *"burial,"* the "continuation" and the "increase" of "mortification." This is understood as the factual decaying and the decomposition of the dead old person, which happens in the afflictions that come to us, in the "exercises" that we must undergo to tame our rebellious flesh, and finally in our bodily death, which ends the battle between flesh and spirit. The third moment of sanctification or rebirth is the *"resurrection of the new person,"* the illumination, strengthening and tutoring of our intelligence, of our will, and of all our capacities through grace.[45]

Barth contends that, however genuinely Reformed Beza's description of sanctification may appear, its presuppositions are dichotomized. "Everything . . . according to Beza, that relates to the attainment of salvation works itself out . . . in the form of a broad depiction of the struggle in which this certainty must assert itself against the 'testing' that 'Satan and our conscience' (!) causes us."[46] Barth indicates that after one has sifted through Beza's Reformed aphorisms, his doctrine of sanctification is presupposed in a very significant way by the subjective response to *Satan's* question: "But *do we have this faith?*"[47] Each facet of Beza's description of sanctification is largely oriented around the *Christian's* assurance of salvation based on the mortification and vivification of the flesh and spirit as a rebuttal to Satan's scorns. Barth says sternly: "A Reformed Christian *is not to direct* his interest toward the psychological subject of religion in this way. Otherwise, the certainty of salvation is *really* jeopardized, because

43. Ibid., 121–22.
44. Ibid., 122.
45. Ibid., 117–18.
46. Ibid., 117.
47. Ibid.

in fact there is in principle no resting in faith. This danger becomes *obvious* in Beza. . . . The soul's life with God cannot and may not become a theme for Reformed thought. Otherwise the theme itself will become dialectic."[48] When that happens, "when one no longer really" knows "how to speak of *God* in Christianity when speaking of religious *relationships*, . . . then all these relationships necessarily had to collapse like so many bowling pins stood on their heads."[49] In Beza, the unity which Barth sought in the doctrine of God appears to be split in two, not dialectically—which would necessarily take up the human question within the context of God's actions—but similarly, so that the human question can be looked at psychologically and analyzed emotionally next to, or apart from the separate action of God. In Beza, the soul's life with God became the central theme of his theology; sanctification was administered as a measure of certainty within the soul against Satan's attacks. In this sense, the doctrine of sanctification could be used as a tangible ethical measuring stick. The certainty of sanctification, the foundation for faithful human action and obedience, however, was then called into question, along with the assurance of salvation as the free act of God. Whenever the *theme* of sanctification is replaced by anything other than God as the foundational principle, Barth explained, the danger that emerges is the breaking apart of that principle. Barth warns that when the foundation of this doctrine shifts from the unity of God's ways and works to the interiority of the Christian soul, it is only a matter of time until sanctification becomes nothing more than a psychology of the Christian soul, an attempted appeasement for the constant questioning and unsettledness of the human experience, or a confused groping about for the assurance of salvation.

The Westminster Confession, along with the Larger and Shorter Westminster Catechisms are perfect examples of what Barth perceives as the tragic result of confusing the *theme* of sanctification with something other than God. "One should note" within these documents, Barth writes, "the intrusion of an historico-psychological way of looking at things."[50] Repeatedly "grace with its gift" is "drawn . . . into the territory of experience and psychologised.... This is how it proceeds, how it *must* proceed when Christian doctrine is no longer quite certain of its subject, of the

---

48. Ibid., 122.
49. Ibid., 125.
50. Ibid., 139.

divine subject in Christianity, so that in spite of all monergistic assertions it must degenerate into the description of possible human relationships to this subject."[51] Of primary significance is the development of the *ordo salutis*. The steady decay of the *theme* of Christian theology—practically speaking, the unity of the knowledge of God—was replaced by the equally steady prominence that the individual Christian received as a theme in his own right. The relationship between God and humanity, as Barth saw it, began to be developed independently, so that the doctrine of God was in a sense mirrored anthropologically. And so, he says, the *ordo salutis* describes the way of salvation from the perspective of the believing individual—the effect of revelation as it takes place over time; "it is thus a religious psychology arranged from the perspective of temporal-biographical sequence of Christian experience."[52]

> So apparently here the action of the Redeemer God has its analogy in the temporal sequence of religious processes, in the continuity of the reflexes of the revelation of grace in the soul of the human person. . . . No longer is a single psychologised moment identified and placed at the centre, a procedure that certainly lends Beza's confession a certain edifying vitality and actuality. . . . Instead, now, it appears that what happens when one becomes a Christian and persists as one shall be *demonstrated*. . . . The earthly analogy of the divine action now begins to become important and interesting. The dark night of objectivism in which the Reformers . . . had remarkably enough remained, now begins to *fade*, and gradually, from very far away, the pleasant morning of that day dawns on which Schleiermacher . . . will discover, as the actual finisher of the work begun by Luther, that the essence of theology is the analysis of the pious self-consciousness. This will be the day on which the Erlangen theologian Hofmann will compose the statement that defines at least two centuries of theology: "I, the Christian, am the most appropriate content of my science as a theologian."[53]

The important point to notice here is that the earthly analogy of divine action now begins to become important and interesting in its own right as distinct and *separate* from the divine work. The unity, which Barth sought in the *theme* of Christian theology—God—is shattered when the

---

51. Ibid.
52. Ibid.
53. Ibid., 139–40.

individual Christian becomes another theme alongside, or apart from, God, or worse, when the Christian becomes the central theme.

> At the moment in which the person who has received grace begins to focus his interest on himself, this swift transition had to become problematic. In accordance with the sequence of human emotions, a reflective passage had to intervene now in which the grace of justification, rather than becoming immediately active as the grace of sanctification, had to be examined and enjoyed for a while as the "grace of adoption."[54]

The intrusion of the emotional and psychological analogy upon divine grace rent a division in the single work of God. Sanctification, rather than immediately following justification—and obedience, rather than immediately following faith as single works of God that necessarily included the very real human aspect, were disconnected from their *theme* in Christian theology and rejoined primarily within the realm of a Christian anthropology.

> *Sanctification* follows then as a second step. It is affirmed with strong language as inseparable from effectual calling. It is defined as universal, comprehending the entire person, but in this life it is imperfect and leads only into the struggle between flesh and spirit. Yes, man's residual "corruption" can "for a time" prevail, but there remains a "regenerate part" in man, thanks to the Spirit of Christ that continually provides help, and this part escapes victoriously so that growth in grace does not cease. But is not sanctification here confused with holiness? It is clear that there is growth in "holiness" but is there in "sanctification" through the Holy Spirit? What should we think of the statement that "sanctification is . . . imperfect," and what are we to imagine the "regenerate part" in man to be? Is regeneration a larger or smaller quantity? And if we are to think of holiness, why is there no discussion here of repentance and obedience? Is this not a concealed naturalism when one speaks of "sanctification," of which there can be more or less, as something that happens to a person without setting that person back on his feet? In what follows, the attempt is made to work out this side of the matter in that the things that mainly happen to man ("vocation," "justification," "adoption," "sanctification") are followed by those things that are to be understood mainly as man's spontaneous action.[55]

54. Ibid., 141.
55. Ibid., 141–42.

The initiating and finalizing reality of sanctification, which Barth sought as a presupposition in *God*, are, in this passage, grounded entirely within the believing Christian, entirely within time, within the realm of rational examination. Despite the recourse to Reformed language, it is clear to Barth that within the Westminster works the doctrine of sanctification is used to rationalize the confusing human experiences of doubt, sin, and struggle in relationship to the grace of God. Barth perceptively realized that the ease with which Calvin could move from divine command—eternity—to human obedience—time, was based on the unity of God. Even Zwingli in his own way iterated the same thing when he said, "Whatever is creaturely, whatever has begun and will end in time, can be neither the object nor the basis . . . of a confident faith."[56] A doctrine of sanctification, Barth contends, foundationally rooted in time cannot help but become just as unconfident, staggering, grinding and halting as the experiences it is supposed to account for. Of course, Barth says, sanctification has to do with humanity and their life and actions; of course, sanctification has to do with time and what appears in some ways as growth (holiness), but his thesis here is that sanctification is foundationally and unceasingly rooted in God and not man.

J. S. Rhee's description of Barth's 1927 lecture "Rechtfertigung und Heiligung" could be enhanced by rightly noting that the ideas of temporality and process found within the lecture are not contrary to what Barth is saying in other places earlier on. Rhee says, "Here Barth makes another significant turn in his understanding of sanctification by affirming sanctification as a process. . . . It is surely a great modification, and even seems to be a reversal back toward the pietistic view of sanctification."[57] Rhee quotes Barth as saying: "Justification is an 'actus purus,' it stands over us with the majesty and clearness of the starry sky" and "once for all, perfect and sufficient," while sanctification is "mulitplex, inchoate, *relativa, inaequalis*". . . . Therefore, sanctification is our temporal reality "where grace sanctifies us."[58] Even here, however, the guiding principle is not that sanctification begins and ends in time and is, therefore, a process; but that sanctification is the temporal description of what *God* does in the human sinner in time. Sanctification begins and ends with *God*; the initiating and finalizing reality is *God*. Sanctification must not be established

---

56. Ibid., 74.
57. Rhee, "Secularization and Sanctification," 76–77.
58. Ibid., 77.

or dependent upon contingent realities for its substance and efficacy, for that which begins in time continually stands under the suspicion that it will just as easily end in time. This is the principle that allows Barth to cultivate in very palpable language his account of sanctification later in the *Göttingen Dogmatics,* from which the lecture "Rechtfertigung and Heiligung" is developed. What emerges in Barth's description of sanctification in that article is not essentially a "great modification" of his earlier work, but a more substantial filling in of positive content within the boundaries set forth here in the *Reformed Confessions* of which the focus on *who* sanctifies, rather than *how* sanctification occurs within the believing individual, is paramount.

This is an extremely important concept to grasp for understanding Barth's work. It means that Barth's doctrine of sanctification is coloured by what it means to say that man is sanctified by *God*; it means that as a formative principle Barth focuses on the initiating and finalizing aspects of sanctification; it means that Barth does not begin with human interests, but will attempt to understand the sanctified person as one who stands before *God* as one has who has been placed within the world, as a human, as a very real part of history. And just for those reasons, it means that Barth really does explore the sanctified person as one who has been placed before God as *human*, in this *world*, and as a very real part of *history*. Rightly perceiving this boundary as one of the essential pillars upon which Barth constructs the doctrine of sanctification may help to clarify the way in which he approaches the "concreteness" of human reality, which has often been the cause of much frustration and of the fear that Barth is essentially unconcerned with human reality.

The Non-Givenness of God

> Religion had to be properly defined as a private matter from the moment it became clear that it was understood solely as a sentimentalized thing inside us. This was the so-called religious experience, which Pietism and the Enlightenment, not without antecedents, moved to the centre, and Schleiermacher made into the holy of holies of official Protestantism.[59]

While the early Reformed confessions characteristically took issue with the Roman Church over the central *theme* of Christian theology, they also

---

59. Barth, "Reformed Confessions," 32.

engaged the Lutheran church in an equally heated controversy with implications, Barth believed, just as crucial for the doctrine of sanctification.

> We have drawn more modest circles here, and while remaining within the narrowly defined theological territory, we have unpacked as the distinctive polemical doctrine against Rome the concept of divine majesty, and as the distinctive positive view of Christianity the parallel relationship, described once more yesterday, between gospel and law, faith and obedience. At both points we have discovered something quite unusual precisely in contrast with Lutheranism, something very important and serious at both points, something that could and should be argued about. The first point would be the contrast between a theological (in the more narrow sense) and an anthropological perspective. The second would be the contrast between an overview that is exclusively religious—whereby the ethical problem is *also* an issue for the latter but only *after the fact* and with greatly diminished power because of the specifically religious formulation of the question. Why did not the two churches battle *about this* if they had to fight about something? In their confessions, they did *not dispute at all* about the second point, which appears to be the more burning issue, the relationship between justification and sanctification. . . . Instead, there were pointed, bitter, and unresolved disputes, lasting long into the nineteenth century, about the *corporal presence of Christ in the Lord's Supper*, linked closely to the Christological question of the importance of the ascension and *Christ's sitting at the right hand of God*.[60]

Though the disagreement between the Reformed and Lutherans, per Barth's second point—the former's characterization of Christianity ethically versus the latter's characterization of Christianity religiously, i.e., ethics—although important, were of secondary concern—did not erupt over the relationship between justification and sanctification, ultimately, it was another way of airing the same concern fuelled by the same central presupposition. The issues Reformed and Lutheran theologians battled over—the meaning of the corporal presence of Christ in the Lord's Supper and the importance of the ascension—were really ways of discussing concretely the "givenness of God" in contingent revelation, an issue that, as Barth stated, is just as foundational and important to discuss today as it was then.[61]

60. Ibid., 155.
61. "Can there be any more urgent task for a theologian than *Christology?*" (ibid., 160).

> What does the Lord's Supper mean for the thought shaped by the Middle Ages? Clearly, it is the proclamation, the objectification of the presence of God "par excellence." This positioned one—as an automatic outcome of the meaning of the Lord's Supper—directly before the special question of revelation: What does it mean that God, God himself in Christ, communicates himself (not in general, not everywhere, not in the entire world, and also not in our ideas, but rather) as the "most concrete thing," that he lets himself be known and enjoyed by us? This is the point from which it is then possible for us to speak about everything else that we are, have, and experience in relation to God. Everything that unfolds between the Word of God on the one hand and the faith and obedience of man on the other must be illumined and proven from this point.[62]

Although the doctrine of sanctification was not the locus for debate between the sister Reformers, the implications that emerge for sanctification from the debate about the Lord's Supper are equally derivative and important. As Barth says, "Everything that unfolds between the Word of God . . . and faith and obedience . . . must be illumined and proven from this point." The Lord's Supper became the topic over which the presuppositions of both issues was fought; simply put: "They fought about *Christology*, for the dispute about the *Lord's Supper* was . . . only the shadow side of the actual dispute about their view of Christ"; and "clearly, Christ is one of the *presuppositions* of . . . sanctification."[63] Again, the differences between the Reformed and Lutheran understanding of how God gives himself in contingent revelation, or, more expressly, what it means to say "God himself in Christ," lay at the heart of the distinctions between them about both the Lord's Supper and the doctrine of sanctification.

The dispute centred around the question: How does God give himself in Jesus Christ?

> It was the differing views of the Lord's Supper, and especially the way in which Christ is present in the elements, that first uncovered the fact that they understood revelation differently. They differed in their understanding of how God warrants his presence as Father and Spirit, outside and inside us, in Jesus Christ. . . . The Lutheran shibboleth in the Lord's Supper question was the thesis of the real presence of the body and blood of the ascended and omnipresent Lord in the visible Communion

---

62. Ibid., 166.
63. Ibid., 161.

> elements.... Both as a continuation and an implication of this for Christology, there was also the thesis of the ubiquity of his body and blood, always and everywhere possible according to the will of Christ.... The Reformed shibboleth in the Lord's Supper question was the interpretation of the Communion elements as symbols... the spiritual eating and drinking with the body and blood of the ascended Lord were happening, parallel to the bodily eating and drinking of bread and wine. This was connected with the Christological thesis of the humanity of Christ, which since Ascension Day and until the second coming is at the right hand of God, and thus is not omnipresent but rather at this particular place in heaven.[64]

The Christological distinction revolves around the way in which Jesus Christ is indirectly identical with God. For the Lutheran, the characteristics of Christ's divine nature are shared with his human nature—*unio personalis*; the emphasis fell on the omnipresence and ubiquity of Christ's body and blood, which were held to be indirectly *identical* with the communion elements. God gives himself *in* the Eucharistic elements, *in* contingent revelation. For the Reformed, however, there could be no sharing of properties between the two natures of Christ; emphasis had to be laid upon Christ's locality in heaven and thus the corresponding work of the Spirit in relating the communion elements with Christ's body and blood—*indirectly* identical with God. God does not give himself *in* the elements, but instead communicates Himself through the Spirit along with the elements. Reformed theologians, Barth writes, "strongly resist the idea that the properties of the one—meaning chiefly the properties of the divine nature—are transferred over to the other, to the human nature."[65] According to Barth, the Reformed church feared that, "by accepting the direct givenness and presence of contingent revelation, ultimately that revelation will merge with contingent reality, so that the Creator might no longer be distinguished from the creature."[66] In short:

> On the *Lutheran side*, it was an *undialectical step forward*, the uninhibited definition of the human nature of Christ with the predicates of deity, a total unifying of revelation with the contingent in which it reveals itself. On the *Reformed* side, it was a *dialectical step back*, the Reformed reservation, the "Calvinist

---

64. Ibid., 164–65.
65. Ibid., 167.
66. Ibid., 184.

extra," according to which the humanity does not participate in the predicates of deity in the full sense.[67]

This sense of reserve comprises the core of everything Barth has to say about the relationship between God and human beings. Reserve here is not meant in a negative way, however, but is shorthand for saying that, "contingent revelation is never and nowhere given to us; there is no human act, no seeing, touching, sensing, that would be directly identical with our relationship to that of revelation."[68] Barth's doctrine of sanctification, therefore, is intrinsically born from the ontological reality that God does not give himself as a possession in revealing himself; in other words, "humanity does not participate in the predicates of his deity" in such a way that those predicates become something attributed to humanity without the continual and sustaining subjective work of the Holy Spirit. Sanctification occurs only in dynamic relationship with Jesus Christ, "the one with whom humanity has to do when humanity has to do with God, with God's *contingent revelation*," in such a way that it does not become a human predicate or possession, and remains in need of divine grace at every moment.[69] This is the presupposition that Barth articulated as "the point from which it is then possible for us to speak about everything else that we are, have, and experience in relation to God."[70]

> Now we turn to the *relationship of the human person* to this contingent but also concealed divine revelation. Calvin proceeds here, again, from the decisive concept that Christ himself is the subject in this relationship. This effectively does away with the psychologism of the Zurich confessors. Christ unites us through faith with his spiritual body in that he justifies and sanctifies us (here the characteristic Calvinist doublet) through the power of the Spirit. But the only way in which this can happen is that he, as our head, shares his "life" with us (Art. 3-4). . . . It is *Christ* who acts and brings about this fellowship, not human faith.[71]

This passage highlights the paradigm in which sanctification occurs; *Christ* is the subject who unites *us* with his own life, who justifies and sanctifies *us*. Because Christ himself is the subject of this relationship,

---

67. Ibid., 202.
68. Ibid., 170.
69. Ibid.
70. Ibid., 166.
71. Ibid., 176.

there is real fellowship, real sanctification "with us." And, as the controversy over the Lord's Supper demonstrated, for Reformed theology and Barth, it is very significant that Christ, "seen from the perspective of human, earthly, and temporal possibilities, is in heaven and remains there," because "*this* contingent entity does not become contingent next to other entities."[72] This fundamental boundary dictates the overall shape of Barth's doctrine of sanctification. It allows Barth to speak quite constructively and concretely of human action and obedience, for within this framework faithful human action "is never thought to be identical with the action of God"; rather it "is shifted so totally into the *light* of God's action"—*insertio in Christum*—that "it is enveloped and filled with ultimate seriousness."[73] Here the Reformed dialectic shines through for Barth. While "not even the smallest portion of our salvation" is transferred from the creator to the creature, even though one really has to do with the actions of man here, "the 'spiritual life'" that Christ grants us consists not only of *"vivification"* by his *Spirit* but also of his making us participants in his life-giving *body through* the power of his Spirit."[74] Sanctification occurs *in Christ* as he shares his life with believers through the power of his Holy Spirit creating real participants.

There is a real danger here in misperceiving Barth's point about the non-given work of Christ. Some, like Anthony Hoekema, have read Barth in this Göttingen period as over-emphasizing the work of Christ in salvation to the extent that there seems to be little or no distinction between justification and sanctification.[75] Others, like J. S. Rhee, contend that Barth's work on sanctification in the 1920's was "radically objectivistic." Even G. C. Berkouwer, who came to appreciate aspects of Barth's work on sanctification, still characterized it as "quietistic and antinomian," judging it "powerless in its historical and subjective implications."[76] Barth's emphasis on the non-givenness of God in sanctification, however, is meant neither to overly objectify the work of Christ, nor to cast

72. Ibid., 170.
73. Ibid., 173.
74. Ibid., 169.
75. "It will be noted that in this article ('Rechtfertigung und Heiligung') Barth's emphasis was almost exclusively on justification—which is typical of his earlier period. As a matter of fact, there does not seem to be much difference between justification and sanctification as he describes them" (Hoekema, "Karl Barth's Doctrine of Sanctification," 4).
76. Berkouwer, *Faith and Sanctification*, 110f., 121f., 186f., 189f., quoted in Rhee, "Secularization and Sanctification," 37.

believers upon a bed of doubt and uncertainty by removing the impact of sanctification from history. For Barth, God's contingent self-giving presence works doctrinally as a type of filter. It is certainly positive content in its own right, but intrinsically it also functions as a boundary marker; it directs the shape and flow of sanctification by indicating what may be appropriately pursued and what is unsuitable for theological discussion for this doctrine. The non-given nature of God means that sanctification is not an infused quality, even if a gracious one, and therefore sanctification must be discussed relationally as an existence in which humanity stands before *God*. Because Jesus Christ is the subject of the "participation" in sanctification, just as He is of justification, faithful human action and obedience can never be discussed apart from "the Spirit from above," who "overcomes the differences in space, making that which is far into something near, uniting us with the humanity of Christ, setting us in relation to the contingent revelation whose local presence we could under no circumstances ever assert."[77] While this at times seems to consign believers to an unimportant, or at best a secondary role it is only in the sense that to look upon a sanctified person means to look upon him sanctified *in Christ*. Barth's emphasis on the non-given nature of God in revelation marks the boundary between authentic Christian discourse and what he ultimately perceives as a self-serving Christian anthropology. As Barth would say a few semesters later in his *Göttingen Dogmatics*, "There is thus, although sanctification itself refers to the *actions* of man and in *certain* actions of man takes the appearance of steps, no *self-sanctification*."[78] Above all, the non-givenness of God in revelation serves Barth's doctrine of sanctification as a type of sieve or watchman, a way of preventing it from becoming another casualty of privatization, of "the so-called religious experience."

A Real Yet Relative Reality

Because Barth's doctrine of sanctification is shaped by focusing upon the work of God the Father who does not give Himself over as a possession— a quality/thing to be handled—but who gives Himself gratuitously and dynamically in His son Jesus Christ through the Holy Spirit, his doctrine

---

77. Barth, "Reformed Confessions," 171.

78. Barth, *Unterricht in der christlichen Religion III, Die Lehre von der Versöhnung / Die Lehre von der Erlösung 1925/1926*, 312.

of sanctification also necessarily addresses its relevance to human life and obedience in response to God. Barth states, "these relationships are not suspended in midair, are not metaphysics and not mythology, but rather this entire 'from God' and 'toward God' that is apparently to be defined by them address the human, plays itself out in and on the human, so that I am justified, sanctified, am a believer and am obedient, whatever that might mean."[79] Pointedly stated: there are indeed real, earthly correlates to God's sanctifying action, even if those correlates are shaped similarly to the Reformed Confessions by notions such as relativity, multiplicity, mutability, and transitoriness.

The dialectic of classical Reformed theology to which Barth consistently refers back to throughout these lectures assures Barth that the content of the first two presuppositions (focus on the work of God, and the non-givenness of God in sanctification) do not negate the concrete, earthly, temporal implications of the third presupposition. Rather, for Barth the reality of God's work in Jesus Christ through the Holy Spirit places the question of human existence and action in a most serious and concrete light, just as it did for Calvin.

> Based on Christianity, especially upon Reformation Christianity, Calvin saw it as possible and necessary to view the great Renaissance problem, "human life" or the problem of humanity . . . a priori together with the problem of God. The issue is . . . simply the person as such in his createdness, with the inescapable question of his *existence*, with his question—What is my purpose as a *human being*?—and the equally inescapable, unheard of, and burdensome answer that must follow. It is the human person in the problematic of his real actions. Calvin dares to take this person seriously, to see him in *relation* to the Christianity whose content is entirely *God's* action, and to relate that Christianity to this question. He does so at the risk that Christianity as God's action might disintegrate when it is placed in *this* context. The further danger is that the human question might explode when it receives this answer. . . . Whatever he is discussing, be it the Ten Commandments or Christ's descent into hell and ascent into heaven, he will always have in view the *totality* of God and the *totality* of the human. . . . This implies, to be sure, what one has called the dialectical character of Calvin's theology.[80]

---

79. Barth, "Reformed Confessions," 161.
80. Ibid., 96–97.

The dialectic is once again, sharply stated: "That at the beginning of all knowledge of God stands no human self-knowledge but God's own knowing, man's being known by God, that is, revelation."[81] Barth affirmed that for the Reformed theologians, God's testimony about Himself not only had profound implications for human life and action, but was the continual *basis* for such implications.[82] Unlike the Catholic, Lutheran, and modern theologies which Barth used as foils, to highlight the significance of the Reformed confessions, the latter, in Barth's estimation, do not transpose the implications for human life and action into themes in and of themselves along side of the knowledge of God. They are instead intrinsically bound up with knowing God in such a way that apart from His continual gracious self-revelation they become corrupt and idolatrous. But Barth also asserted, more positively, that with that knowledge they become the discourse for sanctified human action and obedience.[83] Barth states that, "because the Reformed confession, when it speaks of grace, thinks fundamentally and essentially of what *God* does and sees faith fundamentally only from that side, as God's action upon man, it gains the necessary distance in order then to establish that faith is not God's *only* action upon man."[84] And here the Reformed dialectic ensures, not methodologically, but because it is grounded in the nature of the revealing God, that the concrete, earthly, and temporal facets of sanctification are not stripped of meaning. For "this same God also makes man obedient for his service. . . . Therefore, in the centre of Christianity [lie] *not* only justification, *not* only faith, but without mixture and yet undivided the doublet: faith *and* obedience. The Reformed Christian [is] a child of God *and* a servant of God, certain of his salvation *and* struggling in fear and trembling, his name written by God's finger in heaven *and* on earth."[85]

81. Ibid., 65.

82. "Should not Christianity from the very *beginning*, in its very *essence*, be understood as the truth of *life* and the power of *life*?" (ibid., 97).

83. "One cannot assert that of the *Roman Catholic* confession because of the two-sidedness of the matter, the dialectic of the connection, is blurred by the dominant naturalistic view of infused grace, making sanctification into the outflow of justification and vice versa. It cannot be said of the *Lutheran* confession because there the first side of the matter, justifying faith, is abruptly shifted to the center, over against which the second side, the new obedience, appears to be peripheral if still indispensable" (ibid., 148).

84. Ibid., 148.

85. Ibid., 149.

This is the "problem of life" seen together with the "problem of God," which Barth maintains must not be resolved simply by de-emphasizing or shifting the problem. God's claim upon humanity means that "faith must be joined by something that is not faith; a disciplined pulling of oneself together," and yet all the while "we are and remain the 'pilgrims in mortality'; we remain those with empty hands."[86] The third presupposition of Barth's doctrine of sanctification, put in the language of Trinitarian dogma is, "God *the Holy Spirit*, dwelling in the heart of believers."[87]

The *Scots Confession* of 1560, which Barth found remarkably insightful and trustworthy,[88] offers a concise dogmatic summary of what Barth appealed to as a way of articulating that the work of God in salvation has its correlate in time, in the lives of believers.

> The Scots Confession places emphatically at the centre its view of the free and autonomous action of God over against which everything that happens in and through humanity appears as derivative and secondary. We are *created* by God the Father, *redeemed* by Jesus Christ, *reborn* and *sanctified* by the Holy Spirit. . . . The formation of faith within us through the Holy Spirit is nothing more or less than an awakening from the dead. God relates in the same creative and original way to the *sanctification* that follows after our faith. . . . One sees how independently and necessarily the grounding of *ethics* proceeds from the one overarching principle in Article 13, "*Of the cause of good works*." They have a "cause in us," it says, but this is not based on our freedom of the will but in the Spirit of Christ, who lives in our hearts through true faith, and to that extent gives good works.[89]

The last sentence is of particular importance for this section, especially because its impact, as Barth references several times throughout these lectures, has great potential to lose its significance when shuffled around.[90]

---

86. Ibid., 150, 172.

87. Ibid., 161.

88. "It is truly regrettable that in the seventeenth century the Scots Confession became obsolete and today only has historical significance . . . It is my opinion that . . . the Scots Confession, like few others, may speak to us as a normative and model confession for our pursuit of the question of the positive doctrine of Christianity" (ibid.," 133).

89. Ibid., 130–31.

90. The most notable references reflect the misperceptions that existed between the Reformed and Lutherans who tended to perceive the extremity of inferences from this sentence i.e., "A suspicion hovers in the air that the Reformed Spirit wants to be

And while the initial statement that, "everything that happens in and through humanity appears as derivative and secondary" appears to contradict the significance of temporal human actions, it is not meant to. For, Barth states, in this confession, "the unity and distinctiveness of the religious and the ethical problems are as solid and certain as that of the second and third persons of the Trinity, whose works are recognized in them."[91] This initial statement is intended as an assertion of God's *aseity*, which keeps the question of what happens in and through humanity from becoming a question with "independent significance."[92] And so, the: "but this is not based on our freedom of the will but in the Spirit of Christ, who lives in our hearts through true faith," does not evacuate the veracity of human temporal significance, of the good works that "have a 'cause in us,'" but reflects the notion that the depth of human despair and sin, which remains even after regeneration, does not invalidate God's claim upon humanity as Lord—the one who commands obedience. "Special attention should be given," Barth notes, "to the clear way in which an iron bracket holds together the gift of God and the task of life, without eventuating either into a mystical spiritualism or a rational moralism."[93] In other words, Barth believes that the dialectic between "God and the human" exemplified in the Scots Confession need not rob the seriousness of the human temporal situation by collapsing history into eternity, nor overburden the human creature by allowing it to obtain independent significance.[94]

Thus the unsentimental foundation for discussing real, human, temporal correlates of God's sanctifying reality is established by way of the Reformed fathers as a presupposition for Barth's doctrine of

---

a spirit of a new monasticism and works righteousness, of a moralistic Pharisaisim . . . while the Lutheran Spirit is a spirit of quietism and comfortableness" (ibid., 163).

91. Ibid., 130.

92. Ibid., 131.

93. Ibid., 133.

94. Ibid.," 133. In 1937 and 1938 Barth once again takes up an exposition of the Scots Confession in "The Knowledge of God and the Service of God according to the Teaching of the Reformation," delivered as the Gifford Lectures at the University of Aberdeen. It is worth noting that in these lectures Barth reaffirms the centrality of understanding human work grounded in the person and work of God. He writes, "According to Reformed teaching the knowledge of God and the Service of God do not merely belong together, but like two concentric circles with a common radius, they are one. Knowledge of God is obedience to God. Such knowledge becomes actual by man's becoming a new man through faith in Jesus Christ as his Lord" (Barth, "The Knowledge of God and the Service of God According to the Teaching of The Reformation: Recalling the Scottish Confession of 1560," 114).

sanctification. The characteristically Reformed "awareness of the infinite *distance* between God and human, grace and nature, revelation and reason . . . between God's Word and" the Christian human word gives Barth, just like the early Reformers, "the serene ability to take very seriously the latter within its assigned limits and possibilities."[95] Once one is alerted to the importance of such statements, which highlight the legitimate response of believers to the reality and actions of God, similar notions seem to spill forth from these lectures. Barth genuinely empathises with theologians like Zwingli's co-worker Leo Jud in maintaining that, "Faithfulness on God's side requires faithfulness on our side, that is, faith in his promise and the doing of his *commandments*."[96] With Bullinger, Barth agrees that there is indeed "*no* contradiction between Paul and James. . . . A faith that is not a 'lively and quickening faith' would be a 'feigned faith,' really no faith at all." For, "what God does for man *does not tolerate* any form of passivity, nonparticipation, spectatorship on the part of man."[97] At every point, one encounters not only the inestimable freedom and majesty of God, but along with this, the very real and sedimentary human concern.

At their core, such statements indicate the fabric which comprises the more dogmatically formulated statement: "The 'spiritual life' that Christ grants us consists not only of '*vivification*' by his *Spirit* but also of his making us participants in his life-giving *body through* the power of his Spirit." A legitimate doctrine of sanctification, a doctrine of sanctification faithful to the triune person of God, must truly involve genuine human obedience and action. And Barth contends that there must be genuine "participation" not only spiritually, but physically as well. It must really take place in time, in the history and lives of believers; not because of the independent weight of the human question, but because, as the Eucharistic controversy highlights, "God himself in Christ, communicates himself (not in general, not everywhere, not in the entire world, and also not in our ideas, but rather) as the 'most concrete thing,' that he lets himself be known and enjoyed by us."[98]

Yet Barth remains on guard lest such notions of the Christian life become self-preoccupied. True and requisite language of human action

---

95. Barth, "Reformed Confessions," 83.
96. Ibid., 91.
97. Ibid., 93.
98. Ibid., 166.

and piety can all too easily become self-aggrandizing, spinning the doctrine of sanctification into an independent Christian anthropology "as soon as its moorings to a strong and operative doctrine of grace are loosed."[99] For example:

> Neither the earlier typical medieval nor the later typical modern had counted on the immediate actuality of God's relationship with humanity. . . . Both sides begin with the human person, with nature, with reason in its best sense and build further on this safe and broad foundation, with the help of revelation. Christianity appears as a great pedagogy, a pathway along which the human partly walks, is partly led, and is partly carried along by supernatural power. . . . And as a human person he is obviously the measure of his Christianity as he is the measure of all things.[100]

That Christianity appears as "a pathway along which the human partly walks, is partly led, and is partly carried along by supernatural power" is an implication of the much deeper concern that the human person has become "the measure of his Christianity." A segregation occurs between the reality and work of God and the real but relative human response illustrated here by a *self*-confident human striving and cooperating, whereby the adjective "relative" is essentially dropped, giving the appearance that ultimately human obedience and action is a *self*-secured endeavour. Here the idea of infused grace—that a portion of God's restorative grace is given as a quality or possession to human nature—masks the rift opened between the soteriological and Christological relationship. For although it appears in statements such as these that grace is still a significant feature of the relational equation, in reality, Barth argues, when "grace with its gift is drawn . . . into the territory of experience and psychologised . . . in spite of all monergistic assertions" it degenerates "into the description of possible human relationships," alongside the reality and work of God.[101] In the Westminster Confession, a classic example of such a statement, Barth notes that the theme shifts to "the human person in his receiving and having, accomplishing and presenting."[102] The result: "In *this* context, as was already the case in the doctrine of 'repentance,' it is unavoidable that the Reformed turn to ethics takes on a moralistic and legalistic

---

99. Webster, *Barth's Earlier Theology*, 52.
100. Barth, "Reformed Confessions," 207.
101. Ibid., 139.
102. Ibid., 144.

appearance."[103] Human action, separated from its Christological presupposition here is ironically stripped of its creatureliness, thus forcing itself to take on an air of ultimate responsibility. One can no longer speak of a freedom for obedience here, but rather a pharisaical captivity to specific concrete actions. In the classical Reformed confessions, however, "grace is placed, in principle, over against nature and in the centre. There is no cooperation between God and man."[104] Barth's point is essentially that the anthropological principle must be established and made to depend upon a dogmatic principle; or perhaps even more specifically—the soteriological principle must be developed Christologically.[105] Here the third presupposition functions, similarly to the previous two, as a boundary marker for the doctrine of sanctification.

The pathway that believers travel, guided by this boundary, is not a safe and broad one; it is not a pathway that they tread as ones alongside of God as if infused with grace "as a principle that accompanies and cooperates" with them.[106] Barth is abundantly clear that, "there is *no* equation of divine doing and human having, but rather God remains God. *His* is the Spirit that vivifies us through 'participation' in the body and blood of his Son."[107] It is Christ who "unites us through faith with his spiritual body in that he justifies and sanctifies us (here the characteristic Calvinist doublet) through the power of the Spirit."[108] This is again though, importantly, the hinge which allows Barth's doctrine of sanctification to include the human situation. This communion believers have with *Christ* allows Barth, in his doctrine of sanctification, to clearly articulate the

---

103. Ibid.

104. Ibid., 149.

105. While Barth does not state this explicitly in these lectures, he does lay the foundation with statements such as, "[T]hat God, God himself in Christ, communicates himself . . . as the "most concrete thing," . . . [t]his is the point from which it is then possible for us to speak about everything else that we are, have and experience in relations to God. Everything that unfolds between the Word of God on the one hand and faith and obedience of man on the other must be illumined and proven from this point." Which led him to assert explicitly in his *Unterricht in der christlichen Religion* lectures, "We will also have to keep sharp eyes here, that the soteriological principle can now be a Christological development, the character of an independent Christian anthropology we may never ever accept" (ibid.," 166; Barth, *Unterricht in der christlichen Religion III*, 308).

106. Barth, "Reformed Confessions," 218.

107. Ibid., 172.

108. Ibid., 176.

"communion which [*believers*] have with Christ."[109] That "we are and remain the 'pilgrims in mortality'" allows him to emphasise that "*we* remain those with empty hands." In this way, the soteriological principle that believers are renewed to faithful living is developed Christologically in that "we grasp Christ as the source of all blessings."[110] That Christ is the source and subject of all blessings through the Holy Spirit does not deter Barth from articulating that *we* truly grasp Christ. For, Barth says,

> on the one hand, the human is understood in a sober and rational way, seen in a critically reserved fashion with the possibilities given to him, but then affirmed practically and reasonably in these very possibilities. On the other hand, God as the absolute wonder, God who is God solely in and through himself, especially and most of all when he reveals himself to humanity, is then most to be respected in his deity when the unheard of is to be heard, the unspeakable is to be said: that the human stands in relationship to him.[111]

One could describe this third principle of Barth's doctrine of sanctification, then, as Barth himself described the essence of the Reformed confessions. Human action and obedience, like the Reformed confessions, is a

> *fading* bell stroke, a *falling, streaming* cascade, or, as we said, a *disappearing* shadow. . . . *Yes*, the bell stroke fades and says as it does so that the time is fulfilled [see Gal. 4:4], unrepeatable, but also irrevocable, and the hour has come to arise from sleep [see Rom.13:11] once and for all. *Yes*, the waters stream and fall, "*everything flows*," inexorable, turbulent at all points, and speak with their falling and cascading of the majesty of the mountain heights from which they flow. *Yes*, the shadow disappears and must disappear, and in the very fact of its disappearance it witnesses to the rising light of the sun, an involuntary, vanquished, beaten, teeth-grinding witness perhaps, but still a *witness*. . . . Its centre of gravity, if not in fact its very content, is not in itself but rather *beyond* itself.[112]

Each descriptive feature has its relative purpose. Though the bell, the cascade, and the shadow do not exist in their own right or for their own

---

109. Ibid., 172
110. Ibid., 177.
111. Ibid., 65.
112. Ibid., 38.

glory, that to which they point transforms and fills them with lasting significance; but only as they fade, fall, and disappear. Similarly, Barth would say, human action and obedience "consists in its essential *non-*significance, its obvious relativity, humanity, multiplicity, mutability, and transitoriness," but "the one who knows that this is a *positive* statement . . . should say it loudly and confidently."[113] For though the witness stutters and is at times confused, "the Word of God will stand forever."[114] Similarly, though "*we* are and remain the 'pilgrims in mortality,'" though "*we* remain those with empty hands," nevertheless *His* Spirit really does vivify "us through 'participation' in the body and blood of his Son."[115] To say, "God *the Holy Spirit*, dwelling in the heart of believers" is to say nothing other than "this entire 'from God' and 'toward God' . . . plays itself out in and on the human, so that *I* am justified, sanctified, am a believer and am obedient, whatever that might mean in detail."[116]

113. Ibid.
114. Ibid., 39.
115. Ibid., 172.
116. Ibid., 161.

4

The Resurrection of the Dead

As certain as it is that "if the hope of the resurrection be removed, the whole edifice of piety would collapse, just as if the foundation were withdrawn from it" (Calvin), just as certain is the other thing, that, once the reality of the resurrection, and in it the reality of God, is recognized, man can and may tread the so infinitely narrow path, the knife-edge of Christianity.[1]

Introduction and Significance of Text

ALONGSIDE "THE THEOLOGY OF the Reformed Confessions," Barth also delivered a powerful lecture series on 1 Corinthians 15 in the summer of 1923. And although Barth found himself having "to live from hand to mouth" once again as he taught, he also felt as if he were able to "do it in a better spirit, even when the hour is late."[2] Barth was at home amidst the "astonishing" writings of Paul, which captured his imagination and "fairly lifted [him] right out of the saddle."[3] These lectures allowed Barth to return to the "profound disclosures" he had encountered in 1 Corinthians a few years earlier while still in Safenwil—disclosures that had struck him "like the shocks from an electric eel."[4]

---

1. Barth, *The Resurrection of the Dead*, 212. These lectures, largely unchanged, were first published in 1924 as *Die Auferstehung der Toten. Eine akademische Vorlesung über 1 Kor. 15*.

2. Barth, *Karl Barth-Eduard Thurneysen Briefwechsel*, 2:162.

3. Ibid.

4. Karl Barth to Eduard Thurneysen, 11 November 1919, *Briefwechsel* 1:350, quoted in Grieb, "Last Things First," 50.

Of this series, as well as with his other lectures at the time, Barth remarked that, "first of all the details had to be ascertained, clarified and above all tested."[5] As Busch has rightly commented, "the move from Safenwil to Göttingen was a decisive event" for Barth, and although "in essentials he wanted to say 'the same things as were said in Safenwil,' much had now changed."[6] There had not been a change in Barth's theological agenda *per se*, but rather a shift in the visibility and opportunities placed before him. He had to reckon now with the fact of his renown, and therefore demanded of himself a rigorous specificity in his own theological framework.[7] While his agenda was still clearly rooted in the "essentials" that characterized his pastorate in Safenwil, he recognized that he "had only just begun on a course which . . . one had to follow laboriously in his own sphere."[8] With each new work, Barth further clarified his own theological position. His lectures on 1 Corinthians 15 offer another clear example of his judicious and thoughtful commitment to the task of theology in which he continued to clarify and test his own positions. As Barth returned once again to pore himself over the material on 1 Corinthians his work was characterized by an intensity that mirrored his perception of the importance of this epistle.

Besides the obvious delight which Barth seemed to relish while working with these New Testament texts, the significance of his work on 1 Corinthians 15 is further demonstrated by the fact that these lectures were the only ones from his time at the University in Göttingen that he saw fit to print. For Barth the centrality of the issues raised in these lectures, particularly the incomparable impact of the resurrection of Jesus Christ upon life, could not be overstated, and therefore deserved in his opinion to be more widely disseminated in order for the church to think along with him.[9]

---

5. Busch, Karl *Barth*, 126.

6. Ibid.

7. This is demonstrated for example in Barth's relationship with the "movement" he had unintentionally spearheaded—of which the *Zwischen den Zeiten* was the mouthpiece—which began to break apart even as it was growing in popularity. Throughout the course of Barth's professorship in Göttingen he found himself distancing himself from the "movement" because of the intricate distinctions he perceived lying hid beneath the surface of their similarities.

8. Busch, *Barth*, 126.

9. Barth states in the foreword to *The Resurrection of the Dead* that, "We might even say that this *central* significance of the ideas expressed in the chapter [15] extends beyond the limits of the First Epistle to the Corinthians. Here Paul discloses

As Ingolf Dalferth has noted, "From the publication of his Epistle to the Romans in 1919 to the very end of his life, Barth did not waver on this fundamental point: The reality to which theology refers is the eschatological reality of the risen Christ and the new life into which we are drawn by the Spirit."[10] Dalferth's comments rightly capture the magnitude and lasting consequence that the notions of Christ's resurrection, the work of the Spirit, and an eschatological foundation had on Barth's theology, and it is these notions that comprise the heart of the 1 Corinthian lectures.[11] It is puzzling, therefore, that *The Resurrection of the Dead* has been largely overlooked, particularly in regards to issues surrounding the Christian life, which are so intricately tied up in this work and have often drawn such heavy fire from Barth's commentators. In spite of Barth's own immediate perception of its profitability and the centrality of its message within his overall theological perspective, *The Resurrection of the Dead* remains merely a fringe text.[12] And even when it is treated, as John Webster notes, it is "subject to so many interpretative schemas."[13] In light of the issues surrounding *The Resurrection of the Dead*, this analysis will forgo some of the traditional stalling points such as formal issues relating to methodology and exegesis, and the typical preoccupation with Barth's portrayal of Jesus' resurrection merely as an ahistorical event which fails to adequately engage in its theological implications.

Instead, this chapter will pursue an avenue of thought linked directly to the core material of these lectures: the impact of the resurrection of Jesus Christ upon human sanctification. The centrality of this topic is inherently stressed throughout the work, as Barth continually reminds

---

generally his focus, his background, and his assumptions with a definiteness he but seldom uses elsewhere, and with a particularity which he has not done in his other Epistles as known to us. . . . How vitally important is the chapter, if this be the case, for understanding the testimony of the New Testament generally, I need not emphasize." Barth, *Resurrection*, 5. See also Webster, *Barth's Earlier Theology*, 67.

10. Dalferth, "Karl Barth's Eschatological Realism," 20–21.

11. The 1 Corinthians lectures will be referred to throughout as *The Resurrection of the Dead*.

12. As John Webster has pointed out: "Yet though *The Resurrection of the Dead* has been published for over eighty years, the work has by and large been passed over, not only in studies of Barth's theology of the resurrection, but even by those interested in his exegesis or hermeneutics. . . . When it is treated, [it] is usually handled as a merely ancillary text" although more recent works "have pushed its reception in a more fruitful direction" (Webster, *Barth's Earlier Theology*, 68).

13. Ibid.

his audience that "the Resurrection of the Dead is the point from which Paul is speaking and to which he points. From this standpoint, not only the death of those now living, but, above all, their life *this side* of the threshold of death, is in the apostolic sermon, veritably seen, understood, judged, and placed in the light of the last severity, the last hope."[14]

The resurrection of the dead and the life of believers this side of death are placed in such close proximity that the essence and scope of the Christian life is only truly grasped when viewed through the lens of the resurrection. Barth's whole premise in this work is that, contrary to the predominant interpretation of his day, which saw the resurrection chapter as simply one more "doctrinal pronouncement" along with many other disparate "exhortations" and "rebukes," Paul's analysis of the resurrection of the dead forms not only the binding thread throughout 1 Corinthians, but offers the lens with which to rightly perceive the entire Christian existence.[15] The resurrection of Jesus Christ points not only to an aspect of death; it also, as this text makes clear, forms the material basis through which the Christian life is rightly "seen," "understood," and "judged." The resurrection chapter, Barth wrote, "is admirably suited to clarify what Christianity as a whole involves," for "the shadow which Christ casts over the whole of life on this side of the grave cannot be forgotten."[16] This theme—the resurrection of Jesus Christ and its impact within the world—taken up in various ways throughout *The Resurrection of the Dead* is significant in further understanding Barth's doctrine of sanctification. As Barth reflects: "This other new thing, which is here asserted ('but ye are washed, but ye are sanctified, but ye are justified in the name of the Lord Jesus, and by the Spirit of our God') is, according to Paul, an unheard-of, boundless promise under which the Church is placed. Nor should this positive side of the matter be here over looked."[17] Sanctification is demonstrated in Barth's work here as a surprising, hopeful, and extremely positive identity—albeit an identity born in "unrest"—which believers share in Christ.[18] For as Barth alludes in the opening quotation of this chapter aptly quoting Calvin: In the hope of the resurrection lie

14. Barth, *Resurrection*, 101.
15. Ibid., 6.
16. Ibid., 111, 67.
17. Ibid., 28.
18. Barth states, "Christianity brings not peace but unrest into the natural life; it transforms it into the members of the body of the risen Lord, which, as such, shall be sanctified" (ibid., 33).

equally the foundation and possibility for man's sanctification. Indeed, there can be no right understanding of Barth's doctrine of sanctification, or any other doctrine for that matter, without taking into account this eschatological orientation.

Specifically, this chapter will briefly examine Barth's characterization of eschatology and the resurrection of the dead as developed in 1 Corinthians, and then move on to explore its subsequent impact on the doctrine of sanctification—notably rendered as an existence of struggle and hope. These themes are finally drawn together under a description of Barth's doctrine of sanctification that clearly prioritizes a conception of God's claim upon human life over a more narrowly construed account of spiritual and moral development.

Outline of Text

The Resurrection of the Dead is grouped into three rather unequal sections. The first section, "The Trend of First Corinthians I-XIV," takes up nearly half the length of the entire work; yet, as its title indicates, Barth has assembled almost all of 1 Corinthians into it, devoting the remainder of the book to chapter 15 alone.[19] Barth passes rather quickly through the first fourteen chapters, as he connects and draws together the seemingly haphazardly linked issues surrounding the Corinthian Church. As Barth reads Paul, the main defect in the Christian community in Corinth is that "the testimony of Christ is threatening to become an object of energetic human activity, a vehicle of real human needs."[20] Against "the boldness, assurance, and enthusiasm with which" the Corinthians "believe, not in God, but in their own belief in God," Paul decries (according to Barth) that "the truth and the worth of the testimony of Christ lie in what in them *happens* to the man, happens from God; not what he is as man, nor what he makes of it, not in the word or the 'gnosis' in man's acceptance of it."[21] "Clearly," Barth asserts, "the secret nerve of this whole (and perhaps not only this) section" is this "of God" found in 4: 5.[22]

Section Two, "The Resurrection Chapter," acts as a hinge in this book and smoothly transitions between the two larger sections by joining

---

19. Strangely, Barth does not incorporate 1 Corinthians 16 into this work.
20. Barth, *Resurrection*, 15.
21. Ibid., 15, 16.
22. Ibid., 16.

the threads of the first fourteen chapters with the content of chapter 15 by way of an extended introduction. Although this section is only twenty-four pages long, it is extremely important to Barth's interpretation of 1 Corinthians. Here Barth articulates clearly what he believes Scripture speaks of when it addresses "The Resurrection of the Dead" and "last things." For example, Barth writes, words and ideas typically associated with the doctrine of eschatology, such as "last things," "the ends of history," and even the word *eschatology* itself, involuntarily evoke images "of events and figures belonging to a future of the world."[23] But, "in the sense of the New Testament generally," those descriptions "are *not* such final possibilities, however real they may seem to our eyes."[24] Instead Barth sees Paul rendering "The Resurrection of the Dead" and "last things" as the in-breaking power of God at every moment, "the most positive thing that exists, which looms behind" each instant.[25] As such, the Christian life is determined not by what it may possess here and now this side of the grave, but by the end of all earthly ways. That is—the resurrection of Jesus Christ—life given in faith and hope.

Section Three, "Explanation of I Corinthians XV," comprises the remaining portion of the work. It is divided into four subsections: "The Resurrection Gospel as the Foundation of the Church," "The Resurrection as the Meaning of Faith," "The Resurrection as Truth," and "The Resurrection as Reality." Each subsection in its own distinct and profound way settles around the notion of what it means, "to think from the standpoint of Christ."[26] The focus throughout section three is the eschatological impact of Christ's resurrection on the Christian life. And as Bultmann rightly interpreted Barth's analysis, this very specific rendering of the Christian life—in an eschatological manner—determines "the *whole* of the Christian's existence and bring[s] him into a particular relation to the world. Consequently every question which arises in the area of his existence in the world can be rightly dealt with only from the point of view of eschatology."[27] Properly understood, Barth claims that the message of chapter 15 and all of 1 Corinthians is that the end of all things instituted by God is also the beginning and proclamation of new life—"the mean-

23. Ibid., 103.
24. Ibid.
25. Ibid., 124.
26. Ibid., 184.
27. Bultmann, *Faith and Understanding*, 67.

ing of the resurrection of Jesus consists in this, that the resurrection is the divine horizon also of our existence. Life and the world are finite. God is the end. Hence he is also the beginning."[28]

The Eschatology of 1 Corinthians and the Resurrection of the Dead

Barth begins his reflections on 1 Corinthians with a telling snapshot of the Corinthian Church in light of Paul's remarks. He writes, "Here the new religious matter, brought by the apostolic preaching, must have been accepted with passion, and although not immediately assimilated, was yet absorbed in large understood-misunderstood lumps, and made available for that Church's own needs."[29] As Barth understands Paul, the entire Epistle to the Corinthians addresses the single unequivocal bedrock misunderstanding assimilated by the Corinthians, which laid riotous claim to their ecclesial community: "What was disputed was the fundamental radical application of the 'resurrection of the dead,' the treatment of *this* point of view as 'the main thing.'"[30] The Corinthians did not see death as unnatural or the end to human experience, let alone a foe to be conquered. "To them death is something inevitable which overtakes man, all men must die (verse 51). It is not an enemy.... For them the overcoming of *sins* is not inseparably connected with a victory over death."[31] The Corinthian Church could not, therefore, understand Paul's emphasis upon complete and total acceptance of the *resurrection* of the dead, because for them death was but a gateway for the soul, which continues to live on.[32]

To be sure, the Corinthians accepted Christ's resurrection, "but they regarded it as an isolated historical event, which did *not*, at any rate, stand to us in the relationship that upon the basis thereof our own resurrection must be affirmed (verse 15)."[33] They did not see Christ's resurrection as the foundation of all Christian existence. Instead, the Corinthians

---

28. Barth, *Resurrection*, 165.
29. Ibid., 13.
30. Ibid., 143.
31. Ibid., 116.
32. Dale Dawson summarizes the Corinthian's perspective well: "The resurrection of the body was thought unnecessary because the eternal blessing of the soul was considered guaranteed, once the soul was freed from its bodily imprisonment." See Dawson, *The Resurrection in Karl Barth*, 41.
33. Barth, *Resurrection*, 116.

apparently held that the soul continued after death as a spiritual and immaterial existence, which did not require the body to be resurrected.[34] The crucial point that Barth perceives Paul drawing out here is that the Corinthians maintained a natural continuity between life enclosed in the body—the temporal—and life after death—the eternal; or perhaps even more pointedly stated they maintained a direct correlation between the human and divine world and work and therefore perceived a type of perfected humanity fulfilled in their midst. The overcoming of sins for example was not tied to a specific future redemption imparted here and now through the Spirit of the risen Christ, but was hoped for as a general religious truth to be experienced *in toto*.[35]

What they missed in disregarding the resurrection as constitutive for Christianity was the implication that the continuity of this life and the one to come are "not to be directly ascertained, but only hoped for, only to be believed in."[36] The result was that, "For them the Kingdom of God does not fall outside the sphere of flesh and blood; to seek and to find incorruption in corruption does not appear to them to be at all impossible; but they see in it the very Christian possibility 'to be eternal in every moment' (verse 50)."[37] This philosophy of continuity, the direct equation of the temporal and eternal, combined with the Christian message of the Kingdom of God caused a great "flourishing in Corinth in a disquieting fashion." [38] Barth writes that, "a Kingdom-of-God's springtime seems to have been dawning there, such as was hardly to be recorded subsequently in the best ages of revival."[39] The Corinthian's misunderstanding of the import of Christ's resurrection from the dead, which Barth calls an inadequate eschatology, resulted in their also misunderstanding the essence of the Christian life. For them the Christian life was a robust possessing of the fullness of the Kingdom of God; this led, unfortunately, to the eclipsing of Christ's work by their own. One could fairly infer from Barth's comments that in Corinth sanctification, for example, was not conceived as a matter of participation in the life of the resurrected Christ through faith and hope, and confessed in obedience, but was the present

34. Ibid., 117.
35. Ibid., 142.
36. Ibid., 117.
37. Ibid., 116.
38. Ibid., 98.
39. Ibid..

striving after and enjoyment of moral perfection as a natural capacity given along with the Kingdom of God on earth.

The difference of opinion concerning the resurrection was not merely a doctrinal squabble, open to a wide range of theological positions. Barth impresses upon his readers that, "what is involved is the *substance*, the *whole* of the Christian revelation. It was *not a theological doubt*, to be corrected incidentally or even over looked, but an attack upon what made Christianity to be Christianity."[40] What was fundamentally at stake in the Corinthian rejection of the resurrection of the dead, the direct association of the Kingdom of God and Christianity, was the "rule of God"—God's freedom, *aseity*, and glory.[41] And so Paul, in order to reproach his listeners and confront them with the seriousness of the situation, thrusts them into "the light of the last severity, the last hope. . . . The great answer, which, by reason of the fact that it is exactly given *there*, first awakens all the questions of life . . . and in this disguise as question can only be grasped as answer also."[42] That is, in order to correct the Corinthians' misperception of what life and death entail—of the Lordship of God—Paul directs the Corinthians to the doctrine of the *last things*. For it is here that all things religious, human, and penultimate are placed in light of the rule of God and therefore come to an end; and yet also, it is there that they are at the same time given new life and meaning; the basis which the Christian life is developed upon.

As Barth transitions into the heart of his material, he is quite adamant that "last things" as taken up by Paul here, and in the New Testament generally, are not those expressions typically thought to describe "events and figures belonging to a future of the world,"[43] not even if those expressions are "composed of, and constructed with, material taken from the Bible and perhaps even from I Cor. xv."[44] Those conceptions of "last things," that "attempt, after speaking of everything else possible, to bring forward something about death, the beyond and the world perfection," are essentially not in conflict with what the Corinthians themselves believed.[45] The Corinthian Church's vibrant monism—which proclaimed a

---

40. Ibid., 112–13.
41. Ibid., 98.
42. Ibid., 101.
43. Ibid., 102.
44. Ibid., 103.
45. Ibid., 107.

type of "infinity of the world of time, of things, above all of men"—failed precisely because it did not perceive the Christian life in light of the *end of all things*.[46] It must not be forgotten, Barth repeatedly states, that Paul's doctrine of *last things* as such addresses not simply the continuation of the human story, the reality of life beyond the end of time, but "a reality so radically superior to all happening and all temporality, that in speaking of the finiteness of history and the finiteness of time, he is also speaking of that upon which all time and all happening is *based*."[47] The doctrine of *last things*, therefore, addresses the limitation of time, marked by the eternity of God.

Paul's correction to the Corinthians' rank exuberance, which perceived eternity as simply a continuation of human history, points them to the radical truth that eternity is *God's* eternity, "which sets a limit to the endlessness of the world, of time, of things, of men."[48] In a certain sense, the doctrine of *last things* does indeed point to the end of the world, of time, and man, to death and mortality—as Barth states, Chapter 15 "treats of Death and the Dead," precisely "in sharp contrast to the abundance of the possibilities of life which was the theme of chapter xiv."[49] Paul emphasises this aspect though, Barth writes, to virtually yank the carpet from under the Corinthians' feet, for they too are marked by this finiteness. In and of themselves they too may only know of their death and limitation. Their exuberance and religious vitality established upon the assumption of an infinite continuity between Christian life and the Kingdom of God "suddenly appear here in the pale light of the fact that they must die."[50] But, Barth states, one must not stop halfway. God's eternity, "which sets a limit to the endlessness of the world, of time, of things, of men, must be made fruitful."[51] The *last* word, therefore, which is spoken over time and delimits it "must be so understood as the last word that it can at the same time be understood as *first* word, the history of the end at the same time, and, as such, the history of the beginning."[52] Hence, "the recollection of

---

46. Ibid., 105.
47. Ibid., 104.
48. Ibid., 105.
49. Ibid., 107.
50. Ibid.
51. Ibid., 105–6.
52. Ibid., 106.

death is so important, so urgent, so disturbing, so actual because it is in fact really the tidings of the resurrection."[53]

The resurrection, Barth says, is what really generates meaning in Paul's recollection of the finiteness of the world and time. After all, Paul's emphasis is upon the *resurrection* of the dead and not simply the great nothingness of death itself. The resurrection is the point, Barth writes, from which this entire letter, even the entirety of the gospel, flows, and is made meaningful. Barth's words climax in this section as he divulges the significance of the resurrection, the reality of all *res*.[54]

> With the word "resurrection," however, the apostolic preaching puts in this empty place [the finiteness of the world and the nothingness of death] against all that exists for us, all that is known for us, all that can be possessed by us, all things of all time—what? not the non-being, the unknown, the not-to-be-possessed, . . . but the source and the truth of all that exists, that is known, that can belong to us, . . . the eternity of time, the *resurrection* of the dead.[55]

Barth's interpretation of 1 Corinthians comes full circle here as he draws together the entirety of what it means to say *last things*. The doctrine of the Resurrection of the Dead is not simply a matter of variant importance of which one may choose to accept or deny within Christianity; nor is it a way of explicating those ends of histories which peoples and civilizations have been conjecturing throughout the ages, which simply indicate the continuity of life after death. No, Barth says, the resurrection of the dead is the very place, where death appears to have the last word, in which the end *is the beginning*. In the resurrection, God not only marks time as finite, but He marks it in such a way that ushers in new life. God's final word—the word of *God*, of His *Kingdom*—concerning humanity and death is simultaneously a word of limitation *and* restoration.

The Corinthian's misperception of the Christian life was disastrously conceived because it was precisely not born from this word of restoration and life—the resurrection of Jesus Christ. For, Barth emphasised, the Christian life exists "where only the indifferent conception of the non-existent, unknown, inconceivable seems to have room, where only the dissolution of all things and phenomena seems to be in question,

---

53. Ibid., 109.
54. Ibid., 108.
55. Ibid.

where only the contradictory assertion of the infinity of time seems to be left."[56] The Christian life must be established from the *resurrection* of the dead because without that in-breaking power of God's self revelation in Jesus Christ there is only "the dead," people marked only by sin and death. Jesus' resurrection is God's self-proclamation and, therefore, guarantee, that sin and death have also been marked. They have been overcome and will come to an end. Christ's resurrection establishes new life, but precisely as life given in *Christ* as the first fruits for all—not to be possessed or directly correlated with one's present earthly striving. The Christian life is thus established within this tension of divine-historical action. Though man remains characterized by sin and death within time, he is nevertheless also marked by the resurrection of Jesus from the dead, the one who has overcome sin and death and transcends the finiteness of time.

The essence of the Christian life, including the doctrine of sanctification, is as Barth sees it, an eschatological reality established in the resurrection of Jesus Christ. That is to say, the Christian life exists only in so much as it is effected in this work of God which transcends time. The doctrine of *last things* points to the absurdity of any simple continuity between time and eternity—it points to those things instituted by *God*.

> The dead: that is what we are. The risen: that is what we are not. But precisely for this reason the resurrection of the dead involves that that which *we are*: the dead living, time eternity.... All this is not given except in hope, and therefore this identity is not to be put into effect. The life that we dead are living here and now is not, therefore, to be confounded with *this* life, of which we can only ever say that we are not yet living in it; the endlessness of time is not to be confused with eternity; the corporeality of phenomena is not to be confused with *this* reality; ... The sharp, fundamental step which parts the latter from the former, as the impossible from the possible, is not to be removed, but *given* in hope—in hope, in the identification of the former with the latter, the resurrection of the dead already *effected* in God.[57]

Because the resurrection is the act in which God's eternity infiltrates all of time, "the meaning of the resurrection of Jesus consists in this, that the resurrection is the divine horizon also of our existence. Life and the world

56. Ibid.
57. Ibid., 108–9.

are finite. God is the end. Hence he is also the beginning."[58] Though the Christian life is an impossible possibility never to be simply correlated or confused with one's temporal historicity, it is yet identified with the resurrected life of Jesus Christ in such a way that it is also, as Barth puts it, "already *effected* in God." No truer reality exists.

Characteristics of Sanctification

As mentioned earlier, the question looming in the background of this text relates to the *whom* of Christian existence and discourse.[59] Barth's own theological perspective was shaped precisely by what it means to speak of *this* God, *this* Christ, and *this* Holy Ghost; and, as his work on 1 Corinthians underlined, that same focus is also addressed in this *last* word—the eschatological reality.[60] The first three presuppositions—this God, this Christ, and this Holy Ghost—were especially highlighted in Barth's "Theology of the Reformed Confessions," which, in relationship to sanctification, called attention to the initiating and finalizing reality of God, the non-givenness of God in revelation, and the real yet relative earthly human correlate of God's action. The question concerning this *last* word—the resurrection of Jesus Christ from the dead—as addressed in *The Resurrection of the Dead*, offers further insight into some of the characteristic features of Barth's doctrine of sanctification. For, as was also stated earlier, the impact of Jesus' resurrection deals above all with the life of those now living on *this side* of the threshold of death.[61] This section, then, will build upon the presuppositions previously established in "The Theology of the Reformed Confessions" concerning "*this* God," "*this* Christ," and "*this* Holy Ghost" by turning its attention to the relationship between sanctification and "this *last* word"—the resurrection of Jesus Christ in order to more fully understand what Barth means when he speaks about the doctrine of sanctification.

In light of the eschatological reality of Christ's resurrection, spoken in this *last* word, the Christian life is ultimately characterized as "existence in anticipation," an "indirect identity," the "*synchronism of the living and*

---

58. Ibid., 165.

59. "Without any doubt at all the words 'resurrection of the dead' are, for him, nothing else than a paraphrase of the word 'God'" (ibid., 192).

60. Ibid., 111.

61. Ibid., 101.

the dead."[62] Barth states: "We thus stand in the connexion of *salvation history*, which is a real history: the perishing of an old, the becoming of a new, a path and a step on this path, no mere relationship, but history which is not enacted in time, but between time and eternity—*the* history, in which the creation, the resurrection of Christ, and the End . . . are one day." [63]

Christian existence is thus lived out within the arena of what Barth here calls *salvation history*. It is neither a purely temporal historical existence as the Corinthians assumed, nor an inner-spiritual state gradually overcoming human sinfulness within history awaiting the completion of time to be fully realized. This specific form of existence poised between the Easter miracle and the *parousia*, enacted through the Word of God that transcends the boundaries of time, is the realm of the "new man", already accomplished in God, but not yet possessed. The doctrine of sanctification then finds its form within this arena of anticipation poised between promise and fulfilment—the perishing of the old and the creation of the new. As Barth paraphrases 1 Cor 1:30-31, "Of this God, however—that is, of the God who has chosen the things that are not—*are you*; you have your being in Jesus Christ, who was made unto you wisdom from God . . . and sanctification . . . in which only the Lord can be glorified."[64] This is the basis of Barth's doctrine of sanctification: The place where only the sinner stands is, through the eschatological power of God, the exact place where the "new man" exists. Sanctification is a reality perceived only in the resurrection of Jesus Christ—but nonetheless real—and, therefore, as an integral expression of the Christian life assumes a certain mode of existence: one primarily characterized by struggle and hope.

Struggle

To speak of sanctification as a mode of existence uniquely characterized by the term 'struggle' has less to do with any sort of moral edict, and is certainly no *de facto* call to arms against some*thing* or other, but is more appropriately thought of as a way of expressing the truth that, "Ye are not your own."[65] In other words 'struggle,' in relationship to sanctification, is

---

62. Webster, *Barth's Earlier Theology*, 89; Barth, *Resurrection*, 201, 207.
63. Ibid., 201–2.
64. Ibid., 23.
65. Ibid., 32.

a way of addressing Christ's right over man, and, therefore importantly, the corollary that man is not his own. Barth writes:

> Christianity brings not peace but unrest into the natural life; it transforms it into the members of the body of the risen Lord, which, as such, shall be sanctified. Against the life urge of man, Paul opposes the unassailable truth that he cannot do what he wants: the imperious question, whether and how in his actions he will honour or dishonour the Lord. A hand has been held out to man which will not let him go.[66]

Behind Paul's discussion of this or that particular ethical situation there is one unsurpassable truth which Barth repeatedly calls attention to; that is: Christianity as such does not now possess the fullness of its existence, but relies on the life given in Christ through faith. This thread, expressed in many different ways throughout the text, means further that "we are in no sense to regard our earthly existence, our body, as an opportunity to exhaust our vitality. We are not our own masters."[67] The real issue surrounding sanctification here is the Lordship of Christ and the form of Christian existence it entails, over against any sort of moral certainty which may arise in the wake of a supposed self-assured identity, i.e., the Corinthian problem. To address sanctification as an existence in struggle, then, is a way of explicating, in the first place, Barth's idea that the Christian life brings not peace but unrest into the natural life because "the present state of the world, but also our present relationship to God . . . is a provisional state, an episode, an episode indeed of the transition and the struggle."[68] The Christian, therefore, may not rest comfortably with his sanctification, as if the tension between promise and fulfilment were already resolved. And yet, in the second place, it means that the reality of *God's* actions are not to be forgotten, for the members of the body of the risen Lord shall be, or rather, in Christ *are*, sanctified. The term 'struggle' then, further indicates that sanctification is the sure sign that sin and death have been marked for ruin—the struggle points not only to Adam, but also to Christ.

> And thus he places man forcibly in the light, or, rather, twilight, of the truth that he is created by God in the middle between Adam and Christ, and tells him: Thou art *Both*, or rather thou

---

66. Ibid., 33.
67. Ibid., 32.
68. Ibid., 168.

belongest to both, and just as both jointly describe God's way, from the old to the new creature, so thy life also is the scene across which this path leads, so must thou, too, make the journey *from* here *to* there. In other words, he jerks the questioner and spectator out of his comfortable position and sets him right in the midst of the *struggle*, in which the resurrection is truth.[69]

First, Christian sanctification exists within this struggle between life marked by death, life in Adam that is, and the new life given in Christ. As such, sanctification, just like the truth of the Christian's own resurrection, "is not a reality, not something given, that can be perceived or that is possible to be perceived, like all those second things which are cited . . . as proof of the relative miracle."[70] Barth writes: "The error of the Corinthians may be understood this wise: they comprehended what had happened in Christ in the world as something finished and satisfying in itself. In reality it is only a beginning, in fact only an indication."[71] One of the distinctive facets of Barth's doctrine of sanctification emerges precisely at this point. For Barth, sanctification here and now in this life can only ever be an indication of the transitional state of the world in which "Christ has come to deliver the Kingdom to the Father."[72] The finality of the transition from Christ to the Father is not yet complete and, therefore, "there can be no security of an alleged possession in the shadow of the coming; how can it be when their Lord is even in the field?"[73] Stated negatively, this means that one does not in and of himself possess his sanctification, neither as a type of restored righteousness that he may gradually develop or build himself up in, nor as a gracious gift given with which he may battle the vestiges of sin which lurk about. In this sense sanctification is simply a witness to the *struggle* between the old and the new and should remind Christians that any sort of monism which regards "the Kingdom of God as already established, is a pious godlessness. No, the Kingdom of God is in course of coming, and *that* is characteristic for our situation in Christ."[74] The struggle in which the Christian exists informs him that he can in no ways sanctify himself, nor add an ounce to his sanctification, for his sanctification is not his own.

69. Ibid., 202.
70. Ibid., 195.
71. Ibid., 168.
72. Ibid.
73. Ibid., 169.
74. Ibid.

It must also be mentioned briefly that this negative aspect of the term 'struggle' is important for understanding Barth's doctrine of sanctification not just because it highlights the fact that humans cannot sanctify themselves, but also because it offers a window into sanctification's relationship to sin. That sanctification occurs within the transition from old to new means in a practical sense that, "sin is too serious a matter to be overcome by religious protestations and enthusiasms."[75] Barth does not consider sanctification to be a weapon against sin as if it were the restoration of righteousness within human life by which one could gradually, yet effectively, beat back the powers of sin. Barth states that sin "is a dominion over man, not merely a moral defect that attaches to him. It is given with his existence as a child of Adam, and is only to be overcome with his existence."[76] Humanity stands then within the struggle between the old and new, in the middle between Adam and Christ in which God tells them: "Thou art *Both*, or rather thou *belongest* to both." The doctrine of sanctification, therefore, does not describe the vanquishing of moral defects, and/or sins, but rather addresses the fact that the Christian is righteous despite the fact that he is a child of Adam and will remain one until the end.

Secondly, Barth states, because Christ has stripped death and sin of ultimate victory and does indeed stride "from *struggle* to *struggle* . . . approaching the inconceivable supreme *victory*,"[77] sanctification is not simply a theory, an inoperative principle. That sanctification is an existence characterized by struggle also means that the Christian is in no ways simply a spectator. Although he exists only in *anticipation*—exists in the journey from old to new, which, from this side, only ever tells of sin and death—he nevertheless *exists* in that journey. Just as surely the term 'struggle' indicates man's ongoing relationship to Adam, so also it must not be forgotten that this same struggle characterizes the reality of *God's* actions upon that relationship. The first position, Barth warns, must not be so construed that "the godlessness, spiritlessness, and disconsolate state of the human situation give the lie to the resurrection of Jesus and Christianity, but that, on the contrary, the resurrection is the solution, the light of hope which falls on this situation."[78] In other words, the Chris-

---

75. Ibid., 158.
76. Ibid.
77. Ibid., 169.
78. Ibid., 165.

tian not only belongs to both old and new; he has also been removed from his comfortable position and set "right in the midst of the *struggle*, in which the resurrection is truth."[79] In this sense, the characterization of sanctification as struggle garners an extremely positive meaning, for the struggle attests to the actions of God and the reality of the resurrection. The struggle, therefore, indicates not only the provisional state in which the christian, in and of himself, is *not* sanctified, but also —and this is imperative for Barth— "God's decisive word to mankind: "In Him they *all* live."[80] Humanity is not now sanctified as they shall be one day, but in the resurrection of Jesus Christ their sanctification transcends the boundary of time. And "precisely for this reason the resurrection of the dead involves that that which *we are not* is equivalent with that which *we are*."[81]

Hope

To define sanctification as an existence characterized by the term "hope" is a way, similarly to the term "struggle," of indicating first and foremost the Lordship of Christ. The difference here is really one of emphasis. While the term struggle highlights the right of Christ over humanity, i.e., they are not their own, and, therefore, sanctification is not directly given, the term "hope" is used by Barth to emphasise the reciprocal truth that humanity belongs to Christ and, therefore, sanctification is thus a reality which exists in spite of their sinfulness:

> Through "our Lord Jesus Christ" God *gives* us the victory. Note the present tense: "which *giveth* the victory"! As God's *gift*, the victory, the "reality of the resurrection," is *present*; is valid word spoken to us, not to be forgotten, not to be dragged down into the dialectic of *our* existence, not to be restricted, not to be weakened, not to be doubted. But just for this reason, everything depends upon this "victory" being and remaining God's gift "through our Lord Jesus Christ" present in *hope*.[82]

The notion of hope, similarly to Barth's description of struggle, is a way of indicating both the anticipatory nature of sanctification and its present earthly reality via the resurrection of Jesus Christ. The emphasis here,

79. Ibid., 202.
80. Ibid., 207.
81. Ibid., 108.
82. Ibid., 211.

however, as Barth indicates, is that the victory, the *reality* of the resurrection—that is, new life and sanctification, *is indeed given*, but only as reality of the *resurrection*, only as *gift*, only in hope. While the term struggle highlights the fact that one's sanctification is not his own, Barth draws on the term 'hope' to indicate the *reality* of sanctification—one who belongs to Jesus Christ. That is, sanctification is a valid word spoken to people encountered by the divine work of God in the Lord Jesus Christ. Or, as Barth stated in relationship to all gifts from God, "the way of all ways must be this: the *divine* possibility in all human possibilities."[83] To say that humanity is given victory over sin and death, that they are sanctified, is to say nothing other than Christ is Lord. For, "behind the impenetrable walls of impenetrable reality in front of which we stand, and whose unmistakable sign is death, stands and awaits the new real life, which has appeared in Christ, but is the very life of all of us."[84]

To address sanctification as an existence of hope, then, means primarily two things for Barth: First, because of the resurrection of Christ, upon which his doctrine of sanctification is founded, human sanctification is grasped as a divine-historical act. This is precisely the point, as was mentioned earlier, that the Corinthians failed to grasp. "We thus stand in the connexion of *salvation history*," Barth writes, "which is a real history: the perishing of an old, the becoming of a new . . . but history which is not enacted in time, but between time and eternity—*the* history, in which the creation, the resurrection of Christ, and the End are one day."[85] In other words, one's sanctification is never *simply* an object available for display and empirical scrutiny—a way to assess one's own sinfulness or perfection. That sanctification is characterized as an existence of hope means that the impossible is not to be removed from the possible—that people in and of themselves are indeed *not* sanctified in this life. This does not mean, however, that sanctification has more to do with resignation than fulfilment. In using the term 'hope' Barth emphasised "that, once the reality of the resurrection, and in it the reality of God, is recognized, man can and may tread the so infinitely narrow path, the knife-edge of Christianity."[86] Writes Barth, "To know the revelation of God in Christ means to place oneself within its promise, not proleptically in a supposed

---

83. Ibid., 83.
84. Ibid., 166.
85. Ibid., 201–2.
86. Ibid., 212.

fulfilment. . . . It is the arrival, nay, the presence, of the hidden Christ and His victory, with which the resurrection even of His own is occurrence."[87] It is unfortunate, although somewhat understandable considering the great tension of thought which Barth himself finds within Paul's work here,[88] that this idea of hope has often been heard only in "strangely muted" tones.[89]

While defining sanctification as an existence characterized by hope does imply limitation, finiteness and an overarching "not yet," the greater sense of the term is shaped by ideas such as: divine possibility, given in Christ, effected in God, identification, emancipation, appearance, miracle, divine horizon, in-breaking, life, victory, and participation. The hope in which the Christian contends with this promise of God is no mere prolepsis as Barth stated, for sanctification rests in the in-breaking eschatological power of God. In other words—that sanctification is considered a divine-historical act means that humanity is indeed now sanctified "in the sense that God has spoken and acted here."[90]

> In fact, the conclusion from Christ to us others is based upon the far deeper-lying assumption that the resurrection of Christ, in that "appeared," to which Paul appealed in the name of the primitive Church and in His own name, was a question of the revelation of God. If that be true, if the end of history set by God is here, if the new eternal beginning placed by God appears here, then that which has appeared from God applies to the whole of history within the scope of this horizon, then the miracle of God to Christ is immediately and simultaneously the miracle of God *to us*, and not a miracle about which it may, at any rate, still be asked: What has it to do with us?[91]

The "not yet" which must immediately round out this present tense description—for, "[w]e are, indeed, still living this life, as yet, we, indeed, only know time"[92]—is no mere sleight of hand though, no taking away with one hand what has been given by the other. Sanctification is not a false hope. The distinction which bears much weight for Barth is: "The ribbon of time which, to our eyes, is unwound endlessly, is in God's view

---

87. Ibid., 167.
88. Ibid., 212.
89. Fergusson, "Barth's *Resurrection of the Dead*: Further Reflections," 71.
90. Barth, *Resurrection*, 152.
91. Ibid., 151.
92. Ibid.

rolled up into a ball, a thousand years as a day.... That *He calls* is what decides the reality of the resurrection, not that we live, and not that we die."[93] Sanctification, then, is given not as the Corinthians upheld—as victory and holiness of flesh and blood enjoyed with full hands now as it always will be—but, is continually received as gift and present only as promise and grasped only in hope. And as Barth indicated in his "Theology of the Reformed Confessions," these notions, which seem to imply a sense of human lack and limitation, are taken up into the work of God and issue a supremely positive meaning. "There is no presence of God fuller, more joyful and stronger than that in the eternal future; there is no having, possessing, and enjoying more real than in the words spoken with empty hands: 'But thanks be to God,' in which *all* right and *all* glory is given to *Him* with whom that which falls to us is abolished."[94]

Second, to characterize sanctification as an existence of hope is a radical confession of sin, a confession that does not fixate on one's own sinfulness, but upon the action of God which transcends the boundary of time. Sanctification is the action of God in which He establishes the sinner as the work of His grace. In the resurrection of Jesus Christ sinful humanity is claimed by God as his own and set apart for obedience. As Barth would later say, in the action of God—specifically the resurrection—one's sanctification means "that he in no way sits with his sin under a glass lid secured against grace."[95] "If this hope is to be taken seriously, it puts a man in a perfectly impossible situation. In doing so, he places himself, in fact, under the judgment of God among his own people. There it is perceived that man is under the dominion of sin, there the fragility of all temporal things is perceived ... there man becomes homeless and troubled, inwardly and outwardly."[96] That one may truly hope for his sanctification in Christ is no cause for any sort of self-inflation—spiritual or otherwise. As was stated earlier, to say that one may hope for his sanctification means that he has been claimed by the Lordship of Christ. As such, he is at once displaced from his sinner's being, for although he lives as one still bound to sin and death as a child of Adam, he is now also a child of Christ and has been set free from the final throws of sin's dominion over humanity. To characterize sanctification as an existence estab-

---

93. Ibid., 208.
94. Ibid., 211.
95. Barth, *Göttingen Dogmatics* I, 316.
96. Barth, *Resurrection*, 160.

lished upon the hope of Jesus Christ then is to bear witness against one's own sinfulness. The emphasis of which is not placed upon humanity's lack and deprivation; rather the marquee feature of this confession is the work of God as the one who, in spite of humanity's sinfulness, makes them the object of his sanctifying grace.

Introduction to the Claim of God

Perhaps one of the most antagonistic features of Barth's doctrine of sanctification throughout his career, but particularly in these earlier years, is a seeming lack of concrete application, a curious dearth of explicit Christian ethical content and action. For many, this apparent lack of concern for Christian moral development and spiritual growth, accented by Barth's alleged disdain for historicity and human temporal existence, as especially punctuated by texts such as *The Resurrection of the Dead*, has become at best a source of contemptuous annoyance. And the problem, however misinformed it may be of Barth's actual writings, is not entirely ill conceived. In actuality, it serendipitously points to what is possibly the most remarkable feature of Barth's doctrine of sanctification. Indeed, Barth's doctrine of sanctification does not focus on moral growth and spiritual attainment as these are discussed in most accounts of sanctification; although it does not necessarily follow from this that Barth is unconcerned with the human response to God in sanctification, including notions of change and growth. For Barth, the doctrine of sanctification is set up and developed in terms of God's claim over humanity's entire existence rather than an extended account of progressive human spiritual and moral transformation. The result is, as H. W. Tribble points out in his insightful assessment of Barth's doctrine of sanctification, that "deeds, habits, and motives must be brought into subjection to this one all-embracing claim of sanctifying grace through which he (the Christian) now belongs to God. He (the Christian) recognizes the fact that he is not to choose his way through life, but that Christ chooses it for him and reveals it to him in concrete acts and situations. He can only obey and follow."[97] The Christian is thereby relieved of the impossible task of self-sanctification whether thought of as a type of meritorious striving, or simply cooperating with the grace of God.

---

97. Tribble, "Doctrine of Sanctification," 132.

For many, Barth's doctrine of sanctification has always appeared to be nothing more than "a protective wall . . . against a real change in man that takes place here in this life," which essentially "leads human beings to put their hands in their lap in despair."[98] As Eberhard Busch notes, the Pietistic community in particular was vexed by Barth's doctrine of sanctification. They rallied around the type of critique offered by Adolf Köberle who, in his work, *Justification and Sanctification,* published in 1929,

> understands Barth as one who merely teaches the holiness and transcendence of God but nothing of his immanence. Like [the Pietists], he believes he can and must complete Barth's theology by speaking of God's immanence, our possession of the Spirit, the nearness of God and ethics. Like [the Pietists], he believes he is actually speaking of *these things* when he speaks of the believer's experiences, of God who is "inward," and of our possession of faith.[99]

Helmut Thielicke echoes this same type of critique in his assessment of Barth's *Resurrection of the Dead.* He states that, "One notes the same lack of historicity in Barth's exegesis when he treats of the resurrection of Christ. All this seems to underscore our assertion that the monistic tendency in Barth's theology . . . leads to timelessness, the elimination of salvation history, and hence a philosophical world view."[100]

Perhaps no one summarized this frustration with Barth as clearly as the Hamburg pastor Gustav Nagel, with whom Barth briefly corresponded on this topic. In his work, *Karl Barth und der heilgewisse Glaube,* Nagel states: "In Barth's teaching the believer is merely said to be one who waits and hopes. He must never make use of his faith to gain an experience. He should abandon all certainty and security, all visions and comforts."[101] The Christian, rather, Nagel states, "is not merely 'someone who waits, but who already possesses, who is sure of a present inner spiritual possession.'"[102] In response to Nagel's letters and critiques, Barth replied: "I can only repeat over and over again, therefore, that I feel a discussion about sanctification with people from your circles too difficult

---

98. Busch, *Barth and the Pietists,* 209.

99. Ibid., 189.

100. Thielicke, *Theological Ethics, Vol. 1: Foundations,* 107.

101. Nagel, *Karl Barth und der heilgewisse Glaube,* 20, quoted in Busch, *Barth and the Pietists,* 212.

102. Ibid., 213.

because the concrete consequences of what you call sanctification (in this case the order of the behaviour in a literary discussion) are largely strange to me."[103] The problem, simply put, is that for many, Barth's doctrine of sanctification seems to undercut the power of God's saving grace as effected in the lives of Christians, because he refuses to detail the order and steps in which humans may grasp and demonstrate their holiness.

God's Claim Rather than Human Experiences

What Barth's detractors often refer to as concrete application or Christian ethical content Barth saw as the inflation of an independent Christian anthropology founded upon an over emphasis on psychologism, of which he dared not conceive any Christian doctrine let alone one as befallen by false piousness as sanctification. Admittedly, Barth wrote, "We all lapse into psychology with that which we would pride ourselves upon as spiritual possessions."[104] In a sense, there always remains that danger when attempting to "paint the bird in flight." The point is, however, that for Barth describing this aspect of the Christian life "is not moral exhortation but pure teaching."[105] Sanctification, therefore, is not an experiential/psychological description of Christ's work in the life of Christians throughout time, although Barth does not deny the reality of such an occurrence; nor would Barth propose the opposite extreme—the communication of bare facts: "It is more than a mathematical function."[106] Rather, as "pure teaching" Barth seeks to locate sanctification as a "reality claim" in the resurrection of Jesus Christ.[107] For Barth then, the doctrine of sanctification seeks to answer questions such as: "What does the grace of God in Christ mean for the man to whom it befalls? What does it mean to be a member of the covenant which God in Christ has made with men?" and "What does it mean to be a man reconciled to God in Christ?" before it considers the more psychologically, yet often preferable and "concrete" question: "How does the grace of God get to man or how does man acquire grace?"[108]

103. Barth, *Offene Briefe 1909–1935*, 135–39.
104. Barth, *Resurrection*, 201.
105. Ibid.
106. Ibid.
107. Webster, *Barth's Earlier Theology*, 87.
108. Barth, "Rechtfertigung und Heiligung," 63, 64.

For Barth, this means that questions surrounding spiritual growth, moral development, and concrete ethical content must not be the driving questions. In fact, traditional concerns and questions surrounding the doctrine of sanctification, i.e., spiritual growth and moral development are redeployed entirely. In light of the resurrection of Jesus Christ, Barth glosses Paul, the historical and temporal questions are not disconnected, but relativised.[109] Barth's seeming under-employment of anthropological superlatives in his doctrine of sanctification does not result from any sort of theological hatred of human temporal existence. On the contrary; Barth notes, "Everything which man, even the man who is inspired and impelled by God, can devise here as means, way, and bridge is insufficient . . . not, indeed, because the earthly, the human, is itself so imperfect, but because the perfect comes: *Because* the *sun* rises all lights are extinguished."[110] As Barth demonstrated through Paul's message to the Corinthians, concrete ethical content should not be disregarded; but it must be subjugated to the fact that "man in Christianity is absolutely no longer his own master, but is confiscated in his creaturehood as God's property."[111] Instead of focusing specifically on the experiential, the transformation of "holiness" within a person throughout life, or the right ordering of religio-psychological terms, Barth is more concerned with teasing out what "the action of God means as God's action on *man*, in *this* man, the h*omo viator et peccator*."[112] The anthropological concern is certainly still present, even important, however it is developed in terms of the action of God upon the one grasped by the grace of God. When he takes up the issue of the human response to God in sanctification, therefore, it is treated as an act of obedience, a response of thanksgiving to God's sanctifying claim.

As Barth states in his *Göttingen Dogmatics*:

> We shall also have to keep sharp eyes here so that the soteriological principle may now become a Christological development, for we can never accept the nature of an independent Christian anthropology. . . . Sanctification is reported up to the *border* of an independent Christian anthropology, up to the point where it could be further discussed only in psychological categories. Christian preaching and dogmatics may not cross that border,

---

109. Barth, *Resurrection*, 131.
110. Ibid., 81.
111. Ibid., 95.
112. Barth, *Unterricht in der christlichen Religion* III, 304.

but it may also not omit to make them visible. They must *not cross this border*, because if they did they would cease to speak seriously about *God*; they must *make them visible*, because if they did not they would otherwise not speak *seriously* about God.[113]

The soteriological principle is thus developed in terms of God's claim upon sinful humanity as they are identified with Christ. Sanctification is therefore concerned with, once again, teasing out what it means to be a reconciled sinner—not only in terms of one's *status* before God, justification, but also in terms of his status *before God* as one who has been placed under the Lordship of Jesus Christ and lives as one who no longer claims authority for himself. Simply stated: for Barth, sanctification is the depiction of one who stands before God—whose life is no longer his own—yet nevertheless truly lives in and through Christ, rather than a confession of one "who is sure of a present inner spiritual possession."[114]

A depiction of this sort cannot help but to affirm a *real* change in those being sanctified. As Barth points out throughout *The Resurrection of the Dead*, it is not merely the spiritual that Christ is Lord of, but also all corporeality, earthly existence and even human bodies.[115] "What else," he writes, "could the Easter gospel be except the gospel become perfectly concrete that God is the Lord?"[116] And Barth pushes this even further:

> God is the Lord of the *body*! Now the question of God is posed acutely and inescapably. Body is man, I am body, and this man, this I, is God's. But now I have no longer a refuge from God; I can no longer plead dualism; I cannot retire to a reality secured against God; I can no longer make the excuse of earthly weakness. Just this earthly weakness is meant, if God will be my Lord. I am this very earthly weak one; I am to be bound to God, to live in God, to be in glory before God. The Spirit, not our pinch of spirit and spirituality, but *God's* Spirit triumphs not just in a pure spirituality, but: it is raised a (God-) spiritual body, the end of God's way is corporeality.[117]

---

113. Ibid., 308.

114. Nagel, *Karl Barth und der heilgewisse Glaube*, 20, quoted in Busch, *Karl Barth and the Pietists*, 213. This distinction applies not only to Pietistic strands of sanctification, but also to other various Catholic, Arminian, and Reformed versions that view sanctification as a manifestation of an innate righteousness.

115. Barth, *Resurrection*, 32–33.

116. Ibid., 192.

117. Ibid., 193–94.

That sanctification is developed christologically means it is necessarily and importantly concerned with humanity's entire existence including his very real, earthly self. This too is placed under the Lordship of Christ. That sanctification is a depiction of the statement, "I am to be bound to God, to live in God, to be in glory before God," as stated above, does not mean however, that it must *eo ipso* be driven by the anthropological experience, by the perception of the God who is "inward," or the Christian's possession of faith. These are examples of a Christian anthropology to which sanctification may only indicate, but never take upon itself.

Barth's unique understanding of sanctification as the claim of God upon human life was not meant to negate the *seriousness* of any real change in humanity. Rather, it emerged from the centrality of the resurrection of Jesus Christ from the dead within Barth's theology,[118] in which, as Barth stated, the reality of the Christian life, "becomes *our* truth, not by our undertaking the hopeless task of going to heaven, but *by its coming to us from heaven.*"[119] In the reality of the resurrection, human sin and "earthly weakness" maintain no refuge from the power of God. For although "I am this very earthly weak one. . . . *God's* Spirit triumphs not just in a pure spirituality," but in such a way that as the reality of God "is recognized, man can and may tread the so infinitely narrow path, the knife-edge of Christianity."[120]

---

118. It should be noted that the essence of the Christian life is developed, for Barth, not simply out of the lens of the resurrection of Christ, it is not simply the logical result of his theological 'system', but indeed by the resurrected Christ himself.

119. Barth, *Resurrection*, 199–200.

120. Ibid., 212.

5

Göttingen Dogmatics and "Rechtfertigung und Heiligung"

General Summary

THUS FAR WE HAVE examined several specific lecture texts from just before and during Barth's tenure as Professor of Reformed Theology in the 1920s, in the hope of understanding his doctrine of sanctification as it took shape during this formative period. These texts, covering ethics and historical and biblical theology, have proven a valuable resource for determining the foundational issues surrounding Barth's doctrine of sanctification as it emerged in his thought and work. The emphasis has been to resist overly systematizing his thoughts about sanctification during this period, in order to gain a more realistic picture of what sanctification entailed for Barth, as well as to perceive more clearly the contours and consistency of his thoughts about this doctrine by offering a close reading of his texts. This approach requires patience; its benefit lies in seeing how the importance and far-reaching significance of the doctrine of sanctification emerges from within Barth's work, as the various texts are linked together. Although Barth did not first fully treat the doctrine of sanctification until 1924, already in his earlier lectures one begins to recognize the outline of the doctrine and its intrinsic value within his work. A quick summary of what has been discussed so far will help to remind the reader of this picture as we move on in this next chapter.

During the period from 1916 through 1922, just before and slightly overlapping his appointment as Professor of Reformed Theology in Göttingen, Barth expressed the content of Christian life in fellowship with God primarily by disabling false constructions of human piety, by emphasising human righteousness grounded and vividly portrayed in *God's* own righteousness. For Barth, the doctrine of sanctification was growing as one of the key theological components for upholding and describing the divine-human relationship that affirmed both God's love for and reconciliation of humanity, and their faithful life-response. In particular, the idea of *encounter*, which Barth used to critically differentiate God and human beings, became the basis for his discussion of that relationship early on. Fundamentally, what Barth began to articulate from the beginning, as we saw in chapter one, was that this encounter between God and humanity is the exposition of a specific relationship in which God draws near to humanity in grace and uniquely transforms their lives. It is the specifics of that relationship which gives shape to his doctrine of sanctification early on.

When Barth took up his teaching post in Göttingen, one of the most important influences upon his theology overall and certainly his notions of sanctification was his turn to the Reformed tradition. Barth saw in the Reformers, especially Calvin, how his own basic instincts about dogmatics and ethics, or human life and living, could in fact be worked out in positive terms, because of the inextricable link between the divine vertical and the human horizontal.

In the discussion of the Calvin Lectures in Chapter 2, we saw how Barth's newfound affinity for Reformed theology helped him clarify his own doctrine of sanctification, helped him find ways of approaching the divine-human relationship doctrinally and constructively. In particular, Chapter 2 examined Barth's analysis of Calvin's use of faith and obedience, and the relationship between time and eternity, as initial ways of underpinning his doctrine of sanctification positively, as well as his inclination to address the inherent danger of moralism within Reformed theology. Which, perhaps to the surprise of some, meant for Barth that one must emphasize the connectedness and relevance of faithful human action and living all the more clearly in order not to lose sight of the independent weight of God that guards against moralism. Barth's appropriation of Calvin's work in these areas allotted him the opportunity to begin a more doctrinally specific account of the divine-human encounter; including, in particular, how it is that that encounter shapes the life and living of human beings.

In Chapter 3 "The Theology of the Reformed Confessions," the overarching theological principles for Barth's doctrine of sanctification were set forth and analyzed.¹ These are the doctrinal principles that maintain the most weight and give shape to all other ways speaking of the divine-human encounter. Succinctly stated, for Barth the doctrine of sanctification is oriented towards and developed around rightly understanding the reality of the divine-human relationship, of what it means to say that God the Father, in Jesus Christ His son, through the Holy Spirit, has drawn close to humanity. Barth's account of sanctification is shaped by focusing on *God's* relational activity, and all that this entails for faithful life and living, rather than a more anthropologically oriented account of moral transformation or a process of gradual perfecting. And because Barth insists that sanctification only exists in dynamic relationship with *Christ*, there is never a moment in which one may cease to highlight the continual and sustaining work of grace within the life of Christians. In and with all of this, because sanctification is localized around this God who sanctifies in Jesus Christ, its relevance is also especially purposeful to human life and living as the ones united with Christ through the *Holy Spirit*.

In the discussion of Barth's *The Resurrection of the Dead* in chapter four it was shown that the impact of Jesus' resurrection from the dead cannot be overstated for Barth's doctrine of sanctification. For in the reality of Jesus' resurrection lie equally the foundation for and the possibility of renewed human existence and action. Indeed, there can be no right understanding of sanctified existence without taking into account what Barth calls this eschatological orientation. Meaning that the essence of the Christian life emerges from the work of God that transcends time. Sanctification, therefore, addresses the Christian life as an impossible possibility. It is never to be simply confused with one's temporal historicity yet it is, nevertheless, identified with the resurrected life of Christ in such a way that entails faithful human life and living. In connection to this the notions of struggle and hope were examined as key forms of sanctified living, rendered as "existence in anticipation". These themes were finally drawn together in a picture of Barth's doctrine of sanctification that clearly prioritizes a conception of God's claim upon humanity and its corollary of faithful human life and living.

Read together, these lectures clearly begin to demonstrate Barth's conception of sanctification in terms of, above all else, rightly

1. They were: (1) the focus upon the initiating and finalizing reality of God, (2) the non-givenness of God in revelation, and (3) the real yet relative earthly human correlate of God's action.

understanding the divine-human relationship. A relationship which is featured more constructively than has been typically acknowledged within Barth's work. A relationship in which God draws close to human beings in grace and transforms them.

Introduction and Significance of Text

By the spring term of 1924, Barth had finally begun to prepare his first lectures on dogmatic theology. "I shall never forget the vacation of early 1924," he wrote. "I sat in my study in Göttingen confronted with the task of giving my first lectures on dogmatics. No one can have been more plagued than I was with the problem, could I do it? and how?"[2] Once again, as his studies in biblical and historical theology had highlighted, Barth found himself in an all too familiar situation—"expelled . . . from the goodly society of contemporary . . . theology and . . . as it were, alone in the open without a teacher."[3] And though Barth still seemed to have felt like a "wandering gypsy . . . with only a couple of leaky kettles to call his own," nevertheless "dozens, nay hundreds" of "the confounded 'Barth-movement' of which the great Heim writes so beautifully . . . want to know where it goes from here and crave to hear from us the B and C that come after A."[4] The steady pace at which Barth found himself moving from "deconstruction to reconstruction" over the past several years required him to step out of his comfort zone yet again and touch pen to paper. He expressed these sentiments in a letter to his dear friend Eduard Thurneysen:

> Yes, good heavens, Eduard, the dog must now take to the water. . . . Had we just kept quiet at the time when we were so close to becoming harmless and orderly disciples of Wernle . . . or much later on, when . . . with pale faces we began to proclaim the deathly wisdom and the hollow centre. None of that involved as yet a Dogmatics. . . . But the trouble is that we have never been *silent* and now we are in for it. . . . The foolish world marvels at my rise from pedlar to big businessman, but at times I, and apparently you, too, feel much more like liquidation. . . . Time moves relentlessly on, and the evening and the morning *will*

---

2. Barth, "Foreword," in Heppe, *Reformed Dogmatics Set Out and Illustrated from the Sources*, v.

3. Ibid.

4. Barth, *Karl Barth–Eduard Thurneysen Briefwechsel*, 2:222–23.

bring us to the day where for good or evil . . . this Dogmatics will be launched.[5]

Thus Barth, ever the hesitant prophet, took up his pen in characteristic style of this Göttingen period to set down "rapid movement of thought, in . . . forceful language," with "many new and bold ideas."[6]

The primal questions "Can I?" and "How shall I?" that continued to worry Barth throughout his career, found their relative answers on this occasion soon enough. In several letters to Emil Brunner, who was faced with the same task of beginning *his* first dogmatic lectures in Zurich, Barth recorded how he had narrowed down his organizational choices for his lectures from seven to four:

> 1. "Loci" in connection with the *Romerbrief* (Melanchthon!) . . .
>
> 4. Scholastic (theology) (in the place of Petrus Lombardus: Calvin's *Institutio* . . .)
>
> 5. "Prophetic," i.e., to be Calvin himself, to pound the table, and under constant check 1. by the Bible and 2. By the early Church and Reformation, to go one's own self-chosen way . . .
>
> 6. Confessional: the material in dogmatics is, in this case, "dogma" . . . We have to ask what dogma was *before* the confessions and would come therefore to the Apostle's Creed.[7]

This much was demanded, wrote Barth, the Bible must be the master of a Protestant dogmatics; and it had become increasingly clear to him that the Reformers must also be taken up again.[8] As Barth pored over text after text in search of a way forward, he stumbled upon Heinrich Heppe's *Dogmatics*. Heppe's work was "a collection of texts on all the loci of dogmatics from the sixteenth- , seventeenth- , and early eighteenth-century Reformed theologians."[9] In Heppe's work, and in a parallel Lutheran text by H. Schmid, Barth found surprising new instructors. Barth describes Heppe's *Dogmatics* as

> out-of-date, dusty, unattractive, almost like a table of logarithms, dreary to read, stiff and eccentric on almost every page I

---

5. Ibid.
6. Barth, *Göttingen Dogmatics* XIX.
7. Barth, *Karl Barth-Emil Brunner, Briefwechsel 1916–1966*, 94–95.
8. Barth, "Foreword," in Heppe, *Reformed Dogmatics*, v–vii.
9. Barth, *Göttingen Dogmatics* I, 18.

opened; in form and content adequately corresponding to what I, like so many of the others had described to myself decades ago, as the "the old orthodoxy."

Well I had the grace not to be so slack. I read, I studied, I reflected; and found that I was rewarded with the discovery that here at last I was in the atmosphere in which the road by way of the Reformers to Holy Scripture was a more sensible and more natural one to tread, than the atmosphere, now only too familiar to me, of the theological literature determined by Schleiermacher and Ritchl. I found a dogmatics which had both form and substance, oriented upon the central indications of the Biblical evidences for revelation, which it also managed out in detail with astonishing richness.[10]

Heppe's *Dogmatics* was for Barth "a doorway into the expanses of the Reformed theological tradition" and of Scripture that he had not expected.[11] It was cut from the same cloth as "the old orthodoxy" that he had utterly rejected while still in school. Yet, he wrote, "I had come to be amazed at the long, peaceful breathing, the sterling quality, the relevant strictness, the superior style . . . with which this 'orthodoxy' had wrought."[12] With the help of Heppe and several other promising discussion partners, such as the early Church Fathers and even Catholic scholastics, and a fair amount of "stubborn persistence," Barth set out in timid excitement upon his own path.

Over the next two years, Barth amazingly churned out this entire dogmatic series while simultaneously delivering exegetical lectures on topics such as Philippians and the Sermon on the Mount, and maintaining an intensely rigorous speaking schedule throughout the region in which he pursued various avenues of thought, clarifying and expanding his core lectures.

The structure of the lecture series that Barth finally arrived at was: "Prolegomena," given in the summer of 1924; "Dogmatics I," given in the winter of 1924-25; "Dogmatics II" (the doctrine of reconciliation,

---

10. Barth, "Foreword," in Heppe, *Reformed Dogmatics*, v.

11. Barth, *Göttingen Dogmatics* I, 19.

12. Barth, "Foreword," in Heppe, *Reformed Dogmatics*, vi. Busch notes that, "Barth's openness to earlier Protestant orthodoxy . . . was something which the others involved in the "dialectical theology" could not share, and they could only shake their heads at this remarkable change of direction made by him." Busch, *Barth*, 154.

including Barth's account of sanctification), given in the summer of 1925; and "Dogmatics III" (eschatology), delivered in the winter of 1925-26.[13]

One lecture in which Barth sought to elucidate a portion of his dogmatics was the important piece "Rechtfertigung und Heiligung," composed after Barth's move to Münster. Eberhard Busch writes of this lecture: "At the very time when [Barth] was occupied with his series of lectures on dogmatics he was preparing once again for some very active outside lecturing. His first task in early 1927 was a new approach to the old Reformation problem of 'faith and works'—in other words, to the way in which the question of ethics was illuminated and clarified by knowledge of the Word of God."[14] "Rechtfertigung und Heiligung" was written precisely as a set of further reflections on the relationship between God's self-revelation and its impact upon humanity—an extension of paragraphs 31 and 32 on "Justification" and "Sanctification" respectively in the *Göttingen Dogmatics*.

In January 1925, the theological faculty of Münster offered its first holiday course for religious instruction. The same course, meant for ministers and religious instructors, was held again, following an initial postponement, in early January 1927, after Barth had joined the faculty. It was during this holiday course that Barth first delivered his lecture on "Rechtfertigung und Heiligung."

Over the next six months, Barth presented this lecture a total of six times throughout Germany, Switzerland, and Holland in venues as wide-ranging as friendly "evening reading groups" in Bremen, whose attendees had been waiting for the opportunity to interact with Barth personally since 1922, when the manuscript of his Calvin Lectures had created such lively discussions amongst them, to the Baltic Sea Conference for the German Christian Student's Union (D.C.S.V.) in Putbus, where Barth reported of "the unexpected fierceness of my latest collision with the Furche Pietists, whose rebukes I lived under like a savage for two days."[15] The lecture also appeared in the important periodical *Zwischen den Zeiten* the same year and was purportedly in hand as Barth worked

---

13. Busch, *Barth*, 155. Barth had already moved to Münster to take up a post as Professor of Dogmatics and New Testament Exegesis by the fall of 1925 when he began the third and final cycle of these lectures.

14. Ibid., 175. "Rechtfertigung und Heiligung" is translated as "Justification and Sanctification."

15. Barth, "Rechtfertigung und Heiligung," 57–62. A more detailed account of each engagement can be found in the introduction to this lecture.

through the section on "justification and sanctification" in paragraph 66 of *CD* IV/2.[16]

In this chapter Barth's *Göttingen Dogmatics* lectures (hereafter, *GD*), specifically paragraph 32, entitled "Sanctification," will be considered in relation to the lecture "Rechtfertigung und Heiligung" (hereafter, *RH*). The importance of *GD* and *RH* for Barth's theology is not hard to see. The *GD* offer invaluable insights into a highly charged period of thought and growth for Barth, a time filled with wonderful new discoveries and maturation of deep-seated theological convictions. As Barth's first full-scale dogmatics, these lectures demonstrate the determination and giftedness of the young professor, who was all too often overcome by anxiety. They also occupy a special place in the corpus of Barth's work as the only dogmatics he ever fully completed. In this sense, they also stand poised, ready to offer some insight into the would-be finishing strokes of Barth's magnum opus, *Church Dogmatics*.[17]

While *RH* is in many ways a restatement of concepts and principles found in the *GD*, these same ideas benefit conceptually in a subsequent lecture. Not only does this lecture provide a sharp, and at times more expansive, rendering of the points presented in paragraph 32 of the *GD*, but it also has the advantage of having been offered to a larger audience and delivered on multiple occasions. Having tested his doctrine of sanctification among friends and foes, and having survived much scrutiny and many outright attacks against its content, Barth remained self-assured of his presentation.

The *GD* and *RH* offer perhaps the clearest and most sustained treatment of Barth's doctrine of sanctification during this period. Together they capture the vivid and stirring account of the divine-human relationship that has been established and presented in Barth's theology thus far. Within them, one begins to see the previous components confirmed and developed. The overarching principle that "Christian proclamation must be proclamation of the *magnalia Dei* [the great acts of God] or it is not Christian proclamation"[18] is finely woven together with Barth's genuine concern for faithful human action and living. Sanctification, writes Barth,

---

16. Barth, "Rechtfertigung und Heiligung," 62.

17. Although Barth "resisted the urging of his friends to publish his work as soon as possible because he wanted more time to refine his ideas and his distinctive approach," nevertheless, they remain an invaluable resource understanding Barth. See Barth, *Göttingen Dogmatics* I, 16.

18. Barth, "Rechtfertigung und Heiligung," 65.

is the work of *God* on *man*. From one perspective this means that, "God asserts His right on us and God has mercy on us. By asserting his right He has mercy on us, by having mercy on us he asserts His right."[19] Or, to put the matter somewhat differently:

> It is all about *his* turning back, *his* decision for God. Only through the strength of God's decision for *him* can his decision be made for God. Nevertheless, it is *his* decision. Only through grace can grace be seized; it is only *seized* by the one who has been given grace. To believe and to obey are acts of man's knowing and wanting, as certain as the power of these acts is the power of God alone.[20]

Rightly stated, these lectures are a magnificent expression of those ideas which coursed through Barth's mind so early on: that one must begin with God's own person and work in order to truly speak about faithful human existence and action; and that in speaking about God one will, or rather must, truly speak about human life and living.

Much of the work so far in this book has given expression to what might be called the boundary markers that surround Barth's doctrine of sanctification. The subject matter has been more or less concerned with laying out the foundational perspectives without which, Barth thought, one ceases to speak seriously about God or humanity. Part of this exploration highlighted the growing clarity of Barth's thought as he became more doctrinally sophisticated, and the shift that proceeded from tearing down the old idols to building a new foundation. While the emphasis throughout has been to underscore Barth's concern for both God and humanity, nevertheless the process of tearing down the old and beginning anew was intrinsically a matter of re-establishing the priority of God in theological conversation. The objective material under-girding Barth's account of sanctification was, therefore, never hard to unearth; the unfortunate result for his doctrine of sanctification was its all too common characterization as a "purely negative description."[21] The reciprocal truth that re-establishing God's priority in Christian discourse also meant the re-establishment of humanity's place as well was not widely heard.

The objective content in the *GD* and *RH* remains an intrinsic component of Barth's doctrine of sanctification. Repeatedly Barth emphasises

19. Ibid., 66.
20. Ibid., 69.
21. Ibid., 61.

that sanctification, just as justification, is an *"actio Dei gratuita"* . . . just as directly and absolutely a consequence of the grace of *insertio in Christum* as is *iustificatio*, the gift of the Holy Spirit. Our holiness on all stages is only possible by divine mercy."[22] This type of refrain recurs regularly throughout these works. The interesting and seldom acknowledged complement to such statements, however, emphasises that, "the knowledge about what should be (and this knowledge we have in faith!) must turn us into displaced, into acting, into *moved* people, into people that always see beyond the presence and existence to the better, people that you find where there is a struggle for the better."[23] This type of positive refrain also recurs throughout these works, not in isolation from the *"actio Dei gratuita,"* but in and with it as its necessary result, not as a sort of synergism, but dialectically, or perhaps even more specifically, as a spiritual reality within human life. Without this concrete effect, Barth says, God has not really "shown up". True sanctification is "not about an act between God and man; much less can man become the centre of attention." Rather, because it is the work of God on humanity, sanctification necessarily concerns human willing, thinking, doing, and being. This chapter will in part seek to formulate a more robust account of Barth's doctrine of sanctification by allowing these themes to be heard.

The first task of this chapter will be to outline the content of the *GD* and *RH*, and then note several key doctrines of *GD* that will have an explicit impact on the content and structure of Barth's doctrine of sanctification: Revelation, Holiness, Election, and Eschatology. Secondly, the chapter will offer a preliminary discussion of God's reconciling activity—the specific context in which Barth discusses sanctification— and the relationship between justification and sanctification as forms of reconciliation. Thirdly, this chapter will call attention to three fundamental aspects of Barth's doctrine of sanctification, without which one cannot hope to understand his work on this topic: (1) the *claim of God*—the key concept around which Barth structures the content of sanctification, (2) *the sinner reconciled in grace*—which is the purpose and limit of sanctification, and (3) *grace in time*—the object and impact of God's sanctifying grace. The discussion of *grace in time* will also briefly incorporate a discussion of the relevant material from Barth's 1928/9 *Ethics* lectures.

---

22. Barth, *Unterricht in der Christlichen Religion III, Die Lehre von der Versöhnung/Die Lehre von der Erlösung*, 311–12.

23. Ibid., 324.

Outline of Texts

Göttingen Dogmatics

The *GD* is organized into seven expansive chapters covering prolegomena (which includes three chapters on the Word of God as Revelation, Holy Scripture, and Christian Preaching), the doctrine of God, anthropology, reconciliation, and redemption; each chapter is in turn comprised of various chapter-length subsections, or paragraphs, thirty-eight in all, constructed around central thesis statements. The unifying theme, running through each chapter like the theme of a great fugue (as Daniel Migliore notes in his insightful introduction to the first-part English translation of the *GD*) is that "God is God."[24] "That God is God means that God is the living, free, gracious, and righteous Lord. All that we think and say about God and the world must take into account that 'we are human and not God'."[25] There is no doctrine within Barth's dogmatics that does not explicitly bear the imprint of this theme. Yet, adds Barth, "the limit that is thereby set for us has nothing whatever to do with a one-sided emphasis on God's transcendence, majesty, or negativity. We have seen that the picture would be the same if we started with God's immanence".[26]

The first three chapters of *GD* examine the basic theme, necessity, and course of dogmatics as the "scientific" reflection on the Word of God. By "scientific" Barth does not mean that dogmatics is merely the science of God, reflections on deity, faith, or religion, for "if we reject the possibility of a science of God in the sense of philosophical or metaphysical speaking about God, then speaking about God can refer only to an original speaking by God, or to the impress of the knowledge of God that God himself has revealed to us in his Word."[27] The Word of God that Barth has in mind here is God's own speaking in three-fold form: revelation, scripture, and preaching. The task of dogmatics, then, writes Barth, is to serve the church as it ventures to speak about God and human beings in relation to God. As Barth points out, what he calls prolegomena were usually presented in earlier times as "Dogmatics I." "A science needs prolegomena when it is no longer sure of its presuppositions . . . when it has to work at showing with what right and with what means it can do what

---

24. Barth, *Göttingen Dogmatics* I, 25.
25. Ibid.
26. Ibid., 134.
27. Ibid., 12.

it wants to do ... when it does not yet understand the self-evident things with which any science commences."[28] While Barth does not begrudge the modern necessity of this first step, his own beginning is very different from many others. Instead of first making a case for his dogmatics based on general philosophical or religious principles, Barth begins with his main concept, "the Word of God." Already, then, as Barth addresses the whence and whither of his dogmatic presuppositions, he leans on doctrines such as the Trinity and Incarnation, and finds himself deliberately borrowing "from the material content of dogmatics proper rather than attempt[ing] to establish principles independent of this content."[29]

The next four chapters are organized around the logical content of Christian preaching which "deals with God, with human beings in their relation to God, or more specifically with what God is to and for human beings, and what they for their part have in God."[30] Following the classical line of dogmatics from "Origen to Wegscheider," the chapters are divided as follows: God, Anthropology, Reconciliation, and Redemption.

Several interesting features related to Barth's doctrine of sanctification call for brief remark here. As has been mentioned thus far in this work, and will be demonstrated more fully in this chapter, Barth's doctrine of sanctification is uniquely connected with his conception of what it means to be a sinner. "When seizing God's grace in faith and obedience a Christian recognizes himself as a sinner," writes Barth.[31] Sanctification, rather than immediately indicating the diminishment of one's sinfulness, means that one only now truly recognizes herself as a sinner standing before God. Sinfulness is thus a recognition given only in grace, in the knowledge of Jesus Christ. In light of Barth's conception of the knowability of one's sinfulness, it appears odd that the two sections on sin as action and nature are dealt with in chapter 5, on *Anthropology*. It is more than likely that this awkwardness is merely a by-product of Barth's organizational decisions rather a complete inconsistency of content. Barth had apparently recognized the issue at some level and offered several measures to address the problem. As Migliore comments, Barth placed a section on the covenant of grace directly before the sections on sin and, as he begins the chapter on *Reconciliation*, he "insists that the doctrines

---

28. Ibid., 18.
29. Ibid., 43.
30. Ibid., 323.
31. Barth, "Rechtfertigung und Heiligung," 68.

of God and humanity are not mere 'preparations' for the doctrine of reconciliation but must be completely saturated with the truth of this doctrine (27.I)."[32] Complementarily Barth's article *RH* is able to make the relationship between grace and sin concerning this matter more explicit, suggesting a fruitfulness of clarification.

Several further features help to situate Barth's doctrine of sanctification within the broader scope of his dogmatics. In paragraph 31 of chapter 6, entitled "Reconciliation," the Doctrine of Sanctification, along with his treatment of the Doctrine of Justification, flows directly out of Barth's treatment of the faithfulness of God and the person and work of Christ. Here, Barth is more or less following an historical pattern of treating sanctification in a general connection with the person and work of Christ,[33] and this signals an important formal concern.

It may be recalled that in "The Theology of the Reformed Confessions" Barth had lamented, among other things, the unfortunate anthropocentric drift in Protestant theology, as demonstrated in particular by certain aspects of the Westminster Confession. He had criticised the way the framers of that confession began to focus on the "spontaneous experience of grace on the part of the person called," because it resulted in a disjunction between the Word and work of God and the immediate implications for human life and living.[34] For example: "The Westminster Confession then inserts between justification and sanctification a special "*grace of adoption*," and understands this to be reception into the number of the children of God."[35] While Reformation theologians like Luther and Calvin typically moved directly from treatments of the divine work to the divine gift (the benefits of salvation), the Westminster Confession seems to have inserted a pause between the work of God and its application in order to reflect upon its impact concerning human experience and emotion. The result for sanctification in particular, stated Barth, was a concealed naturalism.[36]

---

32. Barth, *Göttingen Dogmatics* I, 47.

33. See, for example, Calvin's *Institutes*, in which he moves from the knowledge of God the Redeemer in Book Two, to the benefits of the grace of Christ in Book Three; also Schleiermacher's *The Christian Faith*, whose doctrine of sanctification differed radically from Barth's, which treats sanctification in the same broad section as the person and work of Christ in the *Explication of the Consciousness of Grace*.

34. Barth, *Reformed Confessions*, 140.

35. Ibid., 141.

36. Ibid., 138-44.

In the *GD*, however, the benefits of Christ, justification, and sanctification are treated in direct correlation with the person and work of Christ. Barth's treatment of sanctification, rather than appearing as a distinct albeit connected section of Christology flows directly from the paragraphs detailing the faithfulness of God mediated through Jesus Christ, the one who establishes and fulfils the will of God in humanity's place and testifies to this faithfulness through the sacraments.[37] The result being, as has been stated several times in this work, "that the soteriological principle may now become a Christological development," in order that this doctrine may not fall victim to the possibility of an "independent Christian anthropology."[38] This doctrinal ordering appears to be an attempt to remedy the temptation to focus upon the deeds and acts, experiences and adventures, piety and the services of humans rather than the *magnalia Dei*.[39] "Certainly," Barth writes, sanctification "is about God's act on *man*, but it is exclusively about the act of *God* on man, not about an act between God and man; much less can man become the centre of attention. The dispassion of Christian thought rises and falls with the amount of clarity this is stated."[40]

Finally, it is important to note that in the *GD* Barth rearranges what he considers the traditional Reformed treatment of the sacraments, as summarized by Heppe, so that instead of following on the heels of the Christian life, baptism and holy communion surround it as promise and sign.[41] Here baptism is linked with calling, and communion with perseverance as ways of engaging the delicate relationship between the divine work of reconciliation and the human recognizing and seizing of that work. Within the earthly-human-sinful sphere of existence, the very object of sanctification, "there is the sacramental sphere of divine *signs* and of human *venture* in relation to the grace of the Royal Christ. The sacrament calls, guarantees, and seals for us the immanence of the reconciliation of God. It is the reminder, taking place at the level of human things and events, about grace."[42] Although Barth recognizes that this reordering is "a strong divergence of the usual course of the old dogmatics,"

---

37. Barth, *Unterricht in der Christlichen Religion* III, 74, 176.
38. Ibid., 308.
39. Barth, "Rechtfertigung und Heiligung," 65.
40. Ibid.
41. Barth, *Göttingen Dogmatics* I, 35.
42. Barth, *Unterricht in der Christlichen Religion* III, 314.

nevertheless it is one which he hopes will shed light on the importance and significance of the sacraments, particularly in regards to the existential aspects of the Christian life.[43]

"Rechtfertigung und Heiligung"

In the companion article "Rechtfertigung und Heiligung," Barth analyzes the content and nature of the grace of God as it transpires with humanity. "Justification and sanctification are the execution of grace," and therefore, "are the answers to a special question: What does the grace of God in Christ mean for the person to whom it befalls? What does it mean to be a member of the covenant that God in Christ has made with people? What does it mean to be a person reconciled to God in Christ?"[44] The lecture is structured around nine thesis statements in which the implications of such questions are teased out, beginning with a mini-commentary on the unifying principle of the Word of God, and ending with an eschatological exclamation of hope whose presence pervades the entirety of the lecture.

1. "Justification and sanctification are the execution of the grace assigned to the Christian in baptism, the grace of his election and calling to the community with God through Jesus Christ in the truth of the Holy Spirit."[45] This is the longest sub-section in the piece. In it Barth orients the lecture within the wider and more narrow doctrinal circles. In the larger circle, the doctrines of justification and sanctification find themselves tied within the grand scope of the revealed truth of God spoken to His church. More narrowly, justification and sanctification are an expression of the grace of God as they are given and received—in an intimate encounter between God and people. Barth's summarizes his intent by quoting Psalm 100:3: "It is He who made us, and we are His, we are His people, the sheep of His pasture."[46]

2. "When seizing God's grace in faith and obedience, a Christian recognizes himself as a sinner; and only when he recognizes himself as a sinner, will he seize God's grace in faith and obedience."[47] In this second thesis, Barth addresses the event of grace more specifically as an

43. Ibid., 97–201.
44. Barth, "Rechtfertigung und Heiligung," 63.
45. Ibid., 62.
46. Ibid., 68.
47. Ibid.

encounter that takes place within the life of human beings; grace does not simply happen to people, it involves them. Fundamentally, it means understanding oneself condemned by the judgment of God. But because understanding this is a work of grace it also means standing with Christ, and, therefore, it also means salvation. For this reason, the sinner not only confesses his sin before Christ, but wants to be there with Him too.

3. "The unity of the works of grace is true in the secret of God the Holy Spirit. For us, however, it is a different matter that we as sinners are *reconciled*, a different matter that we as *sinners* are reconciled. One is our justification, the other our sanctification."[48] Here Barth points to what is essentially the problem with all human words about God. While the word of God is singular, unified, and unbroken, as humans "we think two thoughts and say two words according to the reality of the argument into which we fell on account of grace," because we are not God. Thus justification and sanctification point to the one reality of reconciliation and must be seen in connection, but they must not be confused with each other lest the singular truth be convoluted.

4. "Justification is God's overlooking of the sin in the here and now that has not yet been removed. Sanctification is God's claiming of us in our not yet removed sin in the here and now."[49] Barth continues to focus his approach on the topic offering a preliminary distinction between justification and sanctification. It means, plainly, "God for us," and "us for God."

5. "The grace of justification is our *life*; the grace of sanctification is our *death* as a sinner."[50] The dead one called to life is the sinner, and the living one called to death is the sinner once again. It is within these two clauses, Barth says, that the Christian life is lived—"there is no other way."[51] Thus, one is set free in order that he live both *before* God and *for* God.

6. "Justification is the eternal side of God's work of love on the sinner; sanctification is the chronological side."[52] Here Barth addresses formally what he had been indicating specifically. The one work of grace means not only that God makes humanity right with Himself (justification), but

---

48. Ibid., 74.
49. Ibid., 78.
50. Ibid., 83.
51. Ibid.
52. Ibid., 86.

there also corresponds a change within the life of human beings by which God determines them, and in which they determine themselves for God.

7. "It is with the same divine seriousness that grace puts us as justified into the great and absolute decision, and as sanctified into the small and relative ones of faith and obedience."[53] Although justification and sanctification are both continually God's work in and on people in the same sense—from God to humanity—this does not invalidate the real but relative human response. The absolute decision in which God decides to be for humans enables and requires their faithful response in obedience. "The insight that all of our doing is in vain, even in the best lives," writes Barth, "can only become opium of the conscience for the one who has only heard about it (the insight) without ever having had it himself."[54]

8. "The faith and obedience of the justified and sanctified sinner are, in the same way, the praise of God's mercy and the recognition of His steadfast law."[55] God is both merciful and just, and in this way He judges humanity and claims them as His own—He both forgives people and frees them. Above all then the faith and obedience of the reconciled sinner cannot be anything other than the joining in of the "holy, holy, holy, the Lord of hosts" (Isaiah 6:3) with which the angels praise God—the simple recognition of who God is in His majesty.

9. "Hope for redemption, which will complete our reconciliation, is the power of our faith and obedience as sinners."[56] Everything addressed within this article is hedged within the boundary of a rather formidable "not yet"; or, rather, positively stated the Christian life lives on hope. In this final clause, Barth affirms what may have been apparent to many already in his address—that justification and sanctification point beyond themselves to something in which Christians must, in an important sense, look forward to. As Barth was fond of quoting, "If we have hope in Christ for this life only, then we are the most miserable men of all" (1 Cor 15:19).[57]

While this lecture notes the distinctions between justification and sanctification, the essence of what Barth is after is not really a comparison

---

53. Ibid., 89.
54. Ibid., 91.
55. Ibid., 94.
56. Ibid., 97.
57. Ibid., 96.

and contrast of these two doctrines. Barth's purpose in this lecture is to offer a theological picture of how justification and sanctification function as the single work of grace in reconciliation. To understand reconciliation, Barth says, "we will have to face *two* strings of thought which both describe the same truth but do not dissolve into each other. Grace in its execution is our justification from the top down; from the bottom up it is our sanctification. We have to see and describe both of these paths, always bearing in mind that it is the one way of God."[58] The emphasis falls on the single work of reconciliation in this double form. The double gaze of humanity—differentiating between the here and there—is brought together in the single work of God.

This lecture makes it implicitly clear that Barth's doctrine of sanctification is not meant to be neatly parcelled out into objective and subjective categories by which one can easily discern the work of God as one thing, and the work of human beings another.[59] Or put differently, this lecture emphasises that Barth's use of the terms 'objective' and 'subjective' are not simply categories which refer to God and humanity respectively, as if objective means God's work and subjective means human work. There are of course objective and subjective aspects within Barth's doctrine of sanctification—to say that God truly reveals himself to humanity, says Barth, presupposes that humanity stands before God—the point emphasised, however, is that the objective and subjective, though from a human perspective require two words, are inseparable as the single work of God.[60] So while Barth acknowledges that it is one thing when we direct our attention to *God's act* on humanity, and another thing (not for God but for us) when it is remembered that this act of God takes place *in humanity*, "in doing so, however we are not attributing one to God and the other to man."[61] Both are the work of God brought together in the unity of the Holy Spirit. Barth's account is a highly integrated and multi-faceted conception of the relationship between God and humanity attested to by his unique theological style, often said to be more circular than linear, which constantly folds the proceeding argument back upon itself creating an overlapping unity. Similarly to Barth's organizational

---

58. *Göttingen Dogmatics* I, 76.

59. This is not to say that there is a synergistic confusion of the divine and human in which there is no difference between the divine and human work; nor would Barth contend that the opposite were true, that the objective merely subsumes the subjective.

60. Barth, *Göttingen Dogmatics* I, 168.

61. Barth, "Rechtfertigung und Heiligung," 77.

premise of the *Reconciliation* chapter in the *GD* in which the divine work is immediately displayed as divine gift, each thesis in this lecture conveys a particular unity of the divine-human relationship in which the grace and mercy of God continually form the basis and content of its anthropological recognition and consideration.

Doctrinal Connections

In the opening section of the *RH* lecture, Barth remarks on the unity of Christian doctrine. It is a good idea, says Barth, to clearly remember

> that the possibility of attaining clarification [of any one doctrine] is determined by its connection with the whole of which it . . . is part..., especially if one deems a partial question more important and more burning than other people do, as might be the case with ours. It cannot be approached in a useful way without keeping an eye on the others; and one has to be clear . . . that in this circle there is generally nothing that could be seen as less important and less urgent to be treated than another.[62]

Barth's initial task in these introductory remarks is to remind his listeners of the general situation in which they now find themselves as theologians. While the content of the lecture is geared towards specific doctrinal explications, the members of his audience must not forget that they are working within the sphere of the "large circle of the truth of God," and must not cut themselves off from its implications.[63] His point here is twofold.

First, Barth stresses that the content of Christian doctrine is determined by *God* himself. That which dogmatics is concerned with, namely, the outlining of this content, finds its existence and coherence "in the event that God speaks His word in His church."[64] "That the Word of God is *spoken*, that the truth is truth, that is the gift of God by which the church lives, always in the moment, always under the reservation that God gives it."[65] This statement essentially serves as an orientation towards the conditions under which dogmatics functions. It is not simply working with propositional truths, which may be casually developed; rather

62. Ibid., 63.
63. Ibid., 62.
64. Ibid., 63.
65. Ibid., 62.

those who speak about God embark on a dangerous quest and must from the outset recognize this speech as a gift. "The truth then is never at our disposal, neither in the whole nor in the detail; therefore, let us make sure that we are at its disposal."[66] Thus, Barth acknowledges the Lordship of God as a reality claim upon the material content of Christian theology, the fount of and unifying principle of its existence.

Secondly, Barth means to indicate the unity and interconnectedness of Christian doctrine. The truthfulness of individual doctrines cannot be maintained apart from their connection with the whole of Christian truth; essentially doctrines should be viewed as various points on a circle rather than linearly. Each doctrine may be truly understood only in that all the other points on the circle are kept within site and are found to overlap with each other.

> That we are sanctified and hallowed through the grace of God is, therefore, true because, and as, all the before and subsequently mentioned content is also true. It is just as true, and we cannot recognize this truth without seeing the shadow from the light, which falls from all onto all the others in a certain way. We have to consider all those other points even if we cannot dwell on their meaning more deeply.[67]

The fullness and complexity of sanctification, therefore, is only rightly assumed as it is considered in some fashion in relation to the entirety of Christian doctrine. To the extent that sanctification, or any other doctrine, is pursued in isolation, or for its own ends, it finds itself vulnerable and prone to abstraction. Something Barth was convinced sanctification in particular had often fallen prey to.

In heeding Barth's concern that one cannot rightly comprehend the meaning and significance of sanctification without acknowledging the light and shadow cast upon it by other facets of Christian theology, this section will examine several key doctrines that throw a significant light on Barth's doctrine of sanctification: Revelation, the Holiness of God, Election, and Eschatology. The point here is not to summarize these doctrines *per se*, but to discern their impact and relationship to the doctrine of sanctification.

---

66. Ibid.
67. Ibid., 64.

Revelation

In revelation, God makes himself known to humanity. By this, Barth means two very specific things. From one perspective, it means that "when God reveals himself, this means that God himself, known *and* making known, speaking *and* hearing," is present.[68] God is both the one who reveals Himself as the *content* of revelation—it is God himself and nothing else that is made known—and the one whom *makes this knowing possible*. Or, as Barth says, "God is seen, believed, recognized, and known only in the act of his self-revelation. The human act of seeing, believing, recognizing, and knowing is primarily his work."[69] God is the one who reveals himself in the Son and makes this knowing possible through the Holy Spirit. On the other hand, Barth adds that, "if fellowship between God and us is to mean anything, then it must mean that we in our sphere turn no less to God than God turns to us in his sphere. . . . There has to be a recognition, an acceptance, an acknowledgment, a respecting, a bowing down."[70] God addresses himself to individuals in this revelation, and they therefore become hearers of this address. Revelation in both aspects of this single event indicates a relation.

The implications of such statements are far reaching within Barth's dogmatics. Essentially the doctrine of revelation serves as the primary vehicle for elucidating the main theme of the GD: God is God. Further, revelation, this relationship between God and people, means something very specific for sanctification. As Barth writes: "God's address to us means directly the knowledge that God is almighty. Address here means claiming, commandeering, binding to faith and obedience. When addressed by God we know that in our totality we are no longer our own. The act of the living God is *eo ipso* an act of Lordship."[71]

Revelation means sanctification! Revelation is the act of sanctification *par excellence* in which God draws near to humanity and makes himself known as Lord, in which God claims people as his own; and in which they acknowledge that they are no longer their own. One must remember that for Barth the doctrine of sanctification is about conveying just this idea of God's lordship, this specific relationship between God and humanity. Rather than offering an account which explains how

68. Barth, *Göttingen Dogmatics* I, 94.
69. Ibid., 87.
70. Ibid., 180.
71. Ibid., 404.

one becomes incrementally less sinful and more righteous, Barth is concerned instead with what it means to say that the person of sin stands before God in covenant relationship, and recognizes that he is no longer his own master but is claimed by God as a child of God. In revelation, Barth says, "the Lord who is over and in the world makes himself known to me, the person I am, as *my* Lord, that he stands in *my* life, that he is seen by *me* as a factor with which I have to reckon. He is and becomes our own Lord. He places over us the sign of victory which is his own being, and *his lordship becomes the decisive determination of our existence* (emphasis mine)."[72] Sanctification is the dogmatic location in which this specific aspect of revelation, "namely, that he (God) becomes our Lord and we . . . his servants, not belonging to ourselves but to someone else, and that we acknowledge this in obedience," is teased out.[73] At every turn then Barth's doctrine of sanctification will be indistinguishable and unintuitable from this very specific rendering of the relationship between God and human beings.

That one hears God speaking this Word to him means that he now knows that his life is no longer his own; he knows that in Christ, though he remains a sinner in himself, he is a new man. And in hearing this he clings to Christ and his life takes on a new direction, a direction pointed outward away from himself towards God and those around him. Because of the Word of God in revelation such a person is no longer bound to the single droning message that he must be his own lord, his own creator, his own master. Such a person now hears that he has been taken up in Christ, claimed by God, and therefore sanctified. His sanctification means that where he once only heard his own voice clamouring for authority he now hears the voice of Holy Spirit proclaiming Christ's sovereign Lordship. Such a person is thus claimed by his Lord and reckoned unto obedience; and his obedience is also his repentance in that he no longer lifts himself up, but instead submits to Christ in his doing and not-doing.

The Holiness of God

In revelation, God makes himself known to individuals and thus encounters them as Lord. A specific relation is established between God and the one who hears, which, in terms of sanctification, means that he

---

72. Ibid., 125.
73. Barth, *Göttingen Dogmatics* I, 126.

recognizes that he does not belong to himself, but acknowledges in faith and obedience that he is now the Lord's. At once, this event begins to address what Barth calls the divine perfections, or attributes of God, in which God makes Himself known to humanity. The divine attributes are the "conditions under which we know God's Word to us.... Where God speaks his own Word, he is known, and where he is known, his attributes are known. The nature is known in and through the attributes. God's attributes are the eyes with which he sees us."[74] The divine attributes are essentially a further clarification of the relation established in God's self-revelation—they are the conditions by which this relation makes itself known.[75]

To say that a person is claimed by God is more than a statement of mere fact. This relation, says Barth, "forms the point at which God and the creature meet, the means by which they reach agreement, the basis of their dealings with one another."[76] Stated more fully this means that:

> As God addresses us, so incomparably alive and so shatteringly mighty that we have to believe and obey, we are understood and perceived and comprehended and known. In revelation God is not merely manifest to us; we are manifest to God.... As God knows us, we acquire a share in his knowledge of himself.... In his knowing, then we see also his holy, righteous, and merciful will. Our fellowship with God rests on the fact that he regards us, remembers us, knows that we are as his handiwork.[77]

To say God addresses a person in revelation is to say that such a person not only recognizes his situation before God, but that he is confronted by God himself, and thus God's will. "God reveals himself because he wills something from us and with us, and this something, the content of his will, is the content of his revelation."[78] It is here that the relationship between the will of God and Barth's doctrine of sanctification finds its connection. For in revelation God reveals Himself as the one who wills "himself, and for his own sake, creation."[79] In revelation God addresses individuals as the one who is "incomparably alive and so shatteringly

---

74. Ibid., 377–78.
75. Ibid., 375.
76. Ibid., 397.
77. Ibid., 410–11.
78. Ibid., 414.
79. Ibid., 415.

mighty that we have to believe and obey"; this God is the one who wills to be none other than Himself, the one who commands and determines, whose will cannot be exchanged or confused with any other, and therefore, the one who sanctifies.

The will of God is thus, *par excellence*, a holy will. That is to say, "that God's will is his most wise inclination to himself as supreme end, and to creatures for his own sake as means thereto."[80] God's holiness is ultimately a way of describing God's relationship to himself, and, therefore, to humanity. It is a way of expressing God's supreme freedom, existence, power, goodness, and faithfulness to Himself, and, therefore, the foundation of all of God's dealings with humanity. "It is in virtue of his holiness," says Barth, "that God, making his will known to us, brings about in us that change, that leading, that conversion from the bad to the good."[81] In other words because God "must be claimed for himself in the jealous distinction or separation which brings to light" His utter distinction from all else, people too are claimed by God, sanctified by God, in order that they might love and praise Him as the Most High.[82]

God's holiness then, rightly said, is foundational for Barth's doctrine of sanctification. It is both the condition under which a person is confronted by God's sanctifying activity—the Lord who claims, and the reason why God sanctifies unto himself—the holy one whom no one may contend against. The holiness of God is a dreadful thing however. "In his holiness God has the appearance of a Moloch, a Saturn, a consuming fire."[83] For in God's holiness He not only wills to be with "us," but He also wills something from "us"; God's holy will is righteous. Righteousness, says Barth, is a way of clarifying God's holy will from "mere whim or caprice, . . . which justifies the self-love, the sacred egoism."[84] Righteousness is the quality by which God wills the good and hates the evil. God's will is an "ordered and ordering will, a critical power, a power that says Yes and No according to a definite standard, that turns from and to, that punishes and rewards, that judges."[85] Humanity, however, is unrighteous; their rebellious existence is at all times a direct affront to the holiness and

---

80. Ibid.
81. Ibid., 418.
82. Ibid., 419.
83. Ibid.
84. Ibid.
85. Ibid., 420.

righteousness of God. In Jesus Christ, the divine righteousness displays the universal judgment upon humanity. It is for this reason that Barth begins his doctrine of sanctification in both the *GD* and *RH* with a similar question: What does the action of God mean as God's action on *people*, in *this* person, the *homo viator et peccator*?[86] In other words how is it that *sinful* people may stand before the *holy* and *righteous* God? Barth's doctrine of sanctification is an attempt to parcel out this mystery. It is precisely an attempt to show "how man comes into a holy relation with God without compromising the fact of divine righteousness on the one hand, or of human sinfulness on the other."[87]

The disjunction between God's holiness and human sinfulness necessitates one further word needs be spoken here. God is indeed dreadful as the holy one who claims Himself in jealous distinction from all else, and righteous as the one who judges according to a "definite standard, that turns from and to, that punishes and rewards." "Like righteousness," however, Barth says, "we must understand mercy as a closer definition of the holiness of the divine will. The 'holy' needs this closer definition."[88] Without it, one ceases to deal with God himself, but clings instead to an idol, a terrible Moloch, or the impartial goddess *Iustitia*.

> God is so holy, so unique in his willing, that in this willing, as his Word reveals to us, within his turning from and to, within his rewarding and punishing, within the judgment and through the crisis there is revealed a quality of his will that we cannot understand as order, as legislative or distributive justice, . . . but only as something which, although it derives of course from his nature, is as such totally unexpected and free and superabundant, not the remainder in the sum of righteousness, but the subjective element in God in virtue of which, far from being just blindfolded, he is Lord of the scales with which he weighs as the righteous one, and as his command goes out and judgment falls he has pity on the object of his command and judgment, accepting solidarity with it and helping it. [89]

Mercy here is intended in the same manner as grace, or goodness, or even patience. It too possesses the same potential to be idolised if it eclipses

---

86. Barth, *Unterricht in der Christlichen Religion* III, 304; Barth, "Rechtfertigung und Heiligung," 63–64.

87. Tribble, "Doctrine of Sanctification," 38.

88. Barth, *Göttingen Dogmatics* I, 420.

89. Ibid., 421.

the righteousness of God, or forgets the fear and trembling which rightly befalls those who stand before the holy God. Rightly understood, however, mercy is the aspect of God's holiness in which God himself overcomes the impossibility of divine-human fellowship. It is through the power of God's will that He not only turns to human beings, accepting solidarity with them, but also turns them to himself and helps them. The righteousness of God which goes out as a demand for obedience, far from being set aside by divine mercy, is fulfilled precisely in the fullness of God's own holiness by which he claims human beings for himself. Sanctification, therefore, is only possible at all times by divine mercy, and subsists in the holiness of God.[90]

Election

Both the doctrine of revelation and the divine perfections point toward a single truth, namely, "God's relation to us is not accidental."[91] In other words, God did not have to have fellowship with humanity, but willed to have it—from all eternity. Put differently, "God does not will to be without the world."[92] Fellowship with God is, therefore, a matter of divine freedom and love, a matter of divine initiative and fulfilment; it is particularly a matter of divine choosing and election. Election (in the text Barth references the Synod of Dort) is the immutable decree of God before the foundation of the world, whereby in sheer grace He chooses in Christ to effectually call and draw close those to whom He reveals Himself by His Word and Spirit.[93] Fellowship with God is, therefore, not arbitrary, nor is it a general truth accessible to all. Election is always a matter of God's decision, of God's free grace.

---

90. Barth, *Unterricht in der Christlichen Religion* III, 312.
91. Barth, *Göttingen Dogmatics* I, 128.
92. Ibid., 423.
93. Barth, *Göttingen Dogmatics* I, 460. Barth adds that his main discrepancy with the council's statement on election is its insistence that the elect refers to a specific number of people (not quoted in the passage above). It is, he insists, what causes this doctrine, "difficult enough in itself," to suffer needlessly and irrelevantly; and acknowledges in seriousness, "This is the rent in the cloak of my orthodoxy for which undoubtedly I would at least have been beaten with rods in old-time Geneva" (ibid., 453). Instead Barth prefers to focus on God's freedom "not only to elect and reject different people but also to elect or reject a particular individual at different times" (ibid., 454).

To this extent then, Barth writes concerning sanctification, "The sinner is reconciled because he is the one chosen, appointed, loved in Christ."[94] Election is, mildly stated, the foundation for and controlling factor throughout Barth's doctrine of sanctification. To be sanctified is to stand before God as an elected and called sinner. "What does it mean," Barth asks, "to be an elected and called sinner? Answer: *God makes him holy*."[95] In stressing this connection between election and sanctification one aspect that Barth means to highlight is the graciousness of sanctification. And so he writes, "There is thus, although sanctification itself refers to the *actions* of man, . . . no *self-sanctification*, as little as a self-justification."; for as Scripture proclaims, "You are now pure for the sake of the *Word* that I have spoken to you (John 15:3)."[96] Because sanctification is a matter of divine election it is and always remains pure gift.

Yet election is not without its impact upon human life and living. For, again, election is a matter of divine willing and fellowship and, therefore, does not simply mean God's turning toward people, but also means their turning toward God. "In those who are addressed by God not only is faith awakened, but *eo ipso* obedience as well, which is just as much a gift of grace as faith is."[97] While it is true that election means divine choosing, sanctification as gift, and, therefore, no self-sanctification, it also means that in and with the divine choosing "I am summoned to move on to decision the very next moment, i.e., to be the one I am, not to elect but to be elected and to confirm my election, to fulfil in my decision the decision that has been *made* about me, to be the one whom God loves in *my own* decision in virtue of *God's* decision."[98] Election, therefore, is not election to a state or group, or some*thing* that one may control, but to a way of life. It is election to an existence in which the claim of God is raised upon a person that he might turn towards God in fellowship no less than God has turned toward him.[99]

It is precisely because a person has been elected for fellowship with God that his life too must bear the image, not of his own innate holiness, but of God's. "In the Old and New Testaments when Holy is used as is

---

94. Barth, "Rechtfertigung und Heiligung," 81.
95. Barth, *Unterricht in der Christlichen Religion* III, 309.
96. Ibid., 312.
97. Barth, *Göttingen Dogmatics* I, 473.
98. Barth, *Ethics*, 92.
99. Ibid., 472.

predicated to men ... it means his qualification by the effective claim that God has raised upon him" and not by the significance and power found within themselves.[100] A person is sanctified so that he might be the one whom God has elected him to be. He is set apart not primarily from other people, but from his own claim to holiness, his own desire to be Lord, to elect. He is holy, therefore, not because he turns to God in his sphere no less than God turns toward him, but because he has been *elected* for holy fellowship.[101] In that a person is elected for holy fellowship with God, however, he is truly sanctified because his life is set apart and qualified by the effective claim that God has raised upon him. The determining factor of his life is this claim for which he has been elected. This claim is not merely the judgment of God but also and supremely his power which marks a person's existence.

Election, however, though it means many things for Barth's doctrine of sanctification, does not mean, says Barth, that the one sanctified stops being a sinner.[102]

> In this regard, it may be noted that the elect in Christ are not plucked out of the mass of perdition, out of rejection, in such a way that they are no longer sinners or mortal, or that they are totally or even partially lifted out of the darkness of human existence. Election does not give rise to any island of the blessed Pharisaic corner of the righteous in the world. The special thing about the elect, so long as time endures, is the special thing that happens to them through God's Word, the forgiveness of sins that is promised them, not their special possessing and fulfilling. The special thing is that, addressed in truth by God, and no longer left to themselves like the rejected, they can say that in both body and soul they are not their own, but belong to their faithful Savoir Jesus Christ.[103]

This passage highlights a particularly distinct aspect of Barth's doctrine of sanctification, one that often caused great strife between Barth and groups such as the Pietists. Though the goal of election is holiness of life, Barth proclaims, this does not mean that through sanctification the believer becomes qualitatively different from the rest of the world in such a way that he may gradually shed his sinfulness and stride step by step toward

---

100. Barth, *Unterricht in der Christlichen Religion* III, 309.
101. Barth, *Göttingen Dogmatics* I, 191.
102. Barth, *Unterricht in der Christlichen Religion* III, 308.
103. Barth, *Göttingen Dogmatics* I, 465.

perfection. As was seen in the previous section, just as God's holiness is most wonderfully demonstrated by the fact that although he is different from the world he is devoted to it, so human holiness is most clearly portrayed not through mere separation from the world, but by the forgiveness of sins and the Lordship of Christ.[104] In contrast to those like W. Hützen, a Pietist, who taught that for Christians the name "lost sinners" no longer applies, Barth proclaimed that it is only the elect who truly understand their sinfulness.[105] Sanctification then, for Barth, is not a way of describing the *sinlessness* of humanity, but the gracious comprehension of *their* complete and total *sinfulness*. And yet in this confession, incomparably linked with God's gracious electing, which erupts simultaneously as an acknowledgment of utter sinfulness and an acceptance of Christ's Lordship, the boundary and power of sin is marked for destruction.[106]

Eschatology

As the chapter on *The Resurrection of the Dead* pointed out, the doctrine of eschatology is crucial for understanding Barth's theology, particularly his doctrine of sanctification. For Barth, sanctification is, like all biblical terms, an eschatological term.[107] As a doctrine of Christian hope, eschatology "is the basic and final instruction about what it means to say that God has chosen lost sinners" to be his covenant partners.[108] This means that "Christian reflection all along has to reckon with the fact that we do not only hope for Christ in this lifetime."[109] Christian reflection, therefore, must signal the present work of grace through the Holy Spirit, and yet maintain the boundary and limits to which this time is subjected. Christian life stands under a big "Not Yet" on the one hand; on the other, it is placed under the authority of the promises of God.[110] In terms of sanctification, this means that the Christian life is viewed from the standpoint of patience and hope, as those who live in time and yet are called

---

104. Busch, *Barth and the Pietists*, 299.
105. Ibid., 209.
106. Barth, *Unterricht in der Christlichen Religion* III, 313.
107. Barth, "Rechtfertigung und Heiligung," 98.
108. Barth, *Unterricht in der Christlichen Religion* III, 403.
109. Barth, "Rechtfertigung und Heiligung," 96.
110. Barth, *Barth and the Pietists*, 212.

to hasten toward the oncoming Kingdom of God and His righteousness within the positive limits of the resurrection of Jesus Christ.

As Migliore notes, in Barth's estimation many of the errors which have occurred within theology were the result of a "premature eschatology" in which Christians, rather than waiting in patience and hope for the fulfilment of God's promises, believed they had already attained their goal, i.e., the Corinthian church.[111] Or, as Barth perceived to be problematic within Reformed Orthodoxy, eschatology was often detached from the rest of dogmatics so that it was loosed from the central work of God in Jesus Christ, or spiritualized in such a way that its impact on the world was distorted.[112] It is critical therefore to be mindful of the relationship between sanctification and eschatology, and ever conscious of what Barth means when he emphasises the eschatological dimension of sanctification.

For Barth the term "eschatological" means two very specific things. First, "eschatological" means "final" or "consummate"—in essence it refers to the work of God that marks time as such. As opposed to those who see eschatology as simply a discussion of "last things," or of realities to come in the future, Barth uses the term as a way of indicating the comprehensive impact of the Word and work of God in relationship to humanity. "Eschatological" then does not refer to something that is still waiting to become true in its most proper sense; it points toward the all-consuming event of God's reconciliation with human beings. It is God's Word to humanity about themselves. And that means that one's present reality, as he perceives it, is not the entirety his real existence.

As an eschatological term sanctification becomes a distinctive element in defining what it means to be one reconciled with God, one who stands, as it were, in contradiction with himself. As such, it refers to God's command for the reconciled sinner to be the one whom God has created him to be—despite himself. Though the reality of sanctification is not intrinsically-visibly manifest to those sanctified, Barth admonishes believers to trust that the Word and work spoken to them and about them is definitive for their existence. Though a person finds himself living within the shadow of death and sin, his existence is not "forfeited to himself and not to the devil."[113] One's sanctification means that he is given the grace to live in and by that fact that he is no longer his own, but belongs to the Lord.

---

111. Barth, *Göttingen Dogmatics* I, 59.
112. Ibid., 38.
113. Barth, *Unterricht in der Christlichen Religion* III, 318.

Secondly, eschatological means the future in the present. More specifically, Barth is referring not simply to some*thing* that remains to be achieved in the future, but to some*one*—Jesus Christ—who, although awaits a definite time for his *parousia*, is nevertheless present. Meaning, therefore, that one's sanctification is not simply a future reality, but is an existence that meets him presently in Christ.

But what then does it mean, Barth asks, that "Christ bids his people wait like servants for their master [cf. Matt 24:45-51] or the ten virgins for their bridegroom [cf. Matt 25:1-13]"?[114] What can this mean except that eschatology is a future that is also a starting point? What is to come in full measure one day has burst in upon humanity's ever present now in such a way that a new quality is given to their present existence. The essential matter here is the presence of Christ, working in and through the Holy Spirit, which brings about something ultimate. Positively stated this means that in faith one reaches beyond himself, so to speak, and already has what God offers to him in grace. In faith he is who he is not, Christ lives in him, the sinner sanctified by grace.

All of this means, however, and this is the crux of the matter concerning sanctification, that "we are not sanctified for a perfection to achieve now and here and not for a millennial kingdom to build here and now, but for the forever oncoming of the kingdom of God and his righteousness (cf. Matt 5:33), but for waiting and hastening towards him (cf. 2 Pet 3:12), and this waiting and hastening is without doubt now and here our part."[115] This is perhaps one of the clearest examples, if not the clearest, of the eschatological nature of Barth's doctrine of sanctification. It means that the goal of sanctification has nothing to do with establishing an oasis of blessedness in this life, nothing to do with a present perfection that can be read directly off one's life; it is not about moral transformation or confidently possessing holiness, but of being possessed. God's claim upon humanity means that though they are now still bound within the limits of sickness and frailty they are God's own, they are now what they will be someday in full measure.

To the extent that sanctification, or any other doctrine, is pursued in isolation, or for its own ends it will in the end succumb to self-delusion, and, therefore, self-destruction. In heeding Barth's concern that one cannot rightly comprehend the meaning and significance of sanctification

---

114. Barth, *Ethics*, 465.
115. Barth, *Unterricht in der Christlichen Religion* III, 324.

without acknowledging the light and shadow cast upon it by the other facets of Christian theology one must continually manoeuvre in accord with the salient doctrines listed above which not only constantly throw a significant hue over one's conception of the divine-human relationship, but in fact fundamentally determine that relationship. As this chapter moves forward we will see how all of these larger themes come together and shape Barth's doctrine of sanctification.

Preliminary Discussion: Reconciliation, Justification, and Sanctification

The doctrine of sanctification is in part, says Barth, a paraphrase of *insertio in Christum*.[116] It is concerned with the renewed relationship between God and sinful humanity, with the impact of the person and work of Jesus Christ on the sinner who now stands in fellowship with God. Along with justification, writes Barth, sanctification is an answer to the special question, "What does the grace of God in Christ mean for the man to whom it befalls?"[117] Sanctification, in sum, manoeuvres as an aspect or form of God's reconciling activity; it testifies to God's own faithfulness and love for humanity. If reconciliation between God and humanity may be considered essentially the content of the gospel, then sanctification, along with justification, is the event in which God makes this reconciliation known. Sanctification and justification are the grace of reconciliation. The above question, phrased differently, serves to highlight this relationship: What must a person *be* because reconciliation *is*? The answer to this question is taken up in the doctrines of sanctification and justification. Whatever might be said about sanctification, therefore, must pay homage in some way to a preliminary discussion of the doctrine of reconciliation and stand in relation to the doctrine of justification.

The Work of Reconciliation

There is from God, declares Barth, reconciliation between God and humanity. It is the paradoxical new relation between God and the sinner in its totality, including its reality within the world, in time.[118] "The divine

---

116. Ibid., 306.
117. Barth, "Rechtfertigung und Heiligung," 63.
118. Barth, *Göttingen Dogmatics*, 9.

faithfulness triumphs wonderfully over the contrast between God and man, unilaterally and autocratically . . . . Reconciliation proclaims a conclusion of peace, the creation of the possibility of being together in love. This conclusion of peace between God and man has happened."[119] Further, Jesus Christ is the guarantor of this peace with God and the promise of everlasting life. As Prophet, Priest, and King, Christ proclaims the everlasting decision of reconciliation, fulfils the whole will of God in humanity's place, and rules omnipotent in the face of their rebellious nature.[120]

This means that in Christ, *unio cum Christo*, not only is there now peace between God and humanity, but this fellowship is also made known to people and upheld in the face of their constant faithlessness and disobedience. For this reason Barth states that reconciliation further shows itself as "God's reign amid man's conflict with Him and with himself."[121] This is an important facet to remember says Barth. It means that not only is the work of God entirely *self*-giving, i.e., communicative, but it is also self-*giving*, i.e., generative. If the event of reconciliation were to have no bearing on the thought, will and desire of people would it then be anything more than a puppet show asks Barth? What is reconciliation, actually, if one simply answers the question about the reality of the sinner in fellowship with God "with a shrug of the shoulders?"[122] It is precisely here that the doctrine of sanctification is appropriately utilized in response to the question: What must a person be because reconciliation is?

The reality of this renewed fellowship between God and humanity forms the backdrop for Barth's doctrine of sanctification. In other words sanctification is dogmatically oriented precisely where the doctrine of reconciliation proclaims that the event of reconciliation is a real event that has enduringly affected human existence, where the grace of God comes to sinful people. Sanctification is geared towards addressing the particular reality of the *viator hominis christiani* for the *homo viator peccator*, in that the reconciled person is the elected and called *sinner*. The issue is: what becomes of a sinful person through reconciliation in so far as he is also a *sinner* in reconciliation?

---

119. Ibid., 8–10.
120. Barth, *Unterricht in der Christlichen Religion* III, 74–75.
121. Barth, "Rechtfertigung und Heiligung," 96.
122. Barth, *Unterricht in der Christlichen Religion* III, 306.

Here Barth makes a distinction between the judgment of God by which one is justified and the power of God by which he is able to stand before God sanctified. Of course, writes Barth,

> I cannot mean with this distinction . . . that the judgment of God in itself is powerless and the power of God is something other than his Word. I would only like to make clear: the reality of reconciliation means for us now that man, with the sinner *as such*, becomes, in the area of his *sinfulness*, something different. The judgment, the Word, justification puts man under *the truth of reconciliation*. . . . But the truth of reconciliation cannot be without *reality*.[123]

Though the work of God in reconciliation is single and undivided it becomes for human beings, at their level, a double word, two strings of thought "which both describe the same truth but do not dissolve into each other."[124] And so while both justification and sanctification are concerned with the question of what the grace of God means for the sinner, the latter is specifically geared towards comprehending the reality of grace in the *history* of human life.

Justification and Sanctification

Justification and sanctification are the execution of the grace of God on sinful people. They are, as has been mentioned already, the answers to a special question: "What does the grace of God in Christ mean for the man to whom it befalls? What does it mean to be a member of the covenant that God in Christ has made with men? What does it mean to be a man reconciled to God in Christ? How is the grace of God executed?"[125] Essentially, says Barth, justification and sanctification describe how it is that one may stand before God in fellowship, and what this person must look like in doing so. As such justification and sanctification occupy a distinct and significant place within Barth's dogmatics—the point at which the Word of God spoken *about* God and humanity is clearly shown also to be spoken *to* individuals. In the doctrines of justification and sanctification, one gets a clear sense that the divine-human relationship is not simply an

---

123. Ibid., 310–11.
124. Barth, "Rechtfertigung und Heiligung," 76.
125. Ibid., 64; *Unterricht in der Christlichen Religion* III, 304.

afterthought for Barth, but is rather, intrinsic within his theology, robust, and even joyful.

In the opening section of paragraph 32 of the *GD*, concerning sanctification, Barth questions whether or not the reality of reconciliation is not simply exhausted with the idea of justification—with the divine acquittal of sinful human beings and faith as the distinctive human correlative.[126] After all, he asks, is not faith *the* good work which is demanded by the forgiveness of sins? Is it not enough to simply say that the new life is exactly faith as the recognition of the forgiveness of sins?[127] This may suffice, Barth writes, when one questions how it is that a person, the sinner, is able to stand with God in covenant, i.e., forensic justification. But when one questions after the reality of such a person, i.e., What does the sinner who stands in covenant with God look like? then one can see, he says, that there is something quite practical missing from the concepts of justification and faith.[128] If then

> it is not a matter of 1. softening and enlarging the concepts of justification and faith so that they themselves overcome this dualism—because one would for this reason only obscure these concepts, the point of the *sache* [things] in their strength and clarity, if they are, however, 2. un-softened and un-broadened they do not provide an answer to our question, and if they 3. do not begin to simply suppress this (practical) question, if they stand there rightly and must be answered, then we see now the gap which the concept of *sanctification* is appointed to fill. Then we see that the one word of reconciliation in our ears must be a *double* one on our lips. By the word justification, un-muddled with it, without destroying its own logic, is heard the word sanctification.[129]

Sanctification is, therefore, says Barth, that essential aspect of the doctrine of reconciliation in which the truth of the Christian message is shown to be addressed *ad hominem*.[130] There is, therefore, no word about justification without reference to sanctification—the divine acquittal, the forgiveness of sins, does not exist without its impact upon the life and living of sinful people. "Justification by faith signifies *eo ipso* the knowledge

126. Ibid., 305.
127. Ibid..
128. Ibid., 305–7.
129. Ibid., 306.
130. Ibid., 308.

of a claim of man by God."¹³¹ On the other hand, there is also no word about sanctification without reference to justification, for there is never any moment in which those sanctified are no longer bitterly in need of the forgiveness of sins and faith.¹³²

Connection

In paragraph 31 of the GD, the section on justification, Barth writes that justification and sanctification function together "like born again and conversion. Not as if born again and justification, conversion and sanctification coincide. Justification acts to born again, and sanctification acts to conversion such as contents to form, like an act to a condition, like a thing to a word, like *facere* to *vocare*."¹³³ They are, in other words, two facets of the singular reconciliatory grace of God indissolubly linked, each central to the event transpiring between God and humanity.

The initial and overarching emphasis that characterizes justification and sanctification for Barth, then, is their dual function as the *one work of grace*. They must in the first instance, writes Barth, be interpreted as an "*act of God on man*," and as such are an expression of the *magnalia Dei*—the great works of God.¹³⁴ Sanctification, therefore, is just as thoroughly and profoundly based upon and upheld by the sovereign work of grace as justification is. "One cannot note enough," writes Barth, that the older dogmaticians "identified sanctification just as justification an *"actio Dei gratuita"* (Schm. 363, H. 407). Just as direct and absolute is *iustificatio* so also is *sanctificatio* the consequence of the grace of *insertio in Christum*, the gift of the Holy Spirit."¹³⁵ This, Barth feels, is the heart of the matter concerning both justification and sanctification, and the consequences for both doctrines are significant. The ground for the one just as the other is the freedom of God. And for sanctification in particular this means that "Our holiness is on all stages only possible by divine mercy, not our purchase, merit, acquisition, nothing whereupon *we* knock, of that we could boast. . . . There is thus, although sanctification itself refers to the

---

131. Ibid., 311.
132. Ibid., 309.
133. Ibid., 277.
134. Barth, "Rechtfertigung und Heiligung," 65.
135. Barth, *Unterricht in der Christlichen Religion* III, 311–12. Barth refers here to Schmidt, *Doctrinal Theology* and Heppe, *Reformed Dogmatics*.

actions of man and in *certain* actions of man takes the appearance of steps, no *self-sanctification*, as little as a self-justification."[136]

Barth's concern for theology in general, but particularly for justification and sanctification, is the ease with which its focus can be diverted when one is not continually conscious of its proper aim. Keeping in mind that the foundation and content of both justification and sanctification is the one work of God serves then to steer a proper course in Christian proclamation. "It is particularly tempting," writes Barth, "with this our subject to disregard this basic rule of all sensible Christian reflection..."[137] That is, that justification and sanctification are:

> thus . . . not proclamation of deeds and acts, of experiences and adventures, of piety and charitable activities of man, and not indirectly, with the detour or the pretence of the glorification of God as it happens not infrequently in Christian circles. Certainly, it is about God's act on *man*, but it is exclusively about the act of *God* on man, not about an act between God and man; much less can man become the centre of attention.[138]

Undoubtedly justification and sanctification must be concerned with humanity, but not because *they* stand at the centre of these works. As Barth continually stressed, when God becomes the sustaining focus of theological discourse humanity is set free from the impossibility of maintaining their own importance. As the focus is shifted towards the *God* who justifies and sanctifies rather than the human *experience* the significance of the work of grace for people becomes clear: "Within this [God's justifying and sanctifying activity] he believes and obeys, within this he is just and holy, if in this he is within God's doing in such a way that he aims away from himself and towards God who is greater than our heart (1 John 3:20) in all the experienced . . . depths, and in all the active . . . strength of his existence. In this way, through grace, his heart is and *becomes strong* (Heb 13:9)."[139] These great works of *God* are "basically what the entire catechism and dogmatics speak of, whether it is about . . . reconciliation or about redemption."[140] The centre of gravity for both justification and sanctification finds its source in this one work of

---

136. Barth, *Unterricht in der Christlichen Religion* III, 312.
137. Barth, "Rechtfertigung und Heiligung," 65.
138. Ibid.
139. Ibid., 66.
140. Ibid., 65.

grace, and for that reason they truly address themselves to the reality of human life and living.

Following a clear Reformed line of thought Barth stresses that justification and sanctification must be distinguished but not separated. They must not be separated of course because they function as the single work of grace. Not only does this mean that the content of the two doctrines are entirely concerned with the work of God on humanity, but they must also not be construed as temporally separate works—as if they happen chronologically or experientially one after the other, or may occur apart from each other at various points within one's life. There is never any word about justification without reference to the justified *person* states Barth, i.e., "The judgment, the Word, justification puts man under the *truth* of reconciliation. . . . But the truth of reconciliation cannot be without *reality*. The forensic act of justification must, said the old ones (H. 411), correspond to a . . . disposition of the state *within* the human sphere."[141] In other words justification by faith intrinsically denotes the knowledge of God's claim upon the sinner who, for that very reason, not only believes that he is no longer his own, but must also *live* as if it were true.[142] And that is his sanctification. "Both are necessary, neither can be overlooked to the disadvantage of the other. Both have to be looked at in "*conjunctim*" (Calvin) if one wants to see the truth. Both show the truth of one and the same grace."[143]

Distinction

Equally important for Barth is the fact that justification and sanctification must be properly distinguished. "They cannot be identified and confused with each other; one cannot be traced back or cross-connected to the other, as it is the mistake of the Catholics and of all catholicising, but also of all the antinomian doctrines of grace."[144] For it means one thing to say that sinners are *reconciled*, and another to say that *sinners* are reconciled. According to Barth, Augustine "unfortunately . . . sought justification in the immediately perceptible actuality of the new obedience. He not only

---

141. Barth, *Unterricht in der Christlichen Religion* III, 311; Barth, "Rechtfertigung und Heiligung," 75–78.

142. Barth, *Unterricht in der Christlichen Religion* III, 311.

143. Barth, "Rechtfertigung und Heiligung," 78.

144. Ibid.

made justification coincide with sanctification but made justification pass into sanctification, interpreting grace as 'the inspiration of goodwill and of works' and faith as the impartation of man's own ability to will and to perform what was commanded by the law."[145] The problem, as Barth sees it, is that Augustine, rather than offering an account of the *reconciled* sinner based upon a continual graciousness from without—the forgiveness of sins—to stand as a distinct facet of reconciliation, built his concept of the sinner's righteousness instead upon the gradual moral perfection of the Christian by which he, in a sense, grows into a state of merit by cooperating with the grace of God. The implication being that sanctification, or the goodwill and works of the Christian, becomes the basis for justification following the initial act of forgiveness by which the Christian gradually attains moral and spiritual purity. In confusing justification with sanctification, one's own ability to will and to perform what is commanded by God's law, or at least his synergistic cooperation, becomes, to the detriment of God's sovereign grace, the pivot on which his relation to God turns.[146]

Although, therefore, the work of God in reconciliation is single and undivided it becomes for humans, at their level, a double word, two strings of thought "which both describe the same truth but do not dissolve into each other."[147] And so while both justification and sanctification are concerned with the question of what the grace of God means for sinful people, justification is, writes Barth, concerned with the eternal truth—the divine side, while sanctification is specifically geared towards comprehending the reality of grace in human history and life—the *chrono*logical.[148] "The one *actio Dei* is," therefore, "understood now as God acting with regard to humans, now as God acting *with regard to humans*, now in more its objective, now in its subjective meaning."[149] Not as if one points towards God's work while the other to human work, but one describes grace from its execution downwards while the other from the bottom up.

Generally stated, writes Barth, justification means: "As an elected and called sinner man stands there in the judgment of God, as if he was

145. Barth, *The Holy Spirit and the Christian Life*, 21.
146. Ibid., 20.
147. Barth, "Rechtfertigung und Heiligung," 76.
148. Ibid., 86–87.
149. Barth, *Unterricht in der Christlichen Religion* III, 277.

not he, but Jesus Christ. As the elected and called sinner, God adds to him the high priestly work of Christ, as if he himself had done it. But that means: his sin is forgiven him, he is just, he is a dear child of God, he is an heir of everlasting life. He is this only by grace, only in Christ, only in faith, but he is this."[150]

The execution of grace means that God looks on humanity in Christ—*unio cum Christi*. "This was the message which the apostles took into the world: God's pleasure which He felt for the one crucified at Golgotha is the truth about God and man. . . . God thus looks at man as His loved one in Christ."[151] God, therefore, does not consider people as the blasphemers, sinners, and rebels that they are in and of themselves. Or, rather, says Barth, "He *sees* it all, but he *overlooks* it; not because of a disinterest towards sin, but because the sin of man is *known* in Christ . . . and His anger towards sin and the curse of death which has to follow it are *borne*."[152] Justification does not dismiss sin but forgives it; justification does not eradicate sin but overcomes it, and humans, therefore, in and of themselves remain yet sinners. A reconciled person is not made righteous, but in Christ he stands before God in righteousness and must, therefore, constantly throw himself at the feet of the One who has forgiven him. In sum, "justification is God's overlooking of the sin in the here and now which has not yet been removed."[153]

Similarly, sanctification, stated generally means that: "Man stands as elected and called sinner in the power of God as one whose life no longer has honour, but yet still is the object of the royal work of Christ. . . . He lives here and now a new life. He lives it only through grace, only in Christ, only in obedience, i.e., in repentance, but he lives it."[154]

Sanctification signifies that in the face of human rebelliousness and sin people have nonetheless been elected and chosen to be God's own dear children, to stand in holy relation to Him despite their sinfulness. Through His mercy and power, God strips the sinner of all forms of pretentious self-centredness and calls him to faithful obedience; this is God's claiming of him in his not yet removed sin.[155] Whereas justification indi-

---

150. Ibid., 272.
151. Barth, "Rechtfertigung und Heiligung," 79.
152. Ibid.
153. Ibid., 78.
154. Barth, *Unterricht in der Christlichen Religion* III, 304.
155. Barth, "Rechtfertigung und Heiligung," 78.

cates God's treatment of sin, sanctification points toward God's treatment of the sinner.[156] "A reconciled sinner is evidently a sinner whose honour, strength, and independence have been taken because he cannot refuse to see himself as a sinner, he can only look for his justness in God's grace. He no longer belongs to *himself.*"[157] Sanctification is particularly concerned with these implications of the power and grace of God for sinful people. To be a new creature in Christ—to be sanctified, means, therefore, to be a special kind of sinner, one who no longer sits upon his own throne, or freely chooses the course of his own creatureliness. That is to say, the grace of God that befalls *this* sinner frees him from the guilt, misery, and power of sin.[158] He is rather like a tree with an axe laid to its roots, whose situation will never be the same; and this change is not just apparently so.[159] For "what does it mean to be an elected and called *sinner*?" asks Barth.[160] "Answer: *God makes him holy.*"[161] And though "Man is not yet holy under all circumstances as he will be holy in the resurrection of the dead, and he also in the resurrection of the dead and all eternity will never be as holy as God is holy," nevertheless, "the reality of reconciliation means for us now, that with man, with the sinner *as such*, at this level becomes, in the area of his *sinfulness* something different."[162] It is certainly a paradox, certainly a miracle, but emphatically the most significant and authentic reality which grips human existence.

Life and Death

Building upon these general descriptions Barth writes further that: "In justification, God says to the dead one: Live! In sanctification, God says to the one alive: Die! The dead one who should live is a sinner, the living one who should die is a sinner again. It is with these two clauses the Christian life is lived, there is no other way."[163] In other words, justification and

---

156. Tribble, "Doctrine of Sanctification," 113.
157. Barth, "Rechtfertigung und Heiligung," 81.
158. Barth, *Unterricht in der Christlichen Religion* III, 314.
159. Barth, "Rechtfertigung und Heiligung," 81.
160. Barth, *Unterricht in der Christlichen Religion* III, 310.
161. Ibid., 310.
162. Ibid., 310–12.
163. Barth, "Rechtfertigung und Heiligung," 83.

sanctification are the reorientation and reconstitution of one's existence away from the self towards God.

Justification is, writes Barth, a summons to new life. It is the radical undermining of the impossibility of the sinner's relationship with God, which, as it stands apart from the mercy of God consists only of corruption, transgression and complete alienation. "In justification, God says to the dead one: live!"[164] By the grace of God, meaning here judgment and the forgiveness of sins, the sinner may live as if his sin did not exist. And he may do so not merely hesitatingly, as though his justification were in some way a contingent promise based upon a level of cooperation. Rather justification means that "we are allowed to live despite our sin . . . in our folly and malice."[165] And the impact of this grace is a joyful summons to live—for it means that:

> We may breathe as if we were deserving of it, that we may be happy in our work and in our rest as if the accusation did not stand over us for even a minute; love and be loved as if all human love was not vanity; serve each other as if we humans could serve each other; even in the obvious, concrete confinement of our trespasses and guilt we may not despair as if we did not lose. Mercy blesses us, atones daily or even hourly for what we do wrong daily or hourly. This is the miracle of the reconciled sinner, the miracle of our justification.[166]

This summons to life, from the perspective of justification, is a reorientation to the truthfulness of human existence. The judgment of God, which does not merely dismiss sin, but condemns it and overcomes it, means new life. The reconciled sinner has been placed into the absolute divine decision which "does not allow us to know of any decision other than over and over again the great last one established in God's decree and executed in Christ: Son, your sins are forgiven!"[167]

Correspondingly, sanctification is the beginning of the end of the sinner as such, his utter and complete ontological, moral, and spiritual bankruptcy; which is to say, a miracle in which God makes that which is putrid beautiful: "God says to the living one: Die!"[168] Just as justifica-

---

164. Ibid.
165. Ibid., 84.
166. Ibid., 84.
167. Ibid., 90.
168. Ibid., 84.

tion, as a summons to new life, is the reorientation to the truthfulness of the reconciled sinner's existence, so sanctification as the proclamation of the death of the sinner, is the reconstitution of the peculiarity of a person within his sinfulness. The living one in this sense is the sinner by himself, the "old man," as the lord of his own existence. He sins by unbelief against the divine promise, he does not want to wait, but creates his own completion in this world.[169] He maintains a perception of life, therefore, by claiming his own right against God, by establishing himself as lord. Just as justification belongs to the judgment of God in reconciliation, so sanctification does His power by which a person at the level of his sinfulness, in his mortal obstinacy, becomes something different.[170] He becomes, writes Barth, a sacrifice, surrender, and a penance that God accepts by His grace.

Barth's "negative" phraseology here did not help to alleviate the worries of some that his doctrine of sanctification lacked real power for the Christian life. At a conference in Putbus in 1927, Barth's "Rechtfertigung und Heiligung" lecture was critiqued precisely on this point. "Immediately during the first day the essential contradiction started against the purely negative description of sanctification."[171] While the details are incomplete, W. H. Neuser notes that the protest called attention to the perceived difference between Barth's account and "the Word of God which describes sanctification differently than merely the death of the sinner."[172] Although Barth may certainly be guilty of polemically pushing the "death" language to its limits, one can see from his lecture, however, that Barth in fact agreed with his detractors that sanctification does not refer merely to the death of the sinner, or rather, it does not refer to the death of the sinner for its own sake in order to reduce the Christian life to nothingness. He writes: "Here, here, in this space thus created can bloom the freedom and joy of a Christian, in this he knows himself to be just before God as the sinner he was, is and will be."[173] That God says to the living one, "Die!" is not a black parade. It is in a sense a triumphant announcement of the fullness of life. "A reconciled sinner," writes Barth, "is evidently a sinner whose honour, strength, and independence

---

169. Barth, *Unterricht in der Christlichen Religion* II, 399.
170. Ibid., 310.
171. Barth, "Rechtfertigung und Heiligung," 61.
172. Ibid.
173. Ibid., 92.

have been taken because he cannot refuse to see himself as a sinner, he can only look for his justness in God's grace. He no longer belongs to *himself*."[174] Recognizing this claim is certainly not the elimination of sin; it is however, the beginning of the end of the sinner. It is, writes Barth, "a notorious movement in the existence of the sinner as such. It is on him as such that God puts His hand."[175] The sinner's continual summons to death then is not merely a fascination with a prolonged negativity or even an evasion of the power and joy of the Christian life, but a bold word confronting all that stands in opposition to the glory and power of Christ. The death of the sinner is a pronouncement of the royal work of Christ in which the "sinner becomes as such a praise and offering of thanks" because his sinfulness, despite its perceived presence, does indeed not have the consummate word about his existence.[176]

It should be stressed though that the notion that sanctification is a call for the death of the sinner *is* in fact meant to be earnest and shocking, and at times, therefore, even dreadful; for "It is," as Hebrews 10:31 says, "a fearful thing to fall into the hands of the living God." And this is precisely the point Barth is after by describing sanctification as the death of the sinner. To fall into the hands of the living God, to be claimed by Him, is to relinquish all notions of self-ownership or procurement, to fall apart and become unravelled as a sinner. Barth recalls a lengthy and vivid sermon by Kohlbrügge in which the latter describes in detail the implications for the sinner. As Barth reconstructs Kohlbrügge's words one sees

> the last part of his life poured out onto the earth, the last cover is pulled away from him, head and fat, all reason and spirituality are gone. Innards and thighs, heart and liver and every crutch he uses to walk are declared to be impure, have to be washed and are also taken. At the bottom there is a fire, then there is wood and on top is man, his entire self, his mind and everything given by God, his heart and his senses, his power and might; he cannot lament anymore, had I only considered this or that, had I only increased in beatitudes, had I only had a softer heart, had I only done it like this or that, had I only gone this way or that—he is being set on fire and the fire eats away his head and

---

174. Ibid., 81.
175. Ibid., 82.
176. Barth, *Unterricht in der Christlichen Religion* III, 315.

fat, innards and thighs, so that it turns only into dust and ashes before God.[177]

In essence, sanctification means there is no place to flee, there is no escape for the sinner, no place left within the corners of his innermost being that he can reserve for himself. Or rather, as Barth says, there is only one place to flee—headlong into God and His all-consuming mercy. Barth continues with Kohlbrügge's words:

> Man sees and marvels—the calf goes up through blazing flames and takes with it all it was encumbered with, it goes through all heavens—and man sees and marvels. God accepted it and turned the stench into loveliness before him. He sees and marvels: the calf went up with its sin, the flame of wrath turned into a flame of love, the flame of consumption turned into a flame of salvation; it is in this flame that man went up to God, amidst his doom, and he goes home justified and *hallowed*.[178]

And so the dreadful flames of God's all-consuming wrath becomes through love a reprieve for the sinner—his freedom found in his own demise as he relinquishes his crutches and impurities.

Essentially Barth redefines entirely what it means to speak of the death of the reconciled sinner. He writes that this concept must not be used in connection with talk about the new life in Christ, that is, as a "change of the ordinary and sensual humanity into a spiritual, moral, and pious one."[179] Rather the death of the sinner is a surrender of one's right over oneself, a relinquishing of both sin and morality. It means that "our humanity belongs to God in all its ranges and possibilities; that it may finally, finally be brought to Him as a sacrifice, after we have experienced mercy (Rom. 12:1f.)."[180] Instead of being liberation *from* worldly connections, sanctification is the freedom in which the reconciled sinner is rightly ordered *within* those relations.[181] In this sense, the death of the sinner as Barth expresses it would seem in fact to denote the very freedom for the new life in Christ which Barth's critics found wanting in his work. The death of the sinner is freedom from the curse of sin, freedom from not wanting to stand before God as he truly is. In sanctification

---

177. Barth, "Rechtfertigung und Heiligung," 85.
178. Ibid., 85–86.
179. Ibid., 84.
180. Ibid.
181. Biggar, *The Hastening that Waits*, 91.

"the Word and the Spirit free [people] to let go of the disastrous open arrogance as well as the hidden one, to know themselves under God's justice, and not wanting to stand somewhere else. . . . In short, this is what God wants from us here and now. He wants our submission to Him and nothing else, and this is just that submission."[182]

The Contours of Sanctification

As has been demonstrated thus far, Barth's doctrine of sanctification is a multi-faceted theological description of the impossible new relationship established between God and sinful humanity in the event of reconciliation. At each layer of his work on this topic Barth has reiterated, "If the *truth* of the Christian message hangs on the fact that its subject is the actions of *God*, so you hang *seriously* on the fact that it addresses itself *ad hominem* "[183] Eduard Thurnyesen noticed this theme in what Barth wrote early on: "Karl Barth's theological thinking was from the beginning directed to the life of man. The existence, the life of man, on the one side, and on the other the Word of God that meets this life, lays hold of it, and transforms it."[184] Sanctification is precisely the realization of that relationship, the *viti hominis Christiani*, the impossible new life of man wonderfully proclaimed in and through the Holy Spirit as human life is taken hold of and radically transformed by God in Jesus Christ.

In the GD and RH, we have seen that sanctification is for Barth one piece of a much larger picture, and only properly finds its place within his dogmatics in relationship to many other doctrines. Specifically this work has highlighted the integral connectedness of sanctification to revelation, holiness, election, and eschatology. The outline of these foundational principles which continually hover in the background of Barth's work, along with the characteristic concepts of sanctification developed thus far within the other primary sources, have set the stage for a more precise interpretation of, and building upon Barth's writings. This section will further develop the analytical interpretation offered thus far by focusing on three primary and purposive contours that have emerged in the course of this period in Barth's work. These themes will be explored under the headings: *The Claim of God: Nostri non sumus, sed Domini*; *The*

---

182. Barth, "Rechtfertigung und Heiligung," 73–74.
183. Barth, *Unterricht in der Christlichen Religion* III, 308.
184. Barth and Thurneysen, *Revolutionary Theology in the Making*, 13–14.

Sinner Reconciled in Grace: Simul Sanctus et Peccator; and *Grace in Time: the Christian Disposition.*

The Claim of God

Sanctification is, as Barth describes it, the answer to a very specific type of question concerning the divine-human relationship, that is, namely, "What does it mean to be a member of the covenant which God in Christ has made with men?" or differently put, "What does the action of God mean as God's action on *man*, in *this* man, the *homo viator et peccator*?"[185] Generally stated, sanctification is the doctrinal elucidation of what it means for the reconciled sinner, as elected and called by God, to stand before God in restored fellowship—a snapshot of what it means for the *sinner* to be *reconciled* to God in Jesus Christ through the Holy Spirit. At the heart of this scenario, as previously discussed, is God's self-revelation. For in revelation God does not reveal himself generally as one voice among many others competing for one's attention, but rather draws close to humanity in a specific relation. That is, "God's address to us," states Barth, "means directly that God is almighty. Address here means claiming, commandeering, binding to faith and obedience."[186] God draws close to people as their Lord. The result is that, "when addressed by God, we know that in our totality we are no longer our own. The act of the living God is *eo ipso* an act of lordship."[187] God makes himself known, therefore, not simply factually, but as "the Lord who is over and in the world . . . as *my* Lord. . . . He is and becomes our own Lord. He places over us the sign of the victory which is his own being, and his lordship becomes the decisive determination of our existence."[188] Sanctification stated precisely is the gracious and mighty act of God in which He claims the entirety of one's life as His own possession as He declares Himself to that person, and in which that person likewise, therefore, joyfully acknowledges this claim in faith and obedience.[189] The content of which is

185. Barth, "Rechtfertigung und Heiligung," 63; *Unterricht in der Christlichen Religion* III, 304.

186. Barth, *Göttingen Dogmatics*, 404.

187. Ibid.

188. Ibid., 125.

189. Tribble, "Doctrine of Sanctification," 36. "A Christian who shall be the subject of the concept "Christian life" is to be understood as a man on whom God has set His claim. Christians are the people of Israel, God's own possession, from whom on that

the declaration "that he [God] becomes our Lord and we . . . his servants, not belonging to ourselves but to someone else, and that we acknowledge this in obedience."[190]

As was shown in *The Resurrection of the Dead*, rather than an account of moral and spiritual growth, or inner renewal, Barth's focus here falls primarily upon the divine claim over humanity and the decisive determination this has for the reconciled sinner's existence. Sanctification is, therefore, as Barth succinctly states much later on, "not a question of improvement but alteration."[191] The lordship of God over the reconciled sinner becomes as such the guiding force within the sinner's existence in spite of his rebelliousness and every seeming contradiction. In struggle and hope, the reconciled sinner begins to live a new life even now in the power and promise of the Holy Spirit. Because "Man stands as elected and called sinner in the power of God as one whose life no longer has honour, but yet is still the object of the royal work of Christ . . . he lives here and now a new life."[192]

"Nostri non sumus, sed Domini"

Barth, drawing on Calvin, encapsulates this claiming and guiding of the Christian life—sanctification—with the phrase "*Nostri non sumus, sed Domini.*"[193] "What does the action of God mean as God's action on *man*, in *this* man, the *homo viator et peccator*?"[194] It means exactly that the sinner stands before God as one whose life no longer maintains its own existence, honour, and importance, it is instead, incredibly, the object of the royal work of Christ, the object of God's loving mercy and judgment.[195] *Nostri non sumus, sed Domini*, literally *we are not our own masters, but belong to the Lord*, characterizes the intent and captures the content of

---

very account sacrifices are demanded" (Barth, "The Christian Life," 41).

190. Barth, *Göttingen Dogmatics I*, 126.

191. Barth, *CD IV:II*, 560.

192. Barth, *Unterricht in der Christlichen Religion* III, 304.

193. "I say nothing other as regards content, when I summarize the "*summa vitae christianae*" with Calvin (Inst. III 7, 1) in the phrase: "*Nostri non sumus, sed Domini*" (ref. Rom. 14:7f)." Barth, *Unterricht in der Christlichen Religion* III, 314–15; Barth, "Rechtfertigung und Heiligung," 95.

194. Barth, "Rechtfertigung und Heiligung," 63, *Unterricht in der Christlichen Religion* III, 304.

195. Barth, *Unterricht in der Christlichen Religion* III, 314.

Barth's entire doctrine of sanctification, the impact of which can be seen as this phrase is parsed as a whole and in its various parts.

Taken as a whole the phrase *Nostri non sumus, sed Domini* points to the grounds for, and boundaries of, Barth's doctrine of sanctification as detailed in chapter three. That is, sanctification is the work of God the Father who claims humanity in Jesus Christ through the Holy Spirit. And in its parts the phrase highlights the characteristic features of God's sanctifying activity. The first part of the phrase—*Nostri non sumus*—signifies the laying aside of the old, the sinful, and the end of self-sufficiency on the one hand; its second part—*sed Domini (Domini sumus)*—indicates the directing of the sinner towards new life in Christ and active obedience on the other. Each aspect points towards God's gracious claiming and proclaiming of sinners as God's own dear children despite their sinfulness.

With this phrase, "not too much and not too little" is said about the significance of sanctification for humanity.[196] On the one hand, this summation does not overstep the boundaries within which the reconciled *sinner* finds himself. Sanctification does not mean that one "loses his sin like a butterfly loses its cocoon."[197] The historical particularity of human sinfulness is maintained in sharp relief against the eschatological reality that bursts in upon one's existence, guarding against the error of pharisaical righteousness, of the delusion that a person becomes progressively less sinful as he becomes more holy. On the other hand, the phrase does not portend too little, as if sanctification did not actually affirm the *reconciliation* of the sinner, as if within his sinfulness he was not "thoroughly attacked . . . so that *he knows*, existentially knows, that it must come to an end with him [Ps. 39:5]," that in Christ he is an entirely new creature.[198] *Nostri non sumus, sed Domini* is both indicative and imperative—a proclaiming and a summoning, at once the end of the old and the beginning of the new existence of the *reconciled sinner*.

Trinitarian Content

Nostri non sumus, sed Domini points to the basis of Barth's doctrine of sanctification as it was examined, in part, in his lectures on "The Theology

---

196. Ibid., 317.
197. Ibid.
198. Ibid.

of the Reformed Confessions." It is essentially a paraphrase of the work of God the Father, Son, and Holy Spirit in sanctification.

As the work of the Father, *Nostri non sumus, sed Domini* indicates what was earlier called the initiating and finalizing reality of God, the fact, that is, that sanctification is above all geared towards expressing what it means to say that it is *God* who sanctifies rather than an account of the experiences and insights of the one sanctified. In the context of GD and RH, this idea may now be stated more specifically as the Father's work of election and calling. Barth succinctly summarizes the first part of his doctrine of sanctification by saying, "Man stands as an elected and called sinner in the power of God."[199] Sanctification means that human beings are "chosen and appointed" by God "to community with Him."[200]

God's claim upon humanity is at once both a divine whence and whither, an election as well as a calling, and, therefore, indicative as well as imperative. Human beings elected to be *God's* own faithful servants, to live in covenant fellowship with *Him* as *His own* dear children. And because *people* are elected to partake in this gracious relationship, *they are called* to *live* as the ones they have been elected to be. That is, God's claim means both that there is an "important and significant change in your sinner's being," (you are no longer your own) "which you indeed do not justify before God, but in itself *appears*, which you *yourself demonstrate*" (you are empowered by God to be the one you have been elected to be).[201] For people are sanctified "*before* God and *for* God."[202] A person is claimed at once *by* God *to be* His own faithful partner, to live, therefore, in an entirely new form of existence, sanctified by God for God.[203]

As the work of the Son, *Nostri non sumus, sed Domini* indicates what was earlier referred to as the non-givenness of God in revelation, that is, that sanctification occurs as a dynamic event with Jesus Christ and is, therefore, not a state but a relationship. It is in this regard that Barth asserts that just as the priestly office of Christ is the ground for our justification, "so the royal office of Christ is the ground for our sanctification."[204] The power Jesus Christ has won over sin and death through His resur-

---

199. Ibid., 304.
200. Barth, "Rechtfertigung und Heiligung," 68.
201. Barth, *Unterricht in der Christlichen Religion* III, 308.
202. Ibid.
203. Ibid.
204. Barth, *Unterricht in der Christlichen Religion* III, 313.

rection is the foundation for the power He has over the boundary of sin "in our flesh."[205] *Nostri non sumus, sed Domini* means, therefore, that sanctification rests not on human efforts, nor even on genuine desire and emotion, but "on conversion, conversion to the life of Christ in us."[206] Sanctification means nothing other than *insertio in Christum* and *uniti cum Christio*, and this in the sense that the sinner is claimed by the power of God through the life and work of Jesus Christ,[207] so that he may finally acknowledge that he has no rights over himself, because in himself he is nothing but a rebel and a traitor. And yet, somehow, because of Christ this same traitor is called forth in holiness of life and existence so that he may finally and truly say, "I am regarded and acknowledged by God, yes, infinitely far from Him as I am. Not as a second God but as a man who has sinned, is sinning, and will sin, and who can recognize himself as nothing else than lost, I am acknowledged by God in Jesus Christ His beloved Son, acknowledged, chosen, and, when the fullness of time was come, reconciled to Him."[208]

Finally, as the work of the Holy Spirit, *Nostri non sumus, sed Domini* refers to what was earlier termed the real yet relative human response to God in His self-revelation. That is to say, that the objective work of God in His self-address to human beings is graciously given a subjective hearing within the same sinners through the Holy Spirit, and they become, therefore, also doers of the Word. As these present works attest, "the truth of reconciliation cannot be without *reality*."[209] "The object of sanctification is," writes Barth, "exactly the earthly-human-sinful sphere of our existence."[210] But, Barth adds, "we are objects of His Kingly power through *His Spirit*."[211] So, although sanctification concerns the very real, concrete, and historical reality of sinful humanity, they "can only accomplish on earth what He in heaven wants (ref. Matt. 6:10)."[212] "There is no possibility," therefore, "to definitely reassure oneself anywhere and anyhow, to covenant with one's conscience and to applaud oneself. We can

205. Ibid.
206. Ibid., 325.
207. Ibid., 313.
208. Barth, "The Christian Life," 13.
209. Barth, *Unterricht in der Christlichen Religion* III, 310.
210. Ibid., 314.
211. Ibid., 315; emphasis mine.
212. Ibid., 315.

never overestimate our wanting, striving, doing as a movement as such, as if we could reach the end *with it*."[213] *Nostri non sumus, sed Domini* means that genuine faithful obedience is rendered by the reconciled sinner only in and through the power of the Holy Spirit. For the Word which a person hears in and through the Spirit "denotes our being *limited*, set at a boundary line, seeing that this Word is brought to us for us to hear it."[214]

We Are Not Our Own

What appealed to Barth about the phrase *Nostri non sumus, sed Domini* was its dual emphasis on the denial of human self-interest—the laying aside of the old—and the very earthly proclamation of the miraculous—the directing of the sinner towards new life in Christ and active obedience. In regards to the first part of the phrase, Barth says that "sanctification signifies negatively quite certainly the removal and annulment of all self-sanctification, and of all our own honour which could possibly arise from it."[215] What does it mean to be claimed by God? It means confiscation, the end of self-determination, and the mortification of human life and living. Sanctification, summarized as *Nostri non sumus*, means that the Christian is pulled from the dark abyss of a self-imposed form of existence characterized by sin and death, of isolation from God and others, and, that person in acknowledgment of God's work turns his back on this former existence.

As God claims a person as His own, He frees him from the dreadful burden of maintaining his own form of existence before God. As people stand on their own, says Barth, they are disconnected from God. They desire to be, and believe in a way that they are God. "I look for and want myself without God, I myself want to be God in my own world. This is how I fell from God, a rebel against Him. I have done wrong, do wrong, and will do wrong, am guilty of death; and all this in my entire existence, in all I do and do not do, in my entire being."[216] As God claims and sanctifies people, He establishes His right over them, not just in principle, but in reality. In this sense, one is no longer the master of his own destiny, he

---

213. Ibid., 319.
214. Barth, *The Holy Spirit and the Christian Life*, 34.
215. Barth, *Unterricht in der Christlichen Religion* III, 312.
216. Barth, "Rechtfertigung und Heiligung," 70.

is stripped of all forms of self-existence, and his sanctification means that he now stands in the place that God has appointed for him.[217] Sanctification is thus not an empowerment to be a better version of one's self, but a complete reorientation of what it means to be. It is the end of a person's self-interpretation, the end of his utter faithlessness towards God and others, and the end of his existence as simply a sinner before God. What he was is no longer definitive. The old man is put away, not quantitatively, not little by little until non-existent, but completely, *in toto*, in the sense that man's existence as one who stands outside the reach of God's love and power is no longer the scenario that defines his existence. For though he remains a sinner, he is now a reconciled sinner. Thus, "the balance between our sinful determination and us must remain *disturbed*, or else we do not stand in grace. It cannot be said that anyone has a cease-fire with evil, or a peace treaty. As sinners we are judged, in faith in Christ we are surely justified, but that means then immediately also sanctified, in claim taken for obedience."[218] *Nostri non sumus* means that, "we are His contrary to what our heart and conscience tell us about ourselves: that we are *our own* and sinners because of that who are slaves of death, no, 'to be with body and soul, both in life and death not mine, but belong to my faithful Savoir Jesus Christ,' this is the grace granted to us, the grace of . . . sanctification."[219]

Nostri non sumus likewise means that one recognizes God's claim upon his life, and therefore relinquishes all forms of self-control—he gives God the rights over himself. This is his *abnegatio*, his self-denial.[220] Sanctification is thus a disturbed form of existence in which the sinner recognizes his thoroughgoing dissolution apart from the grace of God, and thus his necessary uprising against his own self-preservation. As Barth states, "*Nostri non sumus, sed Domini*," signifies that, "we cannot be at home in ourselves anymore."[221] A person's new form of existence then is characterized by a complete and total lack of *self*-confidence in his own abilities, strengths, and independence before God. These are the very things that have been taken from him, and he cannot, therefore, refuse to see himself as a sinner before God. This self-denial is not simply

---

217. Ibid., 73.
218. Barth, *Unterricht in der Christlichen Religion* III, 323.
219. Barth, "Rechtfertigung und Heiligung," 67.
220. Barth, *Unterricht in der Christlichen Religion* III, 315.
221. Ibid., 324.

a form of dispassionate resignation, however, but rather an explicit form of counter-resistance to a life movement that seeks to usurp the authority of God and maintain its own power and significance; for sanctification, says Barth, "is based on conversion, conversion to the life of Christ in us. Christ in us wants to rule, *we* are the rebels. Sanctification means starting the *struggle* against those rebels."[222] *Nostri non sumus* is thus the battle cry in which reconciled sinners actively, and continually, participate in their sanctification—i.e., faithful obedience—by surrendering to the will and right of God over them; and further, thereby, occupying the place for which they have been elected and called.

In light of what the phrase *nostri non sumus* signifies for Barth, this *abnegatio*—the Christian's self-denial—also refers at once to the concepts previously examined in the section on *Struggle* as developed in Chapter 4 on *The Resurrection of the Dead*. In that section, it was shown that to speak of sanctification as a mode of existence uniquely characterized by the term 'struggle' has less to do with any sort of moral edict, and is certainly no *de facto* call to arms against some*thing* or other. It is more appropriately thought of as a way of expressing the truth that "Ye are not your own." The Christian struggle means, on the one hand, that a person does not possess his sanctification as a "divine quality inhering in the soul,"[223] as a form of perfection to achieve here and now, such that he is uplifted gradually until he is made a non-sinner, or only narrowly a sinner, but on the other hand, it means that the Christian is not simply a spectator in this life. Just as surely the term 'struggle' indicates a person's relationship to his sinful human nature, so also it must not be forgotten that this same struggle characterizes the reality of *God's* actions, and therefore, the divine imperative—"Seek what is above, not what is of earth!" (1 Pet 3:21).

As a form of struggle, then, *nostri non sumus*, according to the *GD* and *RH*, denotes further "to be in *conflict* with oneself, and because of that, and within that, to be in deepest solidarity with our fellow men."[224] God's claim upon humanity not only brings about their election and conversion—the ontic—but also discloses the depth and significance of that change in relationship to the rest of humanity—the noetic. Therefore, as

---

222. Ibid., 325.
223. Barth, *The Holy Spirit and the Christian Life*, 23.
224. Barth, "Rechtfertigung und Heiligung," 93.

the reconciled sinner takes up arms against his subtle and not so subtle self-determination, his preferred egoism

> the way is cleared for *understanding* of the other [fellow human beings/one's neighbour], on the one hand recognizing that he is our fellow sinner, that he is this precisely with his often meddlesome *amor sui*, with his brash Ego-hood, very much related to us, that he and we are ill or sick in the same hospital—on the other hand recognizing: Christ also wants to rule in him, therefore he is fighting the same struggle as we are, it is something in him that we have community with, that we must love, something that is not at all himself with the mask, with the mask he is showing us, but the new man—who finally is one and the same in everyone.[225]

In understanding what sanctification implies for the reconciled sinner, his place before God and his demanded obedience to God, the reconciled sinner is further stripped of any supposed right against, or claim over, his neighbour. Just as the Christian no longer belongs to himself, his sanctification also means, precisely because he no longer belongs to himself, that neither does his neighbour belong to him. His presumed rights and assertions over others in subordination to his own life-desires are thus seen as an empty claim. The reconciled sinner's abandonment of self-rights and claims to power in light of his reconciliation with God is demonstrated further as a reconciliation between himself and those around him. Christ is not only his Lord, but the Lord of all.

The reconciled sinner's sanctification, therefore, his struggle against himself and with that solidarity with those around him, bears witness to the person and work of Christ. "As the men who know that about themselves better than those who have not yet been claimed by God's mercy, we are pardoned, and must regard ourselves as men who are now sacrificed, men who . . . in the midst of this world . . . know that the great sacrifice that had to be made for us, has been made, that we are holy, righteous, pure through Jesus Christ, that we as sinners, as the lost, as living beings among others, are called to bear witness" to the fact that we are not our own masters, but belong to the Lord.[226]

---

225. Barth, *Unterricht in der Christlichen Religion* III, 326.
226. Barth, "The Christian Life," 57.

We Belong to the Lord

Just as *Nostri non sumus* refers negatively to the removal and annulment of all self-sanctification—the laying aside of the old form of human existence—so its corollary *Domini sumus* (*sed Domini*) signifies quite positively that "we are objects of His Kingly power through His Spirit."[227] That is, one's election and calling entails freedom to live with and for God because He is the one who claims humanity. Fundamentally, writes Barth, *Domini sumus* denotes an "important and significant change in your sinner's being."[228] Not "that you stop being a sinner, but to be sure an actual re-orientation and redeployment of your life, a necessary and characteristic displacement of the sinful elements of which your sinner's being consists, a movement, which you indeed do not justify before God, but in itself *appears*—which you *yourself demonstrate*, that you are . . . a sanctified man *before* God and *for* God."[229] God's claim upon the sinner is not only the sinner's confiscation from a form of living characterized by self-aggrandizement and rebellion against God, but his emancipation from such things as well and, therefore, a renewal of the divine-human relationship. Sanctification is, therefore, rightly said, as *Domini sumus*, the purposive new life movement for which the sinner has been reconciled—the directing of the sinner towards new life in Christ and active obedience. In this sense, God's claim declares not only that the sinner no longer belongs to himself, but that wonderfully and powerfully he now belongs to the Lord and is, therefore, set free from the misery and power of sin to live as the Lord's own and glorify His name. God's claim upon the sinner thus binds him for obedience just as it engages and frees him.

Domini sumus is a reflection of the reality that although God should in no way be involved with sinful human beings He has, and does, nevertheless, stand up for them despite their sinfulness. This "God for us" means not only that humans have been the object of God's attention but that they are *continually* the object of God's attention—called, loved, and chosen in Christ within their sin to be God's own dear children. God "looks at us in Christ," writes Barth, "and thus uses His law on us, frees us. This is the power of the Word and the Spirit through which we are called to grace; since both the Word and the Spirit are God Himself, God stands

---

227. Barth, *Unterricht in der Christlichen Religion* III, 315.
228. Ibid., 308.
229. Ibid.

up for us before Himself."²³⁰ And because it is God Himself who represents sinful people before Himself, the beneficence of their sanctificatio is a facet of God's claiming just as surely as it comes only as pure gift.²³¹ A person is thus holy in that he belongs to the Lord, he is sanctified by God that he may live *with* God.

If, therefore, *Nostri non sumus* means that "we don't get the chance to agree with ourselves" because as reconciled sinners we no longer belongs to ourselves, then *Domini sumus* means further that "we must agree with God" about ourselves because we now belong to the Him.²³² As God claims a person as His own, He lays His hand upon him. Such a person is cast before God stripped of all honour, strength, and independence, and yet in grace and mercy he is wonderfully "qualified and drawn on by God in a singular manner."²³³ "This is the sanctification of the sinner, that he, just as he finds forgiveness of sin in Christ through God's grace, is changed as a sinner and becomes God's own."²³⁴ The lordship of God over the reconciled sinner becomes the guiding force within the sinner's existence in spite of his rebelliousness and every seeming contradiction to that lordship. The sinner does not belong to himself, he does, however belong to the Lord. And so here Barth stresses the important point that just as sinful man's sanctification means that he may live with God, it also means that he may and must also live *for* Him faithfully—i.e., in obedience. In that sanctification signals an alteration in the existence of the reconciled sinner, it is consistent further in the way in which God demands a reorientation in the sinner's life movement. As such, however, it must be remembered, and again this is key for Barth, that sanctification is not primarily a question of moral improvement but an exposition of this alteration. In sanctification sinful people are set free from the guilt and power of sin as they are turned to the Lord in freedom that they might glorify God's name; and this entails primarily a chastened and continual turning from the self to the Lord.

The other side of the sinner's *abnegatio* is this purposive life movement to which he is called to live towards, what Barth termed *glorificatio Christi*—the glorification of Christ in active obedience. *Glorificatio*

230. Barth, "Rechtfertigung und Heiligung," 95.
231. Ibid.
232. Barth, *Unterricht in der Christlichen Religion* III, 323.
233. Barth, "Rechtfertigung und Heiligung," 81.
234. Ibid, 82.

Christi signifies quite positively that all of one's humanity in all of its ranges and possibilities belongs to God and is, therefore, given to Him in obedience.[235] As Barth stated much earlier in the *GD*, "If fellowship between God and us is to mean anything, then it must mean that we in our own sphere turn no less than God turns to us in his sphere."[236] Essentially God's claim upon a person is at once both an act of appropriation and a demand for faithful obedience, i.e., surrender to this claim. God's claim upon a person is simultaneously an act of emancipation and, therefore, a call for affirmation, of acknowledgment displayed in submission. *Glorificatio Christi* is as such the life movement of the sinner as he continually acknowledges God's claim upon his life and submits to the will and direction of the Holy Spirit. Again, *glorificatio Christi* is the reconciled sinner's self sacrifice in which he not only hears the Word of reconciliation spoken about and to him—of confiscation and emancipation, but also becomes engaged in the process. Specifically "(t)his is what the Word wants of us," writes Barth, "this is the demand it puts on us, not to become a triumph, not an ambition and a success, but a penance, an acknowledgment of the truth, a demonstration of the glory of mercy which brought us to this sacrifice, good work on the run to the One who is good."[237] And

> this is the sinner's obedience, that he believes when *put in his place*. Good works are the works of people put in this place. We are thus not describing piety and spirituality, much rather we are describing a qualified worldliness; we are still not describing the experience and works of man but those of God's grace when we . . . sketch in a few words what could definitely be considered as such obedience in sanctification.[238]

Change

The notion that God claims a person within his sinfulness inherently begs the question of change. In what sense does the claim mean something particular for the reconciled sinner, namely, that he is in fact now someone different from the person he used to be? In what sense is the claimed sinner the "*new* man"? Further, this question appears all

---

235. Barth, "Rechtfertigung und Heiligung," 85.
236. Barth, *Göttingen Dogmatics*, 180.
237. Barth, "Rechtfertigung und Heiligung," 86.
238. Ibid., 91.

the more significant in light of Barth's rejection of issues surrounding moral improvement as the most basic or primary ways of articulating sanctification.

In essence, the concept of change has already been addressed in several places within this analysis of Barth's work. In *The Resurrection of the Dead*, for example Barth locates sanctification as a "reality claim" in the resurrection of Jesus Christ. This means that sanctification does not point to the transition into a new state of being, or a possessed holiness, but is an event in which human action and holiness points away from itself towards the corresponding and "simultaneously occurring divine action." In light of the resurrection of Jesus Christ, the historical and temporal questions about the "new man" are not disconnected, but relativised.[239] Sanctification, therefore, conceived as God's claiming a person for renewed fellowship with Him does not address the notion of change as the transition of the "ordinary and sensual humanity into a spiritual, moral and pious one," but points instead toward the reality that "our humanity belongs to God in all of its ranges and possibilities; that it may finally, finally be brought to God."[240]

For Barth then, the historical, tangible notion of change, is not discarded or disconnected from the grace of God in time, but reoriented towards the person and work of Jesus Christ. Its meaning is neither subjected to a certain kind of retrieved human capacity, nor is it based upon human religious feelings. It is derived entirely as a response of the Word of God to humanity. Simply stated, the notion of change means for Barth that *the sinner becomes God's own possession.* The "new man" is the one whose life is now hidden with Christ in God.

As such, the notion of change, is not meant to be employed as a measuring rod for one's tangible "holiness," or further as an instantiation of the invisibility of heaven. And yet, writes Barth, to become God's own possession, to be changed in the power of the Holy Spirit does in fact entail "an actual reorientation and redeployment of your life, a necessary and characteristic displacement of the sinful elements of which your sinner's being consists, a movement, which you indeed do not justify before God, but in itself *appears*—which you *yourself demonstrate*."[241] The important point for Barth is that beyond and within this notion of "change," to what-

---

239. Barth, *Resurrection*, 131.
240. Barth, "Rechtfertigung und Heiligung," 85.
241. Barth, *Unterricht in der Christlichen Religion* III, 308.

ever extent one actually speaks of the "new man," its meaning is only valid by the testimony of God. To whatever extent there may be a tangible and visible change in the reconciled sinner—and Barth does not deny that this may happen—the true meaning of this change is ascertained only in hope; it subsists purely in the promise and judgment of God.

That said, within human life, says Barth, "there is the sacramental sphere of divine *signs* and of human *venture*" in relation to the grace of God.[242] Though human actions do not explicitly demonstrate one's sanctification or offer reassurances of the reality of the new man in Christ, there is, nevertheless, proclaims Barth, something which alludes to this change above all else. Within Scripture baptism above all other visible signs and gestures "is the reminder about grace taking place at the level of human things and events. Hence its special relevance for the problem of sanctification."[243] Within this life "the sign of freedom is baptism, raising itself . . . amongst the visibility and concreteness of our existence, a demonstration before God in Christ concerning our agreed change, that in just this existence, within these possibilities, the boundaries that are existence, must come to us for execution."[244] It is, simply put, the visible promise recognized in faith of the radically new existence of the reconciled sinner.

It is not that baptism, as a sacrament, offers inherent power for new life or mediates grace in an authentically tangible way. Its importance lies not within it, but beyond it. It is the sign under which reconciled sinners look away from themselves, in which they acknowledge their own dying along with Jesus Christ, his resurrection to new life, and as such his power over death and the grave. Baptism, as the sign of Christ's triumph over sin and despair, then, becomes the visible mark of those who have been claimed by God. Pointing above all towards Christ and away from the sinner, baptism is the epitome of the meaning of "change" for Barth.

The Sinner Reconciled in Grace

As Barth states throughout his work both early and late, sanctification is concerned with the reconstitution of the peculiarity of people *within their sinfulness*. In his reflections on Paul's words to the Romans, he says

---

242. Ibid., 314.
243. Ibid.
244. Ibid.

that Scripture does "not speak to the perfect and the redeemed, but to the reconciled, to men who have heard the word of faith but who, dwelling in this temporal state, have not yet taken down the tent, who still await the habitation which is in heaven."[245] Paragraph 32 on *Sanctification* in the *GD* begins: "We emphasise now the other point [concerning an account of sanctification] in this paragraph about the calling as *insertio in Christum*, as rebirth and conversion in the content described: that the reconciled man is the elected and called *sinner*."[246] Or put differently: the point to be addressed now is, What does it really mean for the *sinner* to have *grace*, to have new life in Jesus Christ? The issue being: What becomes of a person through reconciliation in so far as he is still a sinner in his temporal reality? And it is this idea that people continually stand as elected and called *sinners* in the power of God—that Christians are radically, as Barth quoted Luther, "*caro et spiritus, peccator et justus, reus et non reus*, both completely and at the same time"—that has been both widely admired and deplored.[247] In particular, it is Barth's description of the relation between sin and grace most notably expressed in his appropriation of Luther's phrase *simul justus et peccator*, that has drawn such reactions.

At the heart of this discussion lies the fact that for Barth, once again, sanctification is about the altered state and condition in which *sinful* man now finds himself reconciled with God in grace and mercy, rather than an account of the moral and spiritual transformation of man throughout which man becomes less sinful over time. As Barth repeatedly wrote, "election and calling do not mean at all that you stop being a sinner," rather they entail "a necessary, important and significant change in your sinner's being."[248] Essentially, any notion of sanctification must include a description of how it is that a sinful person may stand before God in fellowship; it must depict who the sinner is because of grace, and what this person looks like within it all. In justification, God does not dismiss sin but judges and forgives it. In this sense, God does not eradicate sin but overcomes it, and each person, therefore, in and of himself remains yet a sinner. While justification points towards how it is that such a sinner is able to stand *with* God in covenant fellowship, i.e., the forgiveness of sins, sanctification describes the reality of such a person, i.e., how the grace

---

245. Barth, "The Christian Life," 19.
246. Barth, *Unterricht in der Christlichen Religion* III, 304.
247. Barth, "Rechtfertigung und Heiligung," 81.
248. Barth, *Unterricht in der Christlichen Religion* III, 308.

of God affects this person in his sinfulness, in his life. Sanctification is precisely for Barth a depiction of the *sinner reconciled* "in the power of God as one whose life no longer has honour, but yet still is the object of the Royal work of Christ."[249]

One of the primary concerns raised about Barth's depiction of sanctification at the conference in Putbus where he delivered his RH lecture and elsewhere, was the issue of the relationship between grace and sin, the sinner and reconciliation. In essence his detractors believed that Barth did not seem to take the grace of God seriously enough in his account of the Christian life. Principally because they supposed that Barth erroneously down played the idea of the *death* of the sinner in light of their own emphasis on the "experiential reality" of grace. That is to say that for Barth's sceptics, in general, "the difference was that in their opinion human beings under grace have only *been* lost sinners, whereas for Barth they *are* always 'lost sinners.'"[250] His critics felt that sanctification ought to be oriented towards an account of the sinner, to the extent that this becomes a delineated line of thought, in which that person is shown to be diminishing in his sinful capacity while simultaneously emerging strongly and confidently in righteousness as the "new man". The same critique sometimes expressed with a more Reformed flair retained a more nuanced place for the *simul peccator*, but would nonetheless reiterate that, though the Christian remains a "sinner" in some sense until the day he dies, it is a lesser and declining part of his existence, rather than a "disposition of the *entire* human" always and continually.[251] This was one of the key issues for those who disagreed with Barth's doctrine of sanctification. They felt that in effect he allowed the term *sinner* to carry on improperly, fatally corrupting any notion of the new life in Christ.[252]

Eberhard Busch highlights a basic alternative concept of sin in relation to Barth's doctrine of sanctification espoused by some of his opponents as represented in Putbus, which in effect asserts "an earthly existence as *justus* that has essentially left the *peccator* existence behind."[253] Quoting W. Hützen, an outspoken critic of Barth, Busch writes:

---

249. Ibid., 304.
250. Busch, *Barth and the Pietists*, 207.
251. Barth, "Rechtfertigung und Heiligung," 75.
252. Busch, *Barth and the Pietists*, 206.
253. Ibid.

> Thus the divine descends into us in such a way that "this [grace] becomes a reality in us through our historical experience so that the line of death runs here [within this experience], separating our former life from our new life in the present." It works in us a "rebirth" defined as a "change of reality that takes place in our present life," by virtue of which "*we* have really become new men and women" and by virtue of which we can talk about a state of being in sin that is now in the past for certain human beings.[254]

The argument highlighted here being that the power of God is a reality in the life of believers in such a way that it demonstrates itself through tangible experiences and modifications in their existence as human beings. In this sense the *death* of the sinner highlights the fact that the line between believers and unbelievers is quite distinct. Whereas the accusation made against Barth's doctrine of sanctification was that there appeared to be "practically no difference between the person outside of grace and the person inside of grace."[255] Because, for Barth, nothing appears to have really, i.e., historically/experientially, changed.

Perhaps somewhat surprisingly there is a level of relative agreement between Barth and Hützen, and others like him, within the concepts expressed above. For example Barth was not averse to using the notion of "rebirth" as a way of expressing the extent to which sanctification as an alteration in reality presently affects the life of the believer. The difficulty between Barth and his critics, therefore, was not simply about the necessity in which the notion of change must be examined within one's doctrine of sanctification. Rather the underlying difference presented itself within the relationship between sin and grace regarding the extent to which the believer was experientially aware of, and could tangibly/historically verify grace in the form of a "new birth," particularly in such a way as to likewise experience an "overcoming" of one's sinfulness. For Barth the divisive idea expressed by Hützen in the above paragraph is that sin and grace are related in such a way that "we can talk about a state of being in sin that is now in the past for certain human beings."

Barth took great exception to the sort of interpretation of the experience of God's grace as rendered in Hützen's comments. That is, as an impartation or *gratia infusa*, which in Barth's estimation diminished the force of human sinfulness. He disagreed primarily because he felt that this

254. Ibid.
255. Ibid., 209.

type of exposition of the grace of God and human sinfulness, amongst other things, proffers an essential break in the history of the Christian by which the sinner's death in sanctification entails the rise of a synergistic co-operation between God and humanity—an opportunity for a person to, in essence, start from square one and thereby uphold his end of the "bargain" before God, to establish himself as a faithful covenant partner. The idea that the grace of God working upon sinners in sanctification was a sort of enabling of a *summum bonum*—the ascertainment of a person's highest good here and now, or his enablement to become a morally superior version of himself more or less by simply setting him back on his feet—was for Barth the epitome of "hostility toward grace and is sin in its proper nature and total seriousness."[256]

Barth was quite persistent in teasing out the impact of this argument in his lecture *The Holy Spirit and the Christian Life* in which he scrutinized the root of this problem in the works of Augustine. He writes there, "The Protestant doctrine of grace in the new age is almost entirely a variety of the Augustinian theme, so that man's reconciliation with God *ex utroque fit id est et voluntate hominis et misericordia Dei*. Put into modern speech this means, 'It is divine gift and man's creative action combined in one.'"[257] When the work of the reconciled sinner is elevated, even if attributed to the hand of God, to participate in the eradication of his sinfulness, writes Barth, "it is a simple fact that man has been handed over and left to his sins."[258] Because in this sense:

> Sin is not taken in deadly earnest when it is regarded as something that can be radically overcome by the enthusiasm of "good intentions," and then, by and by, can be removed by practical activity. You may cure a wound by such treatment but you cannot restore a dead man to life. And Augustine's view of sin was that it was really only a wound, a derangement within the undisturbed continuity of man with God.[259]

Ironically it was the notion of the "death of the sinner" that both Barth and his opponents felt the other had failed to take *seriously* enough.

As Barth saw it this sort of experiential emphasis on the death of the sinner as "an ethical change of course (which) takes place at the

---

256. Barth, *The Holy Spirit and the Christian Life*, 25.
257. Ibid., 22.
258. Ibid., 23.
259. Ibid.

heart of the personality," was exacerbated by a conception of grace and sanctification as quantitative capacities which gave rise to a "step-by-step release from poisonous, self-centred instincts," albeit a process said to be achieved only as the new self puts on the Lord Jesus Christ.[260] In this sense talk about the death of the sinner, i.e., "a state of being in sin that is now in the past for certain human beings," marks the entrance of what Barth deemed the misguided contemplation of Christian reflection. That is, an account of sanctification which inherently disregards what Barth called "the basic rule of all sensible Christian reflection,"[261] and focuses instead on the "proclamation of deeds and acts, of experiences and adventures, of the piety and charitable activities of man," with the "pretence of the glorification of God."[262] The result being that sanctification becomes primarily a way of discussing some type of disconnected Christian anthropology, the entrance of synergism into the divine-human relationship, and/or a cloaked pharisaical righteousness rather than an account of the divine-human relationship as revealed in the reconciling work of Christ.[263]

In that Barth's doctrine of sanctification is meant to get at the reality of the *grace* of God within the life of *reconciled sinners*, over and against for example an account of moral and spiritual progress, it is important to explore the meaning and connection of grace and sin within these works in order to spell out more clearly what Barth means when he questions what becomes of a person through reconciliation in so far as he is yet a sinner in his temporal reality.

Grace

For Barth the grace of God is an event or encounter—one might say the reality—in which God overcomes a person's unbelief, self-destruction, and disobedience by claiming him as His own in love and mercy. God reveals Himself to humanity. And as was mentioned earlier, the reality of this renewed fellowship between God and humanity forms the backdrop for Barth's doctrine of sanctification. Sanctification, rightly understood,

260. Busch, *Barth and the Pietists*, 206.
261. "Christian proclamation is the proclamation of the *magnalia Dei* or it is not Christian proclamation" (Barth, *"Rechtfertigung und Heiligung,"* 65).
262. Ibid., 65. This is similar to the argument that Barth made against the post-reformation doctrine of the *ordo-salutis* as examined in the section "Initiating and Finalizing Reality" within the analysis of "The Theology of the Reformed Confessions."
263. Barth, "Rechtfertigung und Heiligung," 65.

is oriented theologically precisely where the doctrine of reconciliation proclaims that the event of reconciliation is a real event that has enduringly affected human existence, where the grace of God comes to sinful people. Sanctification is geared towards addressing the particular reality of the *viator hominis christiani* for the *homo viator peccator*, in that the reconciled person is the elected and called *sinner*. The issue is, What becomes of a sinful person through reconciliation in so far as he is also a *sinner* in reconciliation?

And, again, this revelation is not simply a disclosure of facts about God by which person could possibly decide for or against God, but is the act of sanctification *par excellence* in which God not only draws near to human beings, but in so doing draws them near to Himself, thus freeing them from the bonds of their sinfulness. In this way, God makes Himself known as Lord. He not only freely elects and calls people but also claims and commands them as well; He is the sovereign reconciler and judge. In this claiming and commanding God discloses to these people this reconciliation and judgment, his true situation and its implications for human existence. God's grace reveals to humanity that they are fundamentally in opposition to God; that they are entirely disobedient, and, furthermore, want nothing less than to be their own lords and masters. Two distinct elements of God's self-revelation and, therefore, important elements of Barth's doctrine of sanctification are God's sovereignty as reconciler and judge and, directly correlated to that, an invariable exposing of human sinfulness.

It is also important to recall the extent to which grace and, therefore, sanctification are eschatological terms for Barth. To the measure that grace not only signifies the Word and work of God spoken to humanity here and now, but also in and with that the boundary and limitation of human existence in this world it indicates that which is ultimate and final in Christ. In other words, grace is an eschatological term because it signals both the present work of God through the Holy Spirit, and yet maintains the boundary and limits to which humanity in this time is subjected. "It is only in Christ that man has grace in his temporary reality."[264] And this means that grace is given to those within the struggle between this life and the next, it is the present hope for those who cling to the God who transcends even the boundaries of time. Christian life stands under a big "not yet" on the one hand, and on the other, it is placed

---

264. Ibid., 89.

under the authority of the promises of God. As Barth was often fond of saying, "Mark it well: we are not sanctified for a perfection to achieve here and now, and not for a millennial kingdom to build here and now, but for the forever oncoming kingdom of God and His righteousness (Matt. 5:33), but for waiting and hastening towards Him (2 Peter 3:12), and this waiting and hastening is without doubt our part as the determination of our *particular concrete* steps here and now."[265] Grace and, along with it, sanctification mean, as eschatological terms, that "we endure living a life which takes place balancing on a knife's edge between being allowed to live and having to die, between eternity and time, in the freedom of the great decisions and the crowd of the small ones. Not only do we endure, but we realize that it is right and good and beneficial."[266]

Sin

In the *GD*, Barth initially treats the doctrine of sin under two headings: "Sin as Action" (paragraph 25), and "Sin as Nature" (paragraph 26). In the first section, Barth outlines the sinfulness of human action as the infidelity of their decision to live inherently against God.

> The free decision of the person is as his own decision, an infidelity against God his creator, his archetype, his ally. He sins by unbelief against the divine promise while he does not want to wait, but rather to create his own completion in this world. And he sins by disobedience against the divine demand in wanting that. He denies the right knowledge and position of himself in his relation to his Lord. He makes himself guilty before God, i.e., he states and establishes towards God his own right, and this is an outrage.[267]

Human sin exists essentially in unbelief and disobedience towards God as people long to, or attempt to, be other than that which they were created to be—God's faithful creatures and partners. In this longing and isolated up-building human actions are continually bent egotistically toward self and are, as such, self-destructive. Within this unbelief and disobedience, however, a person's sins are not self-evident, i.e., they are not specifically this or that act; rather they are the entirety of one's actions as he strives to

---

265. Barth, *Unterricht in der Christlichen Religion* III, 324.
266. Barth, "Rechtfertigung und Heiligung," 99.
267. Barth, *Unterricht in der Christlichen Religion* II, 399.

be his own lord. His sins, therefore, are characterized in sum as resistance to God's grace and judgment—to the truth and reality in which a person exists in relationship to God.

In the second section, Barth writes that humanity's continual resistance and opposition to God are characteristics that define their very existence apart from God. "God is not mocked (Gal. 5:7): What the person does in his own free decision has consequences for who he is. By this sin, his nature has operated and been transformed: He becomes God's enemy; he loses with his original right posture that which connects him with God; his creaturely being becomes his disgrace. His freedom has become the freedom to continue sinning, i.e., to un-freedom."[268]

Barth maintains that a person's sinful nature is not simply a condition of his creatureliness. His existence as a sinner is not based in the fact that he is a finite creature and not as the Creator Himself. This sinfulness, as an enduring characteristic of his being, is, therefore, notes Barth, not simply something that befalls him, of which he is more or less a victim. Neither is it simply indicative of his poor choices and the poor choices of others compounded over time, of a grievous misstep, or deep wound simply in need of "medicine" which once applied would set him rightly upon his feet again. No, Barth says, human sinfulness is a characteristic of their thorough and complete rebellion and resistance towards God. A person sins not because he is a finite being, but rather because he is not content to be this way, he seeks instead to be God, and, therefore, in a sense determines himself to be this way. One's sinful nature roots itself within his continual striving against God's claim as Lord, of his constant attempt to overcome the distance between himself and his Creator.[269] A person's sinful nature, Barth writes, is "not merely the creature's spirit in its lack of openness to his Creator, but also in its unbelief, in its stubbornness, in its meek self-righteousness, in which it wishes to remain by itself, and does not wish to hear of something radically different from its own working and its possible changes: this is the spirit of hostility toward grace and is sin in its proper nature and its total seriousness."[270] Who and what this person is, is the result of his determination not to be the one whom God created him to be.

---

268. Ibid., 415.
269. McConnachie, *The Barthian Theology and the Man of Today*, 299.
270. Barth, *The Holy Spirit and the Christian Life*, 24–25.

Grace and Sin

On the one hand then, for Barth human beings with their life-movement are continually set against God in both nature and deed. Within their unbelief and resistance towards God, both overtly and slightly, humans set themselves up as their own most proper end and authority. And on the other hand grace is the encounter in which God draws close to humans and makes them His own, overcoming their belligerence, both overt and slight, and determining their life in judgment for freedom and love. The point to be addressed now is, What does it really mean for the *sinner* to have *grace*, to have new life in Jesus Christ? What becomes of a person through reconciliation in so far as he is yet a sinner in his temporal reality? It is this idea, that fundamentally sanctification means that one continually stands as elected and called *sinner* in the power of God—that Christians are radically, as Barth quoted Luther, "caro et spiritus," "peccator et justus," "reus et non reus," both completely and at the same time"—that must now be explored in more detail.

"E MIDIIS REBUS"

Barth makes two moves here, concerning the relationship between grace and sin, that play a significant role in his doctrine of sanctification. First, he grounds the doctrine of sin within his doctrine of revelation. That is, for Barth, sin is only known through grace. "The truth," Barth writes, "can only be recognized by someone who has to think and talk *e mediis rebus*, whose thinking and talking has been stripped of all objectivity and consideration, because he stands *in the middle* of the discussed experience."[271] Human sinfulness is not something about which a person may simply ponder and deduce from his historical experiences and perceptions of this world. Neither may he deduce his own holiness or the significance of his works in the same way. These things are precisely those that are and must be continually told to him about himself as he is encountered by God. To know, therefore, means first and foremost to be known, claimed, loved, judged, and stripped of any supposed self-resiliency.

This is a noteworthy feature of Barth's doctrine of sanctification because, as Barth states, "the reality of the occurring grace depends on the fact that the truth about ourselves not be diminished, especially not by

[271]. Barth, "Rechtfertigung und Heiligung," 70.

appealing to Christ, reconciliation, or the Holy Spirit; because all of this *is* the truth about ourselves."[272] Structuring his account of the relationship between grace and sin in this way further emphasises the foundational fact that for Barth there is for the person in Christ, even within his sanctification, never anything beyond grace. There is thus never anything found within human beings to merit grace "not only *before* but also *during* and *after* their reception of grace."[273] For Barth, "God's grace is not an alternative to his judgment, but is itself God's judgment because it rules out all human claims and merit *as* grace. Thus God's grace is at the same time *free* grace, and it is free not only *until* it is bestowed on human beings but also in that it is bestowed on human beings."[274] Grace is not a possession given to the sinner, not a force that simply sets the person of sin back on his feet. It is God's continual freedom and faithfulness to Himself and, therefore, to humanity. As such, it is always a disturbing grace for them. Barth writes, "If the *truth* of the Christian message hangs on the fact that its subject is the actions *of God*, so you hang *seriously* on the fact that it addresses itself *ad hominem*, that it says to him: being reconciled, your election and calling does not mean, not at all, that you stop being a sinner."[275] He remains a sinner within this life. All are and remain in need of grace every moment of this life—and this is exactly what reconciliation speaks of. One's sanctification, therefore, means that despite his sin the sinner is elected and called in the power of God as one whose life, though it does not possess any honour or righteousness, is still the object of the work of Christ.

It must be emphasised again that what a person hears about himself are not certain facts that he may analyze based on prior experiences; rather his sinfulness is known within God's judgment and power, His righteousness and mercy. Within this encounter, he is in no way an observer or bystander. "'The Word' spoken to sinful man 'concerns him'. He only seemingly stands *across* from Him; in reality, it *has* him, and that is why he must ceaselessly follow Him. This compulsion over him and this his obedience is his holiness."[276] Consequently for Barth where the depth of human sin is not rightly understood in some sense as an enduring

---

272. Ibid., 72–73.
273. Busch, *Barth and the Pietists*, 204.
274. Ibid.
275. Barth, *Unterricht in der Christlichen Religion* III, 308.
276. Ibid., 321.

quality of the entirety of human existence it implies a misunderstanding of the grace of God and the content of sanctification, and reciprocally points back toward the curse of sin addressed in reconciliation which humanity continually seeks to avoid hearing—"that we do not want to be who we are, but want to be like God."[277]

In the *RH* lecture, Barth illustrates his position by employing a hypothetical dialogue revolving around four questions. He begins by explaining that, when truly confronted by God, "you will say 'this means for me that I recognize myself as a sinner, i.e., as one who disconnected himself from God. . . . I don't know what I could say or predict for my own good. That's what it means for me so stand before God. That is how I know I'm standing before God. That is how I want to stand before God.'"[278]

Then the observer asks whether grace is really needed for all of this. "Shouldn't [I] know this already"? The interlocutor answers: "No, it is just that which I do not know without grace. Otherwise, I compare myself constantly with others; and this comparison, because of all kinds of lucky circumstances, always makes me look good."[279] It is only when one stands before God without any recourse or possible excuses that one may actually begin to understand the extent of his rebellion towards God. "When His law comes over me, I know I'm a trespasser; when I experience charity, I know I'm a wretch. Not before and not otherwise do I know this."[280]

But, the observer asks, is that all I can know about myself? Does grace not tell me anything other than I am a sinner? Does it not at least tell me "about a partial justification before God, a friendly little beginning of non-sin, of well-being, of good works, even if not in deed, so at least in heart and mind, of a beginning which could amount to a sizeable little nest egg by the time of my death?"[281] The interlocutor responds, "I know full well what God does to me," and that is certainly the point.[282] Of myself, however, "I know nothing . . . other than that I am lost, sick from head to toe, and will be sick up to my last hour, 'semper pecator,' as young

---

277. Barth, "Rechtfertigung und Heiligung," 73.
278. Ibid., 70.
279. Ibid..
280. Ibid.
281. Ibid., 71.
282. Ibid.

Luther never tired of saying, even in my new beginnings, even at the best stages of my journey with God."[283]

"But," the observer replies, "you believe and obey. You abide by your God with your knowledge and your will. Is doing so not good? Should you recognize yourself as a sinner even in doing so?"[284] The interlocutor responds, "Certainly, even in doing so! As long as believing and obeying are my doing, my knowledge and will, my religion and my moral. . . . I will not bring about any glory but the opposite. . . . Seen in itself, aside from God's pleasure which may stem from it, the sacrifice of my faith and obedience are a real sacrifice of Cain [Gen. 4:3-5]."[285] It is God who decides about purity and impurity, about holiness and profanity.

Finally, the observer asks: "But how does grace play into this? The above described is the typical condition of the un-reconciled man!"[286] The interlocutor answers in return: By no means! This is exactly the point. "It is when I am reconciled that I know of myself, that 'God cannot get involved with me.' It is in Christ that I recognize myself as lost and doomed. It is just when reborn to a living hope through His resurrection from the dead (1 Peter 1:3) that I have to give myself up completely."[287] And here is the reconciled sinner's hope, the hope that despite his sin the grace of God really avails,[288] that he is claimed by God despite his sin, within his sin, that God "does not regard [him] as to unimportant to use again to-day as He used [him] yesterday."[289] And with this the sinner is set free from the curse of Adam in which he does not want to stand before God with empty hands. He is sanctified that he may truly live as the dear child of God. Again, sanctification according to this way of thinking is the breaking of the curse and power of sin in which the sinner does not want to stand exposed before God in unbelief and wretchedness, does not want to wait upon God but rather to create and establish one's own rights over and against God and others. Sanctification means, for the reconciled sinner, recognizing one's place before God in both judgment and mercy and wanting this to be so.

283. Ibid.
284. Ibid..
285. Ibid., 71-72.
286. Ibid., 72.
287. Ibid.,.
288. Barth, "The Christian Life," 33.
289. Ibid., 33.

While many of Barth's critics accuse him of overemphasizing the implications of human sinfulness and underplaying the experience of the grace of God Barth claims precisely the opposite about them, that they make too little of sin because they do not take the implications of the reality of the grace of God seriously enough. If grace, as it concerns sinful people in their reconciliation and sanctification, is everything and remains everything throughout their lives and relationship with God, then there is never a moment in which any of these people might be someone other than one who is always in desperate need of grace.[290] H. W. Tribble notes the implications of this line of deliberation for Barth's doctrine of sanctification and summarizes his thoughts nicely here. He writes:

> The fact that we are righteous in Christ leads [Barth] to emphasise the fact that we are [ever] sinful in the flesh. . . . [a person's] sinfulness in the flesh is not set aside, but he is claimed by God in spite of his sin. . . . The reconciled sinner sees that he is thrown completely on the mercy of God and therefore belongs to God. He does not claim that he has overcome, or is overcoming, sin. He confesses only that Christ has justified him, and that now he belongs entirely to God. Sanctification is God's act in making the sinner to become His own possession, not in making him to become sinless, not even in part or by degree. Paul addressed the Christians in Corinth as "called holy." He did not think of them as approaching sinless perfection, but he did desire to lay upon their hearts the fact that they belonged to God. Christians need to let that fact control their thinking, without forgetting that sanctification throws the believer into the struggle of grace against sin.[291]

To re-emphasise, Barth's direct line of thinking here is that, "reconciliation is *sinner's* reconciliation. The man who would not be a sinner anymore would be the *redeemed* man."[292] Because it takes nothing less than the grace of God, always and continually, to address human beings in their situation, the human situation must necessarily be seen as a radically desperate existence that continually necessitates such extreme measures. Apart from the grace of God the sinfulness of people—their unbelief and self-sanctification—would remain the paramount form of their existence. Barth's radical redirection for the doctrine of sanctification is felt

290.
291. Tribble, "Doctrine of Sanctification," 110–15.
292. Barth, *Unterricht in der Christlichen Religion* III, 322.

here once again—"Man does not become right through sanctification; but God is right after all, even about the man who knows nothing else of himself than that he is always wrong before God. He is right that just this humbled man has to acknowledge that God and only God is right; and in doing so he becomes ready for eternal redemption. It is such saints that God wants on earth."[293] This is how Barth expresses the intricate connection between grace and sin, which though a difficult paradox, must not be taken for granted or deprived of its seriousness. Not because sin is too powerful or remains somehow ontologically rooted in human existence, but because:

> We don't stand at the end of the way of God. We see that we are at least on the way. On the way the paradox holds true. Thus: the sin is still there, but in the sin lays the penance which bows before God's law, which accepts our judgment, which implements the insight and the avowal of sin. *In* the sin are also faith and obedience which now stand in place of the truth in which lies God's pleasure, and *with that* the life in the direction given by the judgment. In the sin!.. Once again, everything is found in grace, in Christ, in the Word and the Spirit, in faith and obedience. But grace *is* everything. All this is the execution of grace, henceforth as sanctification.[294]

"Simul sanctus et peccator"

Rooting his understanding of the Christian life and its various components, i.e., the doctrine of sin, etc., in the knowledge of God in this way leads Barth to make a second important move regarding sanctification. That is, his application of Luther's *simul justus et peccator* to the doctrine of sanctification within which the dogmatic concepts sin and grace converge upon the *homo viator* in striking fashion.[295]

The paradox of the *simul* is felt from the beginning of Barth's doctrine of sanctification, and is centrally utilized in the GD and RH lectures. "What does it mean to be an elected and called *sinner*?" Barth asks. "Answer: *God makes him holy*."[296] Here, *hagiasmos,* meaning holy or sanctified in Scrip-

---

293. Barth, "Rechtfertigung und Heiligung," 89.

294. Ibid., 82–83.

295. Barth's appropriation of Luther's *simul* for his doctrine of sanctification might be rephrased as *simul sanctus et peccator*.

296. Barth, *Unterricht in der Christlichen Religion* III, 309.

ture, connotes for Barth the equation *peccator = sanctus*.[297] A person, he continues, "*is* holy, *made* holy, even if we add immediately that 'to become' and *to be* here, especially where it concerns the *homo viator et peccator*, do not exclude the opposite term."[298] That is, a person *is holy* because of the effective claim that God has laid upon him *in his sinfulness*—he is no longer his own, and despite his sinfulness he belongs to the Lord. He is *made holy* as he is set free in Christ from all latent and exuberant hostility of unbelief towards God, as the person of sin is thrust up against the impenetrable eschatological border of the resurrection of Jesus Christ, and though he tarries in a fashion he is, nevertheless, markedly ruined. To be an elected and called sinner, to be sanctified, means therefore that, "Man is not yet holy under all circumstances as he will be holy in the resurrection of the dead, and he also in the resurrection of the dead and all eternity will never be as holy as God is holy. But within these double borders he *is* or thus he *will be* holy, so really, as it is within these borders only conceivable and possible, he is sanctified by the power of God."[299]

In and of himself, therefore, in his history, this person is and remains a sinner—he maintains the form of Adam in this world. Yet as the object of God's attention he is elected, called, and drawn on towards Christ and becomes something different in his sinfulness. He is holy in Christ and that means in particular that he is given a new direction within which to live (*nostri non sumus, sed Domini*). That is to say, as Barth pronounced repeatedly, "We walk in *time*, by faith and not by sight. We do not see the new creation, but the old, just as it is; but we see it in the light of the promise!"[300] The implication being: "You still live at the level where you bitterly need forgiveness of sins and faith at every moment, you live only by the forgiveness of sins and faith. But you live from there, and that is something remarkable"; that is sanctification.[301]

So Barth employs the *simul* as a way of teasing out the essential seriousness that he believes exists between the doctrines of sin and grace and the resultant implications for the reality of human life and living, i.e., their sanctification. It is a way of confessing the radical nature of the Christian life, of addressing the fact that if the truth is that a *sinner* may

297. Ibid.
298. Ibid.
299. Ibid, 310.
300. Barth, "The Christian Life," 50.
301. Barth, *Unterricht in der Christlichen Religion* III, 308.

believe, that the power of God gives a *human* correlative to divine justification, i.e., a hearing of the Word of God, then such a person is also "afflicted at the same time, that he in his total sinfulness is selected for God, qualified before Him, standing opposite Him (i.e., sanctified)"; and "as a real *hearer* of the Word he cannot help also to be a doer of the Word (James 1:22)"—despite his sinfulness.[302] Despite his sin, says Barth, and even further—within his sin, the reconciled sinner is claimed by God, and, therefore, called and commanded to be obedient to God. Thus the subject "*peccator*" does not cancel out the predicate "*sanctus.*"[303] But in Christ, through Christ, the Word of God spoken to a sinful person brings about his sanctification, a true alteration—he is changed as a sinner and becomes God's own possession. The *simul* indicates this great paradox of the *via christiana*, the fierceness of the knife's edge upon which the reconciled sinner treads. For the believer "acts himself as a sinner, in dust and in ashes, he is not just by what *he* does. But while he believes in the God who makes him just, he" is claimed and, therefore, "also obedient."[304] In this scenario, Barth demonstrates his exacting application of Luther's *simul justus et peccator* upon his doctrine of sanctification.

The fundamental implications of this *simul* for Barth's doctrine of sanctification are twofold. First, Barth stresses that grace and sin are not quantitative qualities of the soul; rather they are both dispositions of the believer's entire being at the same time. Grace and sin are the simultaneous, yet mutually exclusive, determinations of the reconciled sinner. In opposition to the teachings of the Roman Catholic Church and its analogue within modern theology, courtesy of the teachings of Schleiermacher, Barth contends that grace and sin must not be thought of as two quanta—of better and worse parts of people—that are engaged in a process whereby one increases while the other decreases, i.e., what they call the process of sanctification. It is clear, writes Barth,

> that in teaching and in life it has been tried and still is being tried to remove this paradox; to introduce God's grace and man's sin as two quanta and their eventful relationship as a process in which grace increases as sin decreases. But all attempts of this teaching of grace . . . suffer from not satisfying the radical seriousness of that against-one-another. They presume the coexistence of grace and sin in a gathering of the two, which

---

302. Ibid., 311.

303. Barth, "Rechtfertigung und Heiligung," 80.

304. Barth, *Unterricht in der Christlichen Religion* III, 315.

within the concept of the two terms is impossible. Grace and sin are qualitative opposites of the *entire* human.[305]

Thus the *reconciled sinner*, twist and turn as he might, is always the one under the almost crushing contradiction of the other—simultaneously *sanctus et peccator*, wholly sanctified and wholly sinful. Not as part and part, nor as two pieces simultaneously balanced within the one, but in the devastating new form of existence that, "in faith the person reaches beyond himself, so to speak, and already has what God's mercy offers to him. In faith he is whom he is not, Christ lives in him, the sinner (Gal 2:20)."[306] Sanctification is not a matter of degree, but of the grace of God, which penetrates the life of the reconciled sinner.

This is perhaps the central reason why Barth's doctrine of sanctification is not geared towards providing an account of how Christians become less sinful and more holy, or, again, how it comes to be that the term "lost sinner" no longer applies to certain individuals.[307] In actuality, Barth's application of the *simul* means that "sin becomes no peripheral thing in the sanctified person, it becomes no gradually insignificant thing, but remains in contrast to his central and essential determination in the Grace of God."[308] Barth deserts the former notion along with its emphasis on progressive moral and spiritual growth found in many accounts of sanctification for what he deems to be the more theologically appropriate charge regarding the relationship between the grace of God and the reality of humanity. That is the explication of the question variously stated: What becomes of a sinful person through reconciliation, in so far as that he is a *sinner* in *reconciliation*?

Of course Barth recognizes that this is a most difficult paradox. Regarding the concept "reconciled sinner" he states, "the subject wants to exclude the predicate; the predicate wants to exclude the subject. One seems not to be true when the other one is true and vice versa."[309] But, he asks elsewhere, "Do we want to abate somewhat the rigour of the truth—both the truth of man, of the present world, and the truth of God, of the future world? Do we want to make things easier for ourselves—represent

---

305. Barth, "Rechtfertigung und Heiligung," 75.

306. Barth, *Göttingen Dogmatics*, 191. Barth, *Unterricht in der Christlichen Religion III*, 404.

307. Busch, *Barth and the Pietists*, 210.

308. Barth, *Unterricht in der Christlichen Religion* III, 405.

309. Barth, "Rechtfertigung und Heiligung," 74–75.

our situation more simply by saying: There is an intermixture of the two; we are at once old and new, there is a growth of the one into the other?"[310] To do so of course, Barth claims, would be to fall back into an illusion, to suffer a form of Corinthian hastiness that he so readily condemned as an enthusiasm that pushes beyond the promise and work of Jesus Christ. No, Barth says, "there can be no question of our shattering the form of this world, throwing it from us, and anticipating the Resurrection."[311] The grace of God that dawns upon human life in this world is not meant to bring about a completed perfection. The meaning and purpose of sanctification for Barth, therefore, is not demonstrated through the inoculation and gradual healing of people from the sickness of sin; in this sense, even within sanctification, reconciled sinners maintain a form of solidarity with the rest of the world. This "truth holds not only for the unconverted, but for the converted Christians that they are and remain beings who exist in this world and who, in all that they do and are, wear the form of this aeon."[312]

This certainly cannot be the final word about grace and sin, lest the grace of God not be the grace of *God*.[313] Though it is true, Barth adds, that "the phrase 'we are and remain sinners' is a dangerous phrase," that "it can like all true phrases in the mouth of man receive a meaning that turns it into a lie. There is," however, "no possibility to perhaps *be glad* about this 'we are and remain,' as if it were a freedom given to us, so to speak."[314] Barth's pressing of the strict and radical nature of *simul sanctus et peccator* on human life, utilizing the language of claim, means that the Christian is not merely left to languish in or boast about his sins. Though "the horror of sin," as Barth puts it, "may not become debilitated by the thought about forgiveness," Christians "are not driven to despair"; for God's mercy has no end.[315]

310. Barth, "The Christian Life," 55.

311. Ibid.

312. Ibid., 56.

313. Similarly to those at the Putbus conference who opposed Barth for what they perceived to be an overly negative portrayal of sanctification, E. Willis in his work *The Ethics of Karl Barth* likewise suggests that Barth's appropriation of the *simul justus et peccator* reveals an all too consistent negativity in regards to the Christian life. He writes, "Reconciled man is, true enough, always *simul justus et peccator*. The difficulty thus far is that the emphasis falls always on the latter point" Willis, *The Ethics of Karl Barth*, 59.

314. Barth, *Unterricht in der Christlichen Religion* III, 322.

315. Ibid, 323. Barth, "The Christian Life," 31.

Secondly, therefore, Barth continues, though grace and sin are both dispositions of the reconciled sinner's entire being (not as quantitative substances), they are nevertheless qualitative opposites. One is the limit and condemnation of the other. Rightly stated the term *simul* does not indicate the balancing of two separate but equally significant factors—it is not the occupation of two entrenched forces of paralleled strength locked in a stalemate within the human soul. Though sin becomes no peripheral thing in the life of individuals the *grace of God*, writes Barth, testifies that God is "not powerful against us but for us, not because we would deserve this somehow besides our sin, but in the face of our sin in His own interest, because in His consistent incarnation of His Word He Himself stood up for us before Himself and atoned for our ill-doing."[316] Simply stated, grace is opposed to sin and can never be in balance with it.

In further contradistinction to those whom he criticized as holding a doctrine of sanctification based upon the coexistence of grace and sin, Barth writes, "to be reconciled with God does not mean an increase of grace but a clash of grace and sin."[317] Though grace and sin, therefore, are both dispositions of the entire being, they are so only in the sweeping transition from death to life, within the journey from the past to the future, as the grace of God is triumphant over the sin sphere. There can be, therefore, no peaceful existence between the two extremes. As such, Barth calls the grace of God within the life of man as sanctification the "bracketing" of the sinners being—the complete and utter displacement of the sinful disposition within one's life.

Rather than a statement of equality between grace and sin then, the *simul* signifies for Barth, the impossibility of their neutral coexistence. "The balance between our sinful determination and us must remain *disturbed*, or else we do not stand in grace. It can never be said that anyone has a cease-fire or peace treaty with evil." And beyond this, grace is not merely opposed to sin but victorious over it. Ultimately the reality of *simul sanctus et peccator* refers to the powerful judgment of God upon humanity and their sin. "As sinners we are judged," writes Barth, "but that means then immediately also sanctified, in claim taken for obedience."[318] Such a sinner no longer belongs to himself, and though his sin-nature does not simply fade away he is, nonetheless, despite that fact claimed

---

316. Barth, "Rechtfertigung und Heiligung," 79.
317. Ibid., 75.
318. Barth, *Unterricht in der Christlichen Religion* III, 323.

by God and set free from the powers of sin in which he has lived as one completely bent in on himself. For Barth this is the point of the doctrine of sanctification. It is the depiction of that freeing grace within human life, the testimony of how it is that one may stand before God in holy fellowship in the face of his own sin.

Further then this means that the implications of *simul sanctus et peccator* do not simply refer to a state of existence, but begin to refer to what Barth calls, "the determination of sinners through grace in time," sanctification as the *viatores hominis*—the manner in which the reconciled sinner is "qualified and drawn on by God in a singular manner."[319] Contra E. Willis who, similarly to those at the Putbus conference, remarked that the difficulty thus far in Barth's account is that the emphasis always falls on the term *peccator* so that no "meaningful reference can be made to human possibilities and actions within the present immediacies of existence," Barth writes that the reconciled sinner's "existence is not . . . forfeited to himself or the devil" because "there is a *relative* grace that gives meaning to every one of his moments, every one of his steps."[320] Though the term *peccator* certainly remains an uneasy one in Barth's work, the accent of the *simul* ultimately falls upon the grace of God. As a result, *simul sanctus et peccator* cannot simply mean that grace and sin meet within people, but that they clash, and that "clash" is the "victory of grace."[321] The "clash" marks the reconciled sinner's life as "*transitus de morte ad vitam*," the transition from death to life, in which the Holy Spirit reorients a person's life in conversion away from himself towards the life of Christ, which gives new meaning to every moment.

From the beginning then *simul sanctus et peccator*, rather than benchmarking Barth's rejection of "anything in the realm of the relative and temporal that would make for a real and vibrant history of man with his redeeming Lord and God,"[322] is the preface for just such a vibrant history in which the clash between grace and sin becomes

> an *alarm call* to a concern, to a question, to an assault against (the reconciled sinner's) existence, as he realizes that he in *no way* sits with his sin under a *glass lid* secured against grace, but

---

319. Ibid., 317. Barth, "Rechtfertigung und Heiligung," 81.

320. Willis, *Ethics of Karl Barth*, 59; Barth, *Unterricht in der Christlichen Religion III*, 318.

321. Barth, "Rechtfertigung und Heiligung," 75–77. "Transitus de morte ad vitam" translates as the *transition from death to life*.

322. Balthasar, *The Theology of Karl Barth*, 371.

> that his house of sin, as big, and sweeping, and magnificent as it may be, is also *on fire* on all four corners; so that it is high time to abandon the bed as he must begin to say yes to this situation, to appropriately imagine this situation . . . that he did not create, but that is now for him in Jesus Christ . . . and becomes his offering of praise and thanks; and *with it* he loses the ground underfoot, and begins for that reason the thorough and hopeful disruption of the sin-sphere, and for that reason he becomes homeless in it. For that reason he becomes sanctified, i.e., selected and claimed for the service of God.[323]

Rather than stripping human life in time of its essential character as a lived existence, of eradicating the vibrancy and joy of the Christian life in relationship with God, the *simul* actually indicates such possibilities with the hopeful destruction of the sin sphere. The clash between grace and sin, and not the general removal of one in favour of the other, is that which truly begins to address the *positive reality* of grace for the reconciled sinner. As the object of the royal work of Christ this person, the sinner, is set free from the power and shame of sin and begins to live here and now a new life in faith. Within the clash, and not simply as the person becomes less sinful and more holy, the hand of God is laid upon this person to transform him, to alter his existence.

As the axe is laid to the root of the tree, the sinner understands how things really are for him. He begins to see that he stands before God as one who is utterly without honour or strength; he understands now that his life as such must come to an end. And in that way, human life and reality may become truly vibrant, because beyond simple judgment the clash also declares God's purpose with humanity. Within the judgment, there is mercy and power, power for new life. In reconciliation, God not only forgives the sinner, but works upon him as well. Despite his sin, he is not forfeited to himself or the devil. This, Barth says, is not the redeemed life, but it is certainly the "tertium datur—the *new* life, *die nova vitum* of reconciled man, the *vita hominis Christiani*."[324] In the end *Simul sanctus et peccator* means anything but the destruction of the concrete and temporal; of course it only points towards the beginning of its regeneration, a beginning that must continually be renewed, but then again, as Barth was fond of saying, why should one say *only* the beginning?

---

323. Barth, *Unterricht in der Christlichen Religion* III, 316.
324. Ibid., 309.

Grace in Time

One of the important themes throughout this book has been Barth's emphasis on the divine claim over humans and the decisive determination this has for their existence over and against an account of moral and spiritual progress. "Alteration not improvement" emerges as an important functioning concept throughout these early works. As such, the lordship of God over the reconciled sinner becomes the guiding force within the sinner's existence in spite of his rebelliousness and every seeming contradiction. In struggle and hope, the reconciled sinner begins to live a new life now in the power and promise of the Holy Spirit; and this life is characterized by the sinner's continual turning away from himself and towards the Lord. Controversially Barth maintains that within this movement the reconciled sinner does not become less sinful and more righteous, because grace and sin are not quantifiable entities that might exist in equilibrium. There is, he says, never any point in the Christian life in which the reconciled sinner is not in utter need of grace and mercy. The Christian life exists then within the continual clash between grace and sin in which the sinner's being is delayed and imperilled—that is, the sinner is set free from the guilt and power of attempting to maintain his own existence apart from God and begins to live as one who has the promise of new life in Jesus Christ. In this way grace triumphs over sin as the reconciled sinner is claimed for the service of God within his sinfulness.

In a most general and important sense this points both toward the notion that the ground for human sanctification is continually God's being and action, specifically the will and work of the Father, Son, and Holy Spirit, and that, "the object of sanctification is exactly the earthly-human-sinful sphere of our existence."[325] While the reconciled sinner does not complete or compete with God concerning his sanctification in such a way that God does one work and the Christian does another, his participation in the event is nevertheless indisputable for Barth. He "*is there at the same time*, sure enough as the sinner, as the man, at *his* level, with his responsibilities, especially his non-responsibilities, but he is *there*. If *he* is not there, God is not there."[326] Sanctification, then, highlights on one hand then the impossibility of self-determination—as the formation of the self apart from God—and yet on the other the positive value and

---

325. Ibid., 314.
326. Ibid., 307.

necessity of human action in time in correlation to the grace of God and the power of the Holy Spirit.

Interestingly, though, despite Barth's continual clarification of the divine-human relationship, the charge of extrinsicism seemed to cling to him. That is, the way in which Barth depicted the divine-human relationship often led others to question whether God's work merely remains outside the believer as a sort of causal power that never really enters into the believer freeing him for "sanctified" action.[327] Another way to put it is, does a person actually experience the grace of God from within, or is he merely acted upon by a omnipotent power, does he simply exist in total receptivity or passivity? The problem existed partially because of Barth's rejection of terms like "self-determination," which seemed to validate the concern that the grace of God merely affects the "status" of humanity before God, but does not actually impart new life or empower them to freely respond to God. While later on Barth was certainly more comfortable using such phrases throughout the *CD*, in reality he employed the same concept during this earlier period as well.[328] At the core of Barth's doctrine of sanctification lies the affirmation that God does not simply draw near to humanity generally, he does so personally, intimately, as their Lord, and effects a change in people in order that they may also draw close to God. Here, as well as in Barth's later works, he affirms and rejects the same things. He affirms the experience of the grace of God within human life, i.e., a hearing of the Word of God, and the free human response to the Word addressed to him, i.e., obedience. The sanctified person is and remains an integral agent. Yet Barth explicitly rejects the notion that determination of the self in relationship to God is an autonomous action apart from the event of God's self-revelation and claiming.

For Barth, then, sanctified human action, however he expresses it, is a rejection of co-determination along with God, i.e., synergism, and even more so determination apart from God's determination. True human agency is never *creatio ex nihilo*. Humans are not Hercules at the

327. Some of those mentioned already who made this type of critique about Barth: Many of those in attendance at the Putbus conference of 1927, those within the Pietistic circles such as pastors Gustav Nagel and Adolf Köberle, and others like Helmut Thielicke, A. Hoekema, and Robert Willis.

328. For example, Barth writes in *CD I/I* that, "the man who really knows God's Word, as this man comes before us in the biblical promise, can understand himself only as one who exists in his act, in his self-determination. The Word of God comes as a summons to him and the hearing it finds in him is the right hearing of obedience or the wrong hearing of disobedience" (Barth, *CD I/I*, 201).

crossroads neutrally deciding their own course concerning God. In both his early and later works true human agency is a matter of call and response, of deciding for oneself what God has decided before hand. This does not, for Barth, take anything away from the free act of human agency because he does not see the two in competition with each other. And it is quite clear for Barth that the claim of God upon man is not simply a causal power manufacturing some type of robotic response. "The matter does not end with our being set down in this sanctuary, with our raising our hands in praise and adoration that we dare to stand here, rejoicing that God, God Himself, God alone does everything in the fullness of His power and glory."[329]

It is a gross misstatement of Barth's doctrine of sanctification to think that the sinner simply stands before a locked door behind which God negotiates everything for him, as if his place within the scope of the divine-human relationship were merely a formal one. Though the grace of God must be strictly interpreted as the grace of *God*, or perhaps precisely because it is the grace of God, reconciliation must also in part be interpreted as an "*operatio physica*," an "*intrinsica mutatio*," a disposition of the state *within* the human sphere, as Barth was fond of quoting the older dogmaticians.[330] In other words, reconciliation is never without *reality*. The grace of God really does touch human life and living, and not merely superficially. There must be some sort of corresponding movement on the human side Barth contends, to the action of God upon his life. Sanctification is the expression of that total reality for Barth. The expression of the grace of God as it encounters human life and living—the reality the divine-human relationship renewed.

As was stated earlier then, sanctification is dogmatically oriented precisely in this place where the doctrine of reconciliation proclaims that the truth of reconciliation is a real event that enduringly affects human existence, where the grace of God truly encounters sinful people. Barth expresses that same notion within these present works by referring to sanctification as, "the *chronological side* of the incomprehensible one doing of grace," akin to the notion of conversion.[331] Thus within the divine-human encounter the grace of God is not only indicative, but generative as well. As God draws near to human beings He claims them; and God's

---

329. Barth, "The Christian Life," 15–16.
330. Barth, *Unterricht in der Christlichen Religion* III, 311.
331. Barth, "Rechtfertigung und Heiligung," 86. (emphasis mine)

claim upon the sinner means, or establishes, a certain form of existence or orientation in time—it shapes a certain movement within the sphere of one's existence. Sanctification specifies then not only that God turns to people, but that people really and truly also turns to God in their own sphere, of their own volition. This turning between God and humanity, says Barth, is the chronological work of grace as the determination of the sinner within time—the sinner's sanctification.

Of course the idea that the grace of God enduringly affects the *reality* of human life and living, that the grace of God means something specific for the way in which one lives, is not a new notion for Barth. In essence, this has been a resounding theme throughout this entire analysis. What emerges within *GD* and *RH*, and the works surrounding them, in particular then is simply a more detailed depiction of the reoccurring premise that one can and must truly talk about human life and action because of who God is. Within these particular works Barth articulates further what he means when he says that the being and action of God does not merely entail a human puppet show. His previous exposition of the divine perpendicular that meaningfully pierces the human horizontal is complemented by the clarification that this continual penetration of the grace of God within human life enamours a certain orientation or ordering of the reconciled sinner's life towards God and his neighbours.

Though it is fair to say that Barth was always wary of rushing too quickly into accounts of the "*unfolding* of the Christian life," of pushing overzealously on to explanations of "this activity of ours," nevertheless notions concerning how the grace of God plays out in human life and living generally from day to day as an existence in fellowship with God are intrinsic within his account of sanctification.[332] Thus, the "question about the Christian life," as Barth told a group of university students during this period, "as a question about what happens to us, about our little Ego, is a special one that very well deserves to be asked!"[333]

In regards to the preliminary question: What does the grace of God mean for the sinful person? Barth does not now, though, after he has laid the divine foundation for reconciliation, turn his head away from God and begin to set his sights upon human life. Yes, sanctification is from first to last geared towards addressing the particular reality of the *viator hominis christiani* for the *homo viator peccator*. And the object of sanctification

332. Barth, "The Christian Life," 10–11.
333. Ibid., 20–11.

Barth says is "exactly the earthly-human-sinful sphere of our existence." But this is so only within the entire scope of everything that has been said so far—that is, the *viator hominis christiani* is important only as the proclamation of the *magnalia Dei*. Again then, sanctification is not the "proclamation of deeds and acts, of experiences and adventures, of the piety and charitable activities of man, and not indirectly, with the detour or the pretense of the glorification of God as it happens not infrequently in Christian circles. Certainly it is about God's act on *man*, but it is exclusively about the act of *God* on man, not about an act between God and man; much less can man become the center of attention".[334] Sanctification is from first to last about the Word and work of God within human life. Not in such a way that one's life may become interesting in its own right, but as the object of God's loving mercy.

With that in mind Barth's expression "grace in time" may be explored a bit further in order to understand what sanctification means as the determination of sinners within time. In particular, this section will summarize what the grace of God means for the reality of the sinner as the chronological side of grace. It will address the sense in which Barth speaks of a Christian disposition in relationship to the grace of God, and the not unrelated question of growth within the Christian life.

The Chronological Side of Grace

In essence, everything that has already been said in this chapter is an expression of what Barth means when he says that sanctification is the determination of the sinner through grace in time. In the section on "The Claim of God," this reality was expressed as the sinner's *abnegatio* and *glorificatio Christi*, in which the Lordship of God becomes the guiding force within his life, chastening and freeing the person of sin to live with and for God. In the section "The Sinner Reconciled in Grace," this same idea was teased out with the concept *simul sanctus et peccator* in which the clash between grace and sin testifies to the sweeping transition from death to life in which the sinner is transformed by God's reconciling purposes. In both of these important sections Barth's intent to depict the reorientation of human life and living was continually set forth. What remains to be shown here is simply the way in which the determination of the sinner is played out more specifically in this living.

---

334. Barth, "Rechtfertigung und Heiligung," 65.

The Reality of Sanctification

As a point of reference for describing this notion of sanctification as the work of grace in time, Barth again indicates its critical differentiation from the doctrine of justification. Though justification and sanctification are both concerned with the single work of divine grace in reconciliation, justification, he says, is the eternal, or downward glance, while sanctification is depicted as the chronological, or upward look. The meaning here is that on the one hand the way in which God deals with the "*sin of man*" is

> "*perfecta, absoluta, aequalis*," i.e., it is true once and for all according to "*actus purus*," as God is God, it is perfect and adequate in itself, it applies unconditionally, equally for the saint and for the convict, for the enthusiast and for the sceptic. As justification, God's mercy stands over us with the majesty and clarity of the starry sky, it is "*actus forensis*," has nothing at all to do with a natural process.[335]

Reciprocally, however, the way in which God deals with the "*man of sin*", Barth says, in distinction from justification is, "*multiplex, inchoate, relativa, inaequalis*. It may, or even has to be described as a historico-psychological process, or an entire complex of such processes, as *actus physicus*."[336] And further, "sanctification as the determination of sinners through grace in time happens . . . in a row of *steps*."[337] That is, sanctification takes place in human life, and in each person, as he *lives* from moment to moment, as the movement from the past into the future.[338]

It is important to note that Barth does not now contradict himself by describing sanctification as a "process" occurring in a "row of steps." Even here he maintains the position that sanctification does not entail an inherent progression from the worst to the better—these "steps" do not, he says, "lead straight upwards."[339] Rather "process" and "steps" refers to the fact that a person lives only as he does something—life takes place only as action, through choices, as a doing. Sanctification *happens* in time, it is not simply a decree but a turning, the conversion of the sinner. As the reconciled sinner acknowledges the claim of God upon him, as he

335. Ibid., 86–87.

336. That is, "varied, a beginning, relative, unequal or uneven" (Barth, "Rechtfertigung und Heiligung," 87).

337. Barth, *Unterricht in der Christlichen Religion* III, 317.

338. Barth, "Rechtfertigung und Heiligung," 76.

339. Barth, *Unterricht in der Christlichen Religion* III, 317.

continually steps away from himself and towards the Lord he is actually participating in his sanctification. In other words, "God acts in time, in which Man is also acting himself."[340]

This movement from the old to the new then is not a gradual progression from sinfulness to righteous throughout time; rather it is the continual disruption of the sin-sphere in every moment. The "process" that Barth intends refers to the constant clash between grace and sin, the relentless struggle against the self that must take place again and again, because nothing is ever "set up" before God by which a person can rest easy. This sort of "process," this turning "from" and "to," happens continuously with every action, and with every thought, feeling, and desire, every step of the way—again not as the gradual submission of sin to grace, but in their repeated clash, across time, again and again within faithful human life and living. And yet the process of "turning from" and "to" is not the stringing together of separate actions, but the single action of conversion within each moment. It is the life movement of the reconciled sinner. As summarized by Barth,

> Sanctification is on every possible step a conflict between these realities of the beginnings and the ends. It means on every step, even on the lowest step *endless distance of man from that terrible beginning*, because also on the lowest step faith is a belonging of the assigned righteousness of Christ. But it also means on every step, even on the highest step *endless distance from this clear goal* because even on the highest step the obedience of Man is the obedience of a sinner, whose *Gotteskindschaft* has not yet been revealed [1 John 3:2], not been disclosed, whose "*mutatio interior*" does not even in the best case involve innate righteousness of the referred to man.[341]

This life movement is, so to speak, the process of ever fleeing to God with empty hands, which become more and more empty, rather than a "laying up" in righteousness. There is no way for the sinner to become "cured" from sin through this "process" or by these "steps," but he is continually subverted to Christ. The point here is not that the person and work of

---

340. Ibid. The distinction made concerning J.S. Rhee's work on the specific issue of "process" still stands. As the chronological side of grace it is important to remember that the guiding principle is the Word and work of God, sanctification is not dependent upon contingent realities for its substance and efficacy, but does not happen without them.

341. Ibid., 318.

Jesus Christ has not dealt a final death blow to sin, that the Christian as such remains in bondage to sin in this life, but that Barth rejects the quantitative language which seeks to measure one's sinlessness across time based on certain experiential or tangible actions. For Barth Jesus Christ is *the* cure, in him the curse of sin has been "eternally removed," "but the consummation of that removal is *not yet*. We walk in *time*, by faith and not by sight." [342] In this sense there is no measurable cure for the sin whose shadow lies across all human action. Despite the sin, then, grace is still there and, therefore, the reconciled sinner may actually do something that is good and acceptable before God.

Further then the terms "*multiplex*" and "*inchoate*" Barth uses as qualifiers of this "process" do not mean for Barth that the grace of sanctification is less powerful than the grace of justification—as if the claim of God upon one's life could be weaker or stronger from one person to the next, or as if sanctification began slowly, as it were, and grew steadily throughout one's life. As the work of *God*, it rests completely, just like justification, on the grace of God, and it is entirely sufficient. This is, after all, Barth affirms, what it means to "speak as truly Reformed."[343] The difference is that whereas justification is only to be believed, "(One) can only clasp the word through which he is promised grace. *This* is how he has it, this is how he is certain of it," sanctification engenders a new form of human existence.[344] It is essentially a process that must be lived. The reconciled sinner must not only believe what God says about him, but *live* as well; or, perhaps it might be better to say that the "man of sin" must *cease* to live as the person he is always trying to become.[345] Despite himself, then, the "man of sin" must *be* the person whom God is calling him to be. As a hearer of the divine truth this person must also become a doer of the divine command though it seems impossible—he must surrender himself and everything he does, he must acknowledge God's claim upon him in every inconsistent and sinful moment and movement of his life. That is his sanctification.

That Barth also calls this form of grace "*relativa*" and "*inaequalis*," therefore, indicates neither a sense of imperfection in the divine work, nor the possibility that one could potentially do something significant

---

342. Barth, "The Christian Life," 50.

343. Barth, *Unterricht in der Christlichen Religion* III, 305.

344. Barth, "Rechtfertigung und Heiligung," 87.

345. Referring again to the fact that Barth calls the grace of sanctification "our death as a sinner" (ibid., 83).

for oneself before God, in comparison with someone else. Rather, he uses these words to point out that between the *terminus a quo* (the beginning), that in Adam the counter part of God was destroyed, and the *terminus ad quem* (the end or goal), that in Christ the counterpart of God is restored—both of which are absolute—"Our wanting, striving, doing is necessary, is demanded, is promising and worthwhile because it happens in faith and obedience. *BUT between him and achievement, the obtaining, lays the resurrection of the dead, the border of eschatology, the end of time.*"[346] In other words, the determination of the sinner within time is a reality that actually happens, but its decisive meaning is hidden with Christ in God. God's claim upon a person demands his obedience, action, and living for God, but that this truly happens is God's decision and not his own.

The significant point for Barth concerning the determination of the sinner within time then is that there *is* grace for each and every moment of his life. Sanctification is the journey in which God's grace and mercy follows a person all of his days; not in such a way as if "we from our side could live a life for God and in God that could correspond to the great "God-for-us" and "God-in-us."[347] Neither by his actions or intentions can a person do something for himself before God, ironically his sanctification inherently convicts him of his sinfulness, yet the grace of God within time testifies that God is not through with humanity yet. That God journeys with such people throughout life means above all that God has drawn close them, chosen and elected them to new life in Jesus Christ, claims them as his own, and reoriented human life and living away from sin and death towards eternal life and love. And as was mentioned earlier, baptism is *the* sign of this promise of participation in the divine-human relationship rising within the world's arena.

In this sense, then, there is a relative seriousness for the Christian life. That God is *on the way* with reconciled sinners, giving meaning and substance to their lives, indicates that there is in fact a relative good and bad, a comparative better and worse, towards which such people must press on.[348] In this way sanctification points toward the end to which reconciliation tends in the first place—that is, the creation of a holy and faithful people before God. As the chronological side of grace, this means

---

346. Barth, *Unterricht in der Christlichen Religion* III, 340, 319 (emphasis mine).

347. Barth, "The Christian Life," 26.

348. This is the "*divine* possibility in all human possibilities" addressed in Barth, *Resurrection*, 83.

that the reconciled sinner cannot simply remain unmoved before God, nor should he overestimate himself; yet in freedom and love he is compelled to live towards that which he has been reconciled for. The paradox of the reconciled sinner, therefore, is that grace does not simply disturb one's thinking; it must also disturb one's living. The "man of sin"

> *cannot* be happy with what is today, at least he has to reach with all his power for something better in his private and social existence, even if he knows that tomorrow will only be a day, over and over again, a second to last day. He just has to go toward the rising sun, even if he knows full well that his feet won't carry him into the sun. In the world of sin and its orders, he has to be a waif, a man who is moved, who is acting, fighting and hoping.[349]

Within the big picture of grace and sin, Barth asserts, there is of course no such difference between human actions. From God's perspective, all action lay as under a veil before Him. But, he writes, "It is not permitted to use this either or (grace or sin) as a big damper with which one strikes dead everything that is relative, be it an evil, be it good."[350] Beneath the veil, there are differences, things worth pursuing and others worth leaving behind, reasons for joy and sorrow. Beneath the veil, some actions bear witness to the grace of God more than others[351]; and it is towards such things that the Christian life moves.

Growth

The notion of growth then is not discarded completely out of hand. Rather, like the notion of change, it is relativised in light of the person and work of Jesus Christ within the reality of grace in time. Ultimately, it is Jesus Christ who is the sinner's sanctification, it is His life and obedience that is ascribed to the sinner. There is no point within the sinner's life in which he may claim to be further along in his reconciliation with God, or put differently, to be less in need of the grace and mercy of God on this road of struggle. However, the reconciled sinner is also continually called to obedience, to live, to act according to the purposes of God within the relativity of his own existence. He may and must "reach with all his power for something better in his private and social existence." He

---

349. Barth, "Rechtfertigung und Heiligung," 92.
350. Barth, *Unterricht in der Christlichen Religion* III, 318–19.
351. Some actions do not bear witness to the grace of God at all.

may do things which God uses as a witness, there is a pressing on towards a better and the leaving behind of a worse; and within that movement his life may garner a certain form or orientation across time which reflects his repeated "turning from" and "to." Within time these things, which remain hidden as under a veil, may be tentatively discerned within the community of faith and reflected upon across time. Barth utilizes the notion of growth, therefore, to signify the repetition of this "change"—the idea that one's humanity belongs to God in all of its ranges and possibilities and may finally be brought to Him—that has and does occur within the life of the reconciled sinner. That is, to allow oneself to be repeatedly exhorted by the grace and mercy of God to acknowledge God's claim upon one's life.

For Barth, then, the notion of growth refers to the applied "less and less" of human striving before God, and the "more and more" of relying upon His grace and mercy. Rather than a question of elevation or improvement from a worse to better state of being, it refers to the journey in which God continually follows the "man of sin" and in which it becomes evident to the "man of sin" that he may and must continually begin again. That the reconciled sinner understands "more and more" that he must become "less and less" before God reflects something akin to growth for Barth. William Werpehowski sums up the heart of this matter while reflecting on the same issue in the *Church Dogmatics*. He writes:

> For Barth . . . growth is a possibility for the Christian only as it reflects "repetition and renewal." This simply means that growth involves the reaffirmation of oneself in one's present hearing of the command as one who belongs to God. There is a growth (a deepening of the self's determination through the testing of one's current posture against one's central orientation and loyalty) in that in the new ethical event one has the opportunity to apprehend more deeply who God is and what he has done.[352]

---

352. Werpehowski, "Command and History in the Ethics of Karl Barth," 315. David Clough rightly grasps Barth's intention here when he writes that, "The God we have come to know in Jesus Christ is faithful, and knows our nature as creatures with a past and future, as well as a present. Our lives are historically extended, and while there are times when we are called to sudden new realizations of ourselves and our responsibilities, there are many vocations in which we must remain true to commitments we have made. In our existence over time, therefore, there is both continuity and discontinuity. Few crises force us back to square one—though we cannot exclude this possibility—some will leave us concluding we are already heading in the right direction, and most will cause a reorientation of some degree" (Clough, *Ethics in Crisis*, xvii).

Such a notion of growth is more or less unconcerned with pointing towards what the reconciled sinner is striving to become, and is oriented instead towards the repeated joining "in the 'Holy, Holy, Holy, the Lord of hosts' [Isaiah 6:3] with which the angels bow down before God."[353] Barth's revised notion of growth is but a small conversation within the larger context that revolves around the work of God in time; and within that conversation he would rather direct one's attention to God's relentless mercy instead of the reconciled sinner's perception of himself.

The Christian Disposition

Principally then sanctification as the determination of the sinner through grace in time stands in correlation to the concept of offering or repentance—not in the sense of an atonement or debt offering of course, it is not as if such actions are, or may become, mild assurances of God's favour.[354] But in that sanctification denotes God's claim upon a sinful person he may and must offer up to God his life and obedience in every moment with every action, and even non-action, as testimony of his surrender to that claim.

In the old religions, Barth notes, the concept of offering or repentance always meant,

> an act which represented a substitution for what the man would really like to do, is willing to do, and ought to do in relation to God and what is demanded of him. By surrendering his best (e.g., the best of his herd), he shows his good will. He testifies before God that he is in earnest. And if he is in earnest, then God accepts his sacrifice, and this sacrifice is then a living sacrifice, holy and well-pleasing to God! Not because God needs what the man gives Him—God does not need the sacrifice! But because he accepts it as witness to the fact that the man has heard His word, and would like to believe and obey.[355]

As the reconciled sinner acknowledges the claim of God upon him, as he continually steps away from himself and towards the Lord, within the clash between grace and sin, he offers himself up to God through whatever specific action this turning "from" and "to" takes place in. Not

---

353. Barth, "Rechtfertigung und Heiligung," 94.
354. Barth, *Unterricht in der Christlichen Religion* III, 315.
355. Barth, "The Christian Life," 37–38.

with the intent to accomplish something before God, to actually give God something He will without a doubt accept as "good," but because God has commanded it, because the sinner has been claimed. The offering then is not certain specifically "religious actions" over and against other actions; rather one's offering or repentance is nothing other than the submission to the claim of God within every action.

"There is no need," therefore, Barth writes, "for you to grow wings. There is no need for any kind of artificial being to be made out of you. The Christian life is not a superstructure on top of the rest. It is, quite profanely and trivially, that life which each has to live in his situation."[356] In terms of human actions and attitudes, the Christian's offering may not appear as anything different from other human actions and attitudes. Ultimately, then, the difference between what is in actuality an offering, or act of repentance before God, and what is not, is left for God to decide. That we are Cain and not Abel, Barth warns, is for God to judge.[357] That which either affirms or rejects one's offering is neither the Christian, nor the attitude, but God. "We can make sacrifices, but only on the understanding that God is pleased to accept our sacrifice as testimony that we have heard God. No boasting can ever enter into our sacrifice, no sense of assurance, no thought that we have escaped the need of mercy."[358] The reconciled sinner may and must offer up to God such offerings, may and must repent before God with his life, and God may accept such offerings not because they are perfect, but because although imperfect they nevertheless demonstrate that the sinner has heard the voice of God.

The relative uncertainty concerning the status of perceived "Christian" actions and attitudes does not, however, preclude for Barth the possible formation of certain dispositions, character, or the inclination to act in particular ways.[359] In fact, a guarded articulation of such things is deeply rooted within Barth's discussion of sanctification. Even Stanley

---

356. Ibid., 35.

357. "What distinguished the offering of Abel from the offering of Cain? "The Lord looked *graciously* upon it" [Gen. 4:4f]. God decides about pure and impure. God sanctifies the profane." Barth, *Unterricht in der Christlichen Religion* III, 330.

358. Barth, "The Christian Life," 39.

359. The conversation about the formation of character and the Christian life in Barth's later work has been significantly advanced specifically in the works of Webster, *Barth's Ethics of Reconciliation*, and *Barth's Moral Theology*, Werpehowski, "Command and History in the Ethics of Karl Barth," 298–317, Biggar, *The Hastening That Waits*, Mangina, *Karl Barth on the Christian Life*, Migliore, "Participatio Christi," 286–307, and Nimmo, *Being In Action*.

Hauerwas' later, often repeated, criticism that Barth does not allow sufficient space for the formation or development of Christian character or growth in virtue, which is now routinely used as a foil to demonstrate Barth's fundamental concern for human continuity and character, is in the end more of a frustrated complaint that Barth simply does not make these notions central enough in his account of the Christian life, rather than an accusation that they don't legitimately exist within his work. Hauerwas states for example that "the antagonizing thing about Barth's ethics, therefore, is not that he failed to appreciate the importance of the idea of character, but that he really does not integrate it into the main images he uses to explicate the nature of the Christian life."[360] While there is significant emphasis on the passivity of Christian holiness, and Barth's account of sanctification is primarily concerned with describing *who* man is as a reconciled sinner in relationship to God rather than simply *what* he does, nevertheless, his description of that relationship specifically includes the work of grace in time in which the accumulation of wisdom and experience, and the hope for that which is to come, may positively shape one's Christian identity. That these issues appear secondary in Barth's work has always been a cause of frustration for many, that they are actually superfluous is another matter entirely.[361]

The Christian, Barth states, is similar to a soldier, stationed at a post, awaiting the opportunity to perform his duty. This soldier is not defined simply in terms of his "actions," but also by his character or disposition as a soldier, out of which these actions must come.[362] There is of course, once again, no possibility of setting up a program or scheme beforehand by which one can necessarily decide what specific actions God might command in any instance, and the inclination to act in a particular way across time does not indicate that one has achieved something noteworthy before God by which he might praise himself. Dispositions and inclinations like all of human existence and action must also be continually subverted to Christ—these dispositions are expressed also, after all, as forms of offering and repentance. Nevertheless, Barth indicates—acknowledging

360. Hauerwas, *Character and the Christian Life*, 176.

361. David Clough remarks similarly, in relationship to *Romans* II, that Barth's critics "may choose to conclude that [his] depiction of human agency on a knife-edge is finally too uncertain to be satisfactory. They cannot claim simply that for the early Barth there remains no human subjectivity, or that everything is absorbed into the being of God, or that responsible action is out of the question" (*Ethics in Crisis*, 37).

362. Barth, "The Christian Life," 63.

the encroachment of the psychological sphere—there are some ways of living which exhibit, in faith, the event of reconciliation. In essence, the confession of such ways of living, though it does not guarantee anything, offers a more concrete sketch of those who have been claimed by God.

It is important to remember that what Barth is really after, in relationship to any discussion of dispositions or characteristics, is giving further expression to the principle or meaning behind every specific action and attitude—that is, the concrete meaning or expression of Calvin's phrase *Nostri non sumus, sed Domini* in the life, or *living* of the reconciled sinner. "In all acts, in all spheres, in all problems, this," he says, "must be the governing point of view, the objective to which the course must be steered, the line along which one travels!"[363] It is the prolegomenon to every single ethic that may make a claim on the Christian disposition. Because the principle behind every disposition has already extensively been dealt with, it should suffice to simply point towards those dispositions that Barth specifically highlights.

Within GD and RH Barth draws attention to seven sets of attributes or dispositions that are characteristic of the sanctified sinner. It is particularly noteworthy to mention that within GD the section which focuses on "dispositions" takes up roughly half of the entire paragraph dedicated to sanctification, indicating the importance that Barth allows for the concrete expression of the grace of God and the particular shape of the Christian life overall. Sanctification entails:

Attentiveness to the Word: Being continually attentive, bound, or open to the Word of God as it comes to the reconciled sinner concretely in Christ, in the bible, and in the *"viva vox"* of the church above and beyond all other claims that might be made. To submit one's thoughts, will, and desires to this concrete Word again and again.[364]

Daily Suffering for Sin: The balance between one's sinful nature and reconciled existence must remain disturbed. The reconciled sinner feels sorrow about his sin and his conscience does not console him or make him feel secure because of the forgiveness of sins; rather the "good" conscience is an accusing, disquieting conscience.[365]

---

363. Ibid., 46.

364. Barth, *Unterricht in der Christlichen Religion* III, 320–21; "Rechtfertigung und Heiligung," 91–92.

365. Barth, *Unterricht in der Christlichen Religion* III, 322–23; "Rechtfertigung und Heiligung," 92.

Hunger and Thirst after Righteousness: This is the positive counterpart to the previous point. To continually push for and strive after that which Christ wants for the reconciled sinner, not to achieve a sense of perfection, but to wait for and hasten the coming Kingdom of God.[366]

Struggle against Oneself and Because of That Real Community with One's Fellow Human Beings: The first part of this is an intensification of one's suffering for his sin. Above all the Christian is not merely disturbed by something beside himself, but about himself, the sinner. He becomes therefore a rebel against himself and because of this, a positive way is opened up for true fellowship with those around him. The one who has been forgiven much may love much.[367]

Thankfulness Not of the Pharisee, But of the Tax Collector: There is a bad thankfulness and a thankfulness fitting of one who has been claimed by God. It is a deep joy, not excluding the struggle and suffering against oneself as a sinner, but precisely in it, that rejoices in being bound to God, who is faithful.[368]

Patience and Hope: The Christian must always remember that the world he sees and experiences is not the world that God has created it to be. It presently stands under a big "Not Yet" and his hope in Christ is not simply for this life. The action of the reconciled sinner is guided then by a particular waiting or patience that is not merely a resigned stoicism but the bearing of the "bad" as a cross. It is a patience formed by hope of the Risen One who is coming again in glory. Everything which the Christian does is formed out of this disposition.[369]

Fear of the Lord, Which is the Beginning of Wisdom: With this last disposition, Barth essentially summarizes the nature of each characteristic listed above. To fear the Lord is to count on the superior reality of God in opposition to the entirety of one's own thoughts, affections, and desires above all else. To let what is peculiar to God prevail in every aspect, and

---

366. Barth, *Unterricht in der Christlichen Religion* III, 323–24; "Rechtfertigung und Heiligung," 92–93.

367. Barth, *Unterricht in der Christlichen Religion* III, 325–26; "Rechtfertigung und Heiligung," 94.

368. Barth, *Unterricht in der Christlichen Religion* III, 327; "Rechtfertigung und Heiligung," 95–96.

369. Barth, *Unterricht in der Christlichen Religion* III, 327–29; "Rechtfertigung und Heiligung," 96–98.

to replace, so to speak, what is peculiar to the ego. This is the fount to which the reconciled sinner must continually return.[370]

The particular relevance of these dispositions for the Christian life in detail then, writes Barth, are that the consciousness which is prevalent within each disposition would always prevail in this and that concrete action. And yet, within it all the reconciled sinner must ever be mindful that he exists from moment to moment as such only because of the grace and mercy of God. In this way, within the divine-human encounter, the grace of God not only addresses individuals, but directs them as well. Sanctification specifies quite concretely then, that not only does God turn to people, but that they really and truly also turn to God in their own sphere. Not in competition with or apart from God's action, but as the most appropriate and correlate response to the grace of reconciliation. This turning between God and humans, says Barth, as the chronological work of grace is the sinner's sanctification. "I can only each moment turn to God and say: It is Thou, who holdest me, who carriest it through. Thou alone through Jesus Christ, Thou livest in thy Holy Spirit the Christian life—and in consequence of that I will dare, as a man, as Christian upon earth, to live it also!"[371]

The Ethics Lectures

It is appropriate here to incorporate one final section in relationship to the work of grace in time. It comes from Barth's striking *Ethics* lectures of 1928/29.[372] These lectures are in essence a wonderfully creative paraphrase of Barth's doctrine of sanctification, arranged with an eye towards answering the question "What is human good?"[373] Although they span

---

370. Barth, *Unterricht in der Christlichen Religion* III, 329; "The Christian Life," 53.

371. Barth, "The Christian Life," 64.

372. These lectures were presented again, slightly revised, in 1930/1 in Bonn. While these lectures have been largely overlooked in Barth scholarship several interesting studies in particular have emerged over the past several decades offering analyses within the larger corpus of Barth's work and as stand alone accounts of specific topics. See for example Webster, *Barth's Moral Theology*, 41–64, Spencer, "Clearing a Space for Human Action," 239–81, Biggar, *The Hastening that Waits*, 46–97; Nimmo, "The Orders of Creation in the Theological Ethics of Karl Barth," 24–35, Ziegler, "Doing Conscience Over," 213–38.

373. The *Ethics* lectures are in essence a continued and robust alternative to what Barth first rejected around 1915—that is, the rise and development of the Christian life as an independent topic of interest, the existence of a standalone Christian

more than five hundred pages, the *Ethics* lectures do not contain much that would add to the analysis of Barth's doctrine of sanctification offered thus far; they are quite consistent with many of the major theological themes of Barth's work at this time.[374]

In one very important sense, however, theses lectures do offer a more precise clarification of the work of grace in time. Specifically, they present a fuller more detailed description of how the sanctifying claim of God manifests itself concretely in time. And further, significantly, the normative form of the noetic basis of that claim—that is, the distinct *knowledge* of the way in which the claim of God encounters humanity.

This final section, then, is concerned with clarifying in simple form first the way in which the claim of God encounters humanity concretely within life and, secondly, the way in which this is specifically manifest to people in its normative noetic basis.

The Command of God

Plainly stated, the way in which the claim of God encounters humanity concretely within life is as a command. That is, God claims a person as He commands him in a particular way for a particular purpose, and demands his obedience. God's commanding is thus the specific actuality or means through which God encounters a person and claims him, in which the encountered person is sanctified. As such, the command of God, like the claim of God, is not a general moral or religious truth, but the precise determination of one's existence in imperatival form. It is concerned in the first place with "God's speaking and the encounter in which this confrontation takes place."[375] Sanctification, therefore, occurs in the event of God's *imperative* claim. Barth writes:

---

anthropology distorting the reality of the divine-human relationship. Within these lectures an answer is sought to the question of human goodness not as a topic of interest alongside of dogmatics but precisely within the Word of God, which effects a definite claiming of humanity. They offer a sustained reflection on the central premise that, "The question whether and how far (man) acts rightly is thus none other than the question whether he exists rightly" (17). Or in other words, "*Good* means *sanctified by God*"—claimed by Him for fellowship (16).

374. Formally, however, they do divulge the inspiring architectonic arrangement that Barth will use to organize his *CD*, which literally infuses his doctrine of sanctification into the entirety of his dogmatics.

375. Barth, *Ethics*, 50.

> The decision in which we live every moment is a decision for or against *God*. Responsibility to *him* is its point. His judgment is passed on us in it. As we seriously ask about the good, we recognize that we are not on our own but have a *Lord, this* Lord, *the* Lord. We "have" him, as we "have" a master, to the extent that we have his command, that here and now we, you and I, hear his command, that in virtue of the Word of his he "has" *us*. It might be added that we cannot have the Lord, we cannot have God, in any other way.[376]

In the earlier section, on *The Chronological Side of Grace,* the point was made that for Barth the most significant issue concerning the determination of the sinner within time is that there *is* grace for each moment of the reconciled sinner's life. Meaning specifically that God journeys with such a person throughout his life; that God has drawn close to him, chosen and elected him to new life in Jesus Christ, claimed him as His own, and reoriented his life away from sin and death towards eternal life and love. For Barth sanctification refers to the journey in which God's grace and mercy follows a person all of his days. It is dogmatically oriented precisely where the doctrine of reconciliation proclaims that the event of reconciliation is a real event that has enduringly affected human existence. It is geared, therefore, towards addressing the particular reality of the *viator hominis christiani* for the *homo viator peccator*.

At the heart of this scenario, as previously discussed, lays God's self-revelation, for in revelation God does not reveal himself generally as one voice among many others competing for person's attention, but rather draws close to people in a specific relation. That is, "God's address to us means directly that God is almighty."[377] God draws close to a person as Lord. The result is that "when addressed by God we know that in our totality we are no longer our own. The act of the living God is *eo ipso* an act of lordship."[378] God makes himself known therefore not simply factually, but as "the Lord who is over and in the world . . . as *my* Lord. . . . He is and becomes our own Lord. He places over us the sign of the victory which is his own being, and his lordship becomes the decisive determination of our existence."[379] The fundamental issue here is not only that God draws close to humanity and demands something from each

---

376. Ibid., 87.
377. Barth, *Göttingen Dogmatics*, 404.
378. Ibid.
379. Ibid., 125.

person, but that God draws close to each person in a specific way and demands something specific from him. "The truth of God," Barth writes, "is not a general and theoretical and consequently a conditioned truth. It reveals itself in the concrete event of our own conduct as our decision for or against the command of the good that is given to us."[380]

This is not new information, of course. The imperative force of the claim of God has consistently functioned within Barth's doctrine of sanctification. To be claimed by God means inherently that God demands something from a person—in fact God demands one's very life, his obedience within every decision and moment of his existence. This was one of the most important truths that Barth brought to light in his Calvin Lectures. And in the *Reformed Confessions* Barth chided the authors of the Westminster Confession for dividing the unity of the truth of God and human obedience. Nevertheless, within the *Ethics* lectures Barth brings this notion more sharply into focus; particularly by structuring his account of the command of God around "the great orientation points of the whole course of Christian dogmatics," that is, by disclosing what the command of God entails for human life and living as he is encountered by God as his Creator, Reconciler, and Redeemer.[381] In these lectures, Barth creatively arranges his exposition of the divine command, and therefore his description of sanctification, around the three-fold pattern of the divine movement towards humanity. In that God encounters a person as his Creator, Reconciler, and Redeemer, the "concept of man contained in God's own Word understands him as God's creature, as God's pardoned sinner, and as God's future redeemed."[382] Each particular manifestation of the command of God, then, is a paraphrase and clarification of God's claim upon humanity from a different angle.

Of course, Barth adds, this does not denote three different aspects of a person's being or God's commanding, or even three different forms of sanctification, rather it testifies to the one reality from a threefold perspective.[383] The differences are intended logically rather than ontologically. The *significance*, therefore, of the divine commanding is different

380. Barth, *Ethics*, 63.
381. Ibid., 52.
382. Ibid., 53.

383. "It is plain that these relations, too, do not denote stages or parts of man's being, and that these understandings of sanctification are not different stages or parts of God's commanding, but that we are always dealing with the one whole man and the one whole command of God as this is given to him in God's revelation" (ibid., 54).

when considered afresh from each new angle, revealing the various implications of the *one* reality. In structuring his account of the command of God in this way Barth de-interlaces the one reality, logically, in order to clarify more precisely what the claim of God entails for the life and living of human beings—in one frame as the creature of God, in another the pardoned sinner, and in another the child of God.

The Command of the Creator

The command of God the Creator is the command to *live* for God—formally, it is given in and with life itself. It means essentially that at the most basic level of human existence there is no autonomous self-determination; rather the will of the Creator wills the subjection of the creature. Not in a slavish or menial way, but as the most natural and fitting demand that the creature exist meaningfully and flourish, to be what it is—God's created one. Fundamentally, God requires the creature to exist purposefully, to live and live together with other life, in the way God—the Creator of all life—wants life to be lived; to will for one's own life what God wills for every person individually. In this sense, the command of life also implies that human beings respect the lives of others, those whom God has also created and determined to live.

The characteristic way in which one is encountered by the command of the Creator—the normative form of the noetic basis of the command of life—is in and through one's calling or vocation.[384] That is, the creator claims man concretely to live for Him as He commands him to live in and through the limitation of his own life situation—in and through the particularity and specificity that comprise the details of each person's life.[385] "We are not just creation in general," writes Barth, "nor do we just live in general. We live at a *definite* place and as a *definite* work of God's creation. If the command does not come to us in this limitation and definiteness of ours it does not come to us at all.... It is in absolute dependence on God

---

384. For another treatment of *calling* in Barth's *Ethics*, see Webster, *Barth's Moral Theology*, 53–55; and Spencer, *Clearing a Space for Human Action*.

385. Barth explores seven different circles in which the particularities of life are seen as possible signposts to the command of God: Humanity, Sexuality (maleness and femaleness), Friendship, Kinship, Age, Guidance and Endowment (when and where a person exists, and physiological/psychological capacities), Mortality.

that we have our what and how, but we do have this *what* and *how*. And God's command comes to us in this what and how."[386]

That life itself is a command to *live for God*, that human existence itself directs each person towards the claim of God, is perhaps difficult to understand, and certainly seems extremely foreign to human ears now, says Barth. But this is not because the command of the Creator does not boldly stand before humanity in necessity and truth. The problem, rather, is that "at every point we lie outside our calling by creation and we are thus at odds with ourselves as we are at odds with God."[387] Nevertheless, in and through the very existence of life God claims humanity, each person individually as He sees fit, and demands that he live not for himself as his own lord, but from and unto God, and, therefore, with and for those who live with him—*nostri non sumus, sed Domini*. A person is thus sanctified as God's creature, his own existence a means through which God sanctifies him, and moment-by-moment demands his obedience specifically in relationship to the "how" and "what" of his life.

The force of Barth's doctrine of sin is especially felt here where Barth emphasises that the command of the Creator persists throughout the entirety of one's life. The command does not lessen gradually over time, and is not tied to one's "Christian" performance. Apart from the grace of God one's sinfulness—his unbelief and self-sanctification—would remain his paramount form of existence. Despite his sin, says Barth, and even further—within his sin, the creature is claimed by God, and therefore, called and commanded to be obedient to God.

The Command of the Reconciler

The command of God, which from the perspective of the Creator encounters humanity as the command of life, is now taken up from the perspective of the Reconciler and the pardoned sinner. "We do not render that natural obedience" that is commanded in and with life, Barth states.[388]

> Our calling by creation remains, and we still have to think about it. But we cannot do so on the assumption that we are obedient to it. Because we know nothing about obedience to it, we have also to consider that the command, the same command that was

---

386. Barth, *Ethics*, 175–76.
387. Barth, *Ethics*, 359.
388. Ibid.

meant to be nothing but the command for our own life, must now encounter us as something alien that comes from outside, as law, authority, and direction.[389]

The command of the Reconciler, therefore, encounters humanity as the confrontational command of law, the command of the God who has been violated in His holiness.[390]

The command of God the Reconciler comes to each person as a bridle for instruction and formation, something a person must be told and held to because he does not do it. Rather than simply an affirmation of God in one's life, the command of God the Reconciler means judgment and mercy—the one created must be condemned in his disobedience because he has rejected God. But God does not choose to be without this person, and so judges him in love, that is, in light of Jesus Christ. "In this man's existence, God's command is real to us."[391] Therefore, "God's law that is given to us is that this man is set over against us."[392]

Fundamentally, then, the command of law is the person of Jesus Christ—he is judgment and mercy, forgiveness and new life. Rather than a call to simply exist as God's creature, the command of the Reconciler bids each person to look for himself in Jesus. This command is fundamentally a summons to follow Jesus Christ. It means discipleship and conversion. It does not demand perfunctory obligation or performance of religious and moral deeds as a rule, nor robotic imitation; this law demands each person in and through his life to seek his life outside of himself. To be sure, as it was stated earlier, it demands his whole self in and with this and that specific action, but this means to turn away from himself and towards the Son of God, Jesus of Nazareth—and, therefore, others.[393]

The implication of this command, Barth says, is that the primary relationship to Christ becomes concrete in the secondary relationship to one's neighbour. As Christ took upon himself flesh and bound himself to sinful humanity, so God binds the sinner to Himself in the man Jesus Christ by also binding him through and to his neighbours.[394]

389. Ibid.
390. Ibid., 271.
391. Ibid., 323.
392. Ibid., 322.
393. Ibid., 321–30.
394. Ibid., 347–49

The normative form of the noetic basis of the command of law is thus the authority and claim of another, one's neighbour. The way in which the command of the Reconciler encounters a person concretely in his life is through the command of other people. "God's command comes to me as superior direction by a specific fellow man commissioned by him. In this concrete subordination, controlled by God the Reconciler, it claims me and I have to hear it."[395] From the standpoint of Reconciliation then one's neighbour now becomes a witness to the reality of the divine claim; in and through the claim of another the reconciled sinner is claimed by God.

Generally and comprehensively speaking, Barth states, the neighbour's authority means correction. God's claim upon a person as a reconciled sinner is experienced concretely within his life as he is confronted by the God-appointed-witness as a form of disturbance and guidance. The sinner is at once both unsettled and directed; and the meaning of this correction is always the same in whatever form it might take place: you do not belong to yourself but to the Lord. The action demanded by way of response is, as previously outlined, always a form of repentance and sacrifice, acknowledgment of one's place before God, humble service to Him, and, therefore, service to those around him. "We are to do that which at all events means responsibility to those who confront us. We are to do that which at all events means a testimony of deed that we have heard those in whose closer or more distant spheres of life our own life is lived and who, with their own lives, from a lesser or greater distance, impinge upon the sphere of our life. We have to be answerable to them with what we do."[396]

"In this way," Nigel Biggar summarizes Barth, "I no longer live by what I am in myself but by what I am in relation to Jesus Christ, which becomes concrete in my relationship to my neighbour."[397]

Of course, no person bears the authority of the divine command in and of himself. It is not given as a possession and, therefore, not every person is *carte blanche* an authority. The fellow who confronts another

---

395. Ibid., 349.

396. Ibid.

397. Biggar, *The Hastening that Waits*, 63. Barth also writes, "God's command means that my action as repentance before God becomes service to my neighbor. It claims me, and I have to hear it by letting myself be told that my works as those of a sinner who has been reconciled to God in Christ can only be a sacrifice of my life." Barth, *Ethics*, 399.

as an authority does so only as an appointed witness to and against sinful humanity—this same thing is true of one's own calling as well. For example, says Barth,

> Moses is not the mediator of peace between God and man. But Moses is Christ's witness over against man who has fallen but whom, nevertheless, God will not let fall. Moses testifies to what this divine refusal to let us fall means for us who have fallen. Moses represents Christ's kingdom of grace among sinners. And in Christ's church Moses is the neighbour: hence the neighbour's authority and direction.[398]

Further then because the authority is in fact Christ commanding in the claim of one's neighbour, the claim of this other is not conditioned upon him being any less of a sinner than the one confronted—"it is always sinners who confront one another" as the command of the Reconciler.[399] It is Christ alone who rightly wields this authority, and so while it is witnessed to by others it is still in fact a matter of being summoned by Christ himself.

Despite himself, then, the person of sin must be the person whom God is calling him to be. As a hearer of the divine truth this person, the "man of sin", must also become a doer of the divine command though it seems impossible—he must surrender himself and everything he does, he must acknowledge God's claim upon him in every inconsistent and sinful moment and movement of his life; he must do this specifically as he is claimed by the authority of his neighbour within the particularities of his own life. That is his sanctification.

The Command of the Redeemer

The Command of the Redeemer concerns the reconciled sinner as the command of promise. Beyond what each person thinks and knows of himself, the command of the Redeemer, which claims a person as the child of God, tells him "that his reality includes more than that he was created by God and that, in the state of sin which contradicts his divine creation, the inconceivable grace of the same God reconciled him to God. In and with these two elements, in relation to which we have tried to understand God's command thus far, there is a third element:

398. Barth, *Ethics*, 359.
399. Ibid., 363.

the eschatological reality of man."⁴⁰⁰ This reality, as it encounters humanity, becomes the hopeful orientation of human life beyond the present towards the perfect that is coming.[401]

The command of the Redeemer is God's promise to bring the reconciled sinner to a fruitful completion; to finish the good work in him that He first began. "God's command applies to me inasmuch as, being his child, I am an heir of eternal life. In speaking with me, he promises me his presence as my redeemer from the provisional state in which I am here and now his creature, and from the contradiction in which I am here and now a Christian, and he thus bids me wait for this future of his and hasten toward it."[402]

Ultimately what is at issue with the command of the Redeemer, writes Barth, "is the encounter between God and man in a *final* unity between them."[403] This is of course the meaning of the eschatological reality just mentioned indicating the comprehensive impact of the Word and work of God in relationship to humanity, the all-consuming event of God's reconciliation. What should not be missed here, however, is that this reference not only points to the comprehensiveness or finality of the claim of God upon humanity, but also to the freedom that ushers in with the command of promise in which God not only wills something from a person and for him, but in which *that person also wills with* God. In other words, "God's command *frees* me by winning me for God the Redeemer" in order that there may be a unity of wills between God and the reconciled sinner.[404] The command of God the Redeemer, therefore, signifies unlike the previous two commands, "that what we ought to do we now want to do."[405] This does not mean that the sinner no longer stands under the *command* of God in all its forms though; that, for example, he is not contradicted in his sinfulness or accountable to the claim and authority of his neighbour. Obedience is still demanded. Rather, "it means that we stand under the command that we ourselves affirm, that our obedience is our own will."[406] Hence, as was stated earlier, sanctification specifies not

400. Ibid., 461.
401. Ibid., 514.
402. Ibid., 461.
403. Ibid., 498.
404. Ibid., 501.
405. Ibid., 506.
406. Ibid., 502.

only that God turns to humanity, but that each person can and must also turn to God in his own sphere, of his own volition.

Whereas the command of the Creator comes to a person at a determinate point in his particular life, and the command of the Reconciler as the authoritative claim of a fellow human being commissioned by God, the command of God the Redeemer encounters a person as his "own voice as the voice that proclaims God's Word."[407] That is, the normative form of the noetic basis of the command of promise is the conscience.[408] The command of promise comes to a person concretely within his life as his own co-knowledge with God, his own speaking to himself concerning the word of truth which is spoken to him by God.

Barth drastically flips the notion of conscience on its head. It is not, he contests, the "voice of truth immanent in man by nature," no "voice of humanity that sums up supposedly individual voices of conscience."[409] Conscience is not even a graciously renewed natural capacity set back on its feet. Rather to have a conscience, Barth states, is "to have the Holy Spirit."[410] One must be careful, then, to the extent that he claims to "have" a conscience. It is not a possessing of the truth of God, at least "not in virtue of our apprehension and control but in virtue of the voice and inspiration of the Holy Spirit, by the miracle of God himself."[411] In this sense it is more appropriate, as Philip Ziegler notes, to say that conscience "occurs" or "takes place" in the reconciled sinner rather than is possessed by him.[412]

The command of the Redeemer, then, addresses a person concretely in and through his own voice—not merely passively like an echo, but really and truly in testimony with the voice of God, in freedom, as the Lord Jesus Christ encounters him. "When conscience speaks," therefore, writes Barth, "I find that I am on both sides, both listening and speaking."[413] It too sets the sinner within a decision for obedience or disobedience—it is an authority over him, such as the claim of the neighbour, and, there-

---

407. Ibid., 478.

408. For an extended account of conscience in Barth's *Ethics*, see Ziegler, "Doing Conscience Over," 213–38; see also Webster, *Barth's Moral Theology*, 57–60; and Spencer, *Clearing a Space for Human Action*.

409. Barth, *Ethics*, 478.

410. Ibid., 477.

411. Ibid., 492.

412. Ziegler, "Doing Conscience Over," 219.

413. Barth, *Ethics*, 480.

fore, must be obeyed. Through it, he tells himself that he belongs to God unconditionally. From this perspective, a person is distinctly commanded to wait and hasten for the oncoming kingdom of God. And this means concretely, as Barth stated earlier in RH, that one

> *cannot* be happy with what is today, at least he has to reach with all his power for something better in his private and social existence, even if he knows that tomorrow will only be a day, over and over again, a second to last day. He just has to go toward the rising sun, even if he knows full well that his feet won't carry him into the sun. In the world of sin and its orders, he has to be a waif, a man who is moved, who is acting, fighting and hoping.[414]

Here again, says Barth, "we must recognize that we stand with God, that we confess our situation before him, that we must honestly be what we are."[415] From the perspective of the command of the Redeemer one must confess that he is also the child of God—not simply God's creature, and not simply a pardoned sinner, but as both of these he is also elected in Christ for something more. In and through the event of one's conscience he is claimed as an heir of eternal life and commanded, therefore, to press beyond the limitations of his own existence within this life. Not with the intent to accomplish something before God, to actually give God something He will without a doubt accept as "good," but because God has commanded it, because as the child of God his future has broken into his present, because in hope the command of promise orients the thought and will of each person "beyond the present to the perfect that is coming. In hope, we are citizens of the future world in the midst of the present."[416]

As an elaboration of the work of grace in time Barth's doctrine of sanctification consistently pushed against the opposite ideas of 'possession,' as he argued was the problem in Corinth, with modern theology, and the pietists, and 'irrelevancy,' the worry that the new life in Jesus Christ has no significant bearing on faithful human life and living—a charge he often fought himself. On the one hand Barth held that the work of grace in *time* cannot mean that a person experiences his sanctification as the *fulfillment* of his redemption—one's obedience, for example, is hidden in faith and never becomes unequivocally perceptible. Yet on the other hand he was quite explicit that as the work of *grace* in time

414. Barth, "Rechtfertigung und Heiligung," 92.
415. Barth, *Ethics*, 499.
416. Barth, *Ethics*, 514.

sanctification inherently points beyond the provisional state of this life and intends, therefore, the necessary and characteristic displacement of the sinful elements of one's being. Sanctification is as such this journey between the times, life within the eschatological border.

What can this mean, then, except that sanctification, as an eschatological reality, is a future that is also a starting point? What is to come in full measure one day has burst in upon the reconciled sinner's ever present now in such a way that a new quality is given to his existence and actions. The essential matter here is the presence of Christ working in and through the Holy Spirit which brings about something ultimate. Stated positively this means that in faith a person reaches beyond himself, so to speak, and already has what God offers him in grace. Because what God offers all people is not a quality or some*thing* to possess, but God Himself. As God draws near to the reconciled sinner his reality is altered, his life takes on a new orientation of continually turning away from himself towards God. As God turns towards the reconciled sinner—the sinner is called and empowered to turn towards God in his own life and living. He becomes, or rather, is, as the object of grace and mercy, sanctified by God.

Conclusion

THE TASK OF THIS work has been to offer an analytical interpretation of Karl Barth's doctrine of sanctification from 1916 to 1929. Its goal was to both contribute to a more complete understanding of Barth's earlier theology by examining his doctrine of sanctification through specific writings, and highlight his serious concern for and detailed articulation of the divine-human relationship. It was consistently argued that Barth's account of sanctification, from at least the beginning of his break with liberalism, was concerned with a specific exposition of the divine-human relationship—the relationship in which God draws close to humanity as Lord, and thereby establishes genuine human existence and action. From Barth's earliest writings after 1915, such as "The Righteousness of God" of 1916, up through the beginning of the *CD*, we can see that for Barth sanctification was one of the key theological components for upholding and describing that encounter between God and humanity in a positive and concrete manner. As Barth moved from the pastorate into the university, his account of the divine-human relationship became more doctrinally sophisticated, but his fundamental concerns remained the same.

During the period from 1916 through 1922, Barth expressed the content the divine-human relationship, articulated more specifically as Christian life in fellowship with God, primarily by disabling false constructions of human piety, by emphasizing that human righteousness is grounded in and vividly exemplified by *God's* own righteousness. In particular, the idea of *encounter*, which Barth used to critically differentiate God and humanity, became the basis for his discussion of sanctification early on. This theme persisted prominently throughout his work. Fundamentally, what Barth grasped from the beginning was that the doctrine of sanctification is the exposition of a specific relationship in which God draws near to humanity in grace and uniquely transforms human life and living.

When Barth took up his teaching post in Göttingen, one of the most important influences upon his doctrine of sanctification was his turn to the Reformed tradition. Not only did this Reformed distinction critically distinguish his account of sanctification from Lutheran, Roman Catholic, and modern conceptions, but importantly Barth saw in the Reformers, especially Calvin, how his own basic instincts about dogmatics and ethics could in fact be worked out in wonderfully positive terms because of the inextricable link between the divine vertical and the human horizontal. In the Lectures on Calvin, Barth's newfound affinity towards Reformed theology garnered a greater sense of clarity for his own doctrine of sanctification, i.e., ways of doctrinally and constructively approaching the divine-human relationship. What Barth took from Calvin were the appropriate and necessary parameters to give shape to the doctrine of sanctification without turning it into an inherent human quality. He realized that, because sanctification can be discussed only so far in theological terms, it runs the risk of becoming nothing more than a psychological description of religion. While thinking along with Calvin in these lectures, Barth became increasingly more consistent and comfortable in positively describing the actuality of faithful human action and obedience before God. The result was that his doctrine of sanctification also became more distinct and nuanced.

These doctrinal refinements were immediately evident in the following semester's "The Theology of the Reformed Confessions." In these dense lectures, the overarching theological principles or presuppositions for Barth's doctrine of sanctification were set forth and analyzed. Succinctly stated, for Barth the doctrine of sanctification is oriented towards and developed around rightly understanding the reality of the divine-human relationship. Of understanding what it means to say that God the Father, Son, and Holy Spirit have drawn close to humanity in a particular way. Thus, Barth's account of sanctification was shown to be strictly shaped by focusing on the person and work of God in relationship to humanity in stark opposition to accounts centred around moral and spiritual progress. Further, Barth's account of sanctification is intrinsically born from the ontological reality that God does not give himself as a possession in revealing himself; in other words "humanity does not participate in the predicates of his deity" in such a way that those predicates become something attributed to humanity apart from dynamic relationship with Christ through the power of the Holy Spirit. Because the content of Barth's doctrine of sanctification is foundationally shaped by the work of God the Father who does not give Himself over as a possession, but who gives Himself gratuitously and dynamically in His son Jesus Christ through the Holy Spirit, his doctrine of sanctification also necessarily addresses its relevance to human life and living—including the sinner's response to God in obedience. For Barth, God's testimony about Himself not only had profound implications for human life and action, but was the continual *basis* for such implications. Unlike the Catholic, Lutheran, and modern theologies that Barth used as foils for his work, he vehemently resisted turning human life and action into themes in and of themselves alongside the knowledge of God. For Barth, sanctification is so intrinsically bound up with knowing God that apart from His continual gracious self-revelation, human existence and action become corrupt and idolatrous. Positively asserted, however, with that knowing, faithful, or sanctified, human action and obedience become truly possible. The lectures series "The Theology of the Reformed Confessions" clearly demonstrates that the reality of God's person and work places the question of human existence and action in a most serious and concrete light in Barth's theology early on.

At the same time, Barth also lectured on 1 Corinthians 15, in which sanctification was shown by Barth to be a way of describing the surprising, hopeful, and extremely positive identity that believers share in Christ. The essence of sanctification is, as Barth sees it, an eschatological reality established in the resurrection of Jesus Christ. That is to say, the Christian life exists only in so much as it is affected in this work of God that transcends time. The Christian life is thus established within this tension of divine-historical action. Though the Christian remains a being who, in one sense is characterized by sin and death, in another sense he is marked by the resurrection of Jesus from the dead—the one who has overcome sin and death, and transcended the finiteness of time. There can be no right understanding of Barth's doctrine of sanctification apart from this eschatological orientation. For Barth this means that questions surrounding spiritual growth, moral development, and concrete ethical content must not be the driving questions. In fact traditional concerns and questions surrounding the doctrine of sanctification, i.e., spiritual growth and moral development are redeployed entirely. The driving issue for sanctification is instead the Lordship of Christ and His claim upon human life and living. In this sense, the Christian is forever relieved of the impossible task of self-sanctification whether thought of as a type of meritorious striving, or simply cooperating with the grace of God.

All of these themes were finally taken up and enlarged upon in Barth's first full-scale dogmatic treatment of sanctification, in his 1924/5 *Göttingen Dogmatics,* and the related article "Rechtfertigung und Heiligung" of 1927. Barth's doctrine of sanctification benefited from its placement within the larger circle of doctrinal elucidation and seemed to find its stride in his in-depth portrait of the divine-human relationship. In sum, sanctification maneuvers as an aspect or form of God's reconciling activity; it is testimony of God's own faithfulness and love for humanity; and it is supremely concerned with the renewed relationship between God and the reconciled sinner, with the impact of the person and work of Jesus Christ on the sinner who now stands in fellowship with God. Barth's focus here falls primarily upon the divine claim over humanity and the decisive determination this has for the reconciled sinner's existence, specifically as he joyfully acknowledges this claim in faith and obedience. The lordship of God over the reconciled sinner becomes the guiding force within the sinner's existence in spite of his rebelliousness and every seeming contradiction. Along with this, though, Barth's pressing of the strict and radical nature of *simul sanctus et peccator* for the life of the reconciled sinner means that the Christian is not merely left to languish in or boast about his sins. Sanctification is, ultimately, not a question of "improvement but alteration."[1] In struggle and hope, the reconciled sinner begins to live a new life even now in the power and promise of the Holy Spirit. This person stands "as elected and called sinner in the power of God as one whose life no longer has honour, but yet is still the object of the royal work of Christ," and therefore, "he lives here and now a new life."[2]

The period from 1916 through 1929 was an important time in Barth's theological development. While it has often been viewed merely as a foil in which to prescribe a superiority of thought in Barth's *Church Dogmatics,* and, therefore, merely skimmed for proof texts, or a way of establishing significant, or not so significant, shifts and patterns of growth in Barth's work, it is increasingly becoming recognized as a considerable period of theological articulation for Barth in its own right. Of course, the scope and depth of Barth's *Church Dogmatics* makes it impossible to read any of his other works in complete isolation from his *magnum opus,* and it is not as if the earlier works are likely to overturn or eclipse

---

1. Barth, *CD IV:II*, 560.
2. Barth, *Unterricht in der Christlichen Religion III*, 305.

Barth's *Dogmatics*. Nevertheless, it is also becoming increasingly difficult to thoroughly understand Barth's "mature" work, at least in terms of his intentions and the trajectory of his thought, apart from his earlier theology. An account of Barth's doctrine of sanctification in this earlier period then is both suggestive in many respects on its own for contemporary theology as substantial theological work, but also in regards to perhaps better understanding Barth's later works as well. And while this book does not intend to trace these lines of importance they are indeed not difficult to extrapolate.

Through close readings of Barth's texts from Safenwil, Göttingen, and Münster I have sought to respond to the appeal by other recent interpreters of Barth's theology for a more balanced and careful exposition of his work. In doing so I have attempted to address the criticism that the sheer abundance of Barth's depiction of the saving work of God in Christ tends to identify real action with divine action, and leave little room for positive and purposeful human existence and action.[3] I have also tried to fill an important gap in Barth scholarship by extensively engaging Barth's pre-*Church Dogmatic* material in relation to his doctrine of sanctification—a task not undertaken in more than seventy years.

Throughout the course of this exposition the force of Eduard Thurnyesen's wonderfully insightful comments about Karl Barth have shown themselves to be fruitfully born out within his work from very early on. That is, "Karl Barth's theological thinking was from the beginning directed to the life of man. The existence, the life of man, on the one side, and on the other the Word of God that meets this life, lays hold of it, and transforms it."[4] As this book has shown, for Barth the doctrine of sanctification is precisely the description of genuine human existence and flourishing because of and within the sheer abundance of divine grace and mercy, not in cooperation or independence from it, but as the most fitting existence of one who has been reconciled with God. And as Barth reflected upon the magnificent importance of that relationship many years later he happily affirmed that, "To be on the right track here makes it impossible to be completely mistaken in the whole."[5] It seems appropriate to end this work by referring back to the simple confession of faith that Barth offered at the end of his reflections on "The Christian Life" in 1926

---

3. Webster, *Barth's Moral Theology*, 1.
4. Karl Barth, Eduard Thurneysen, *Revolutionary Theology in the Making*, 14.
5. Barth, *Church Dogmatics: IV:I*, 4.

in which faithful human life and living is confidently expressed and the delicate essence of the divine-human relationship is laid bare:

> I can only each moment turn to God and say: It is Thou, who holdest me, who carriest it through. Thou alone through Jesus Christ, Thou livest in thy Holy Spirit the Christian life—and in consequence of that I will dare, as a man, as Christian upon earth, to live it also![6]

---

6. Barth, "The Christian Life," 64.

Bibliography

Anderson, Clifford Blake. "The Problem of Psychologism in Karl Barth's Doctrine of Sanctification." *Zeitschrift für Dialektishe Theologie* 3 (2002) 339–52.

Andrews, James F., ed. *Karl Barth. Christian Critic Series.* St. Louis: B. Herder, 1968.

Balthasar, Hans Urs von. *The Theology of Karl Barth.* San Francisco: Ignatius, 1992.

Barth, Karl. "The Christian Life." Translated by J. Strathearn McNab. London: Student Christian Movement Press, 1930.

———. "The Christian's Place in Society." In *The Word of God and the Word of Man: Lectures 1916–1924.* Translated by D. Horton. London: Hodder and Stoughton, 1928.

———. *Church Dogmatics:I:I.* Translated by G. W. Bromiley. New York: T. & T. Clark, 2004.

———. *Church Dogmatics:IV:I.* Translated by G. W. Bromiley. New York: T. & T. Clark, 2004.

———. *Church Dogmatics:IV:II.* Translated by G. W. Bromiley. New York: T. & T. Clark, 2004.

———. "Das Halten der Gebote." In *Gesamtausgabe, III: Vorträge und Kleinere Arbeiten, 1925–1930.* Zurich: Theologischer Verlag, 1994.

———. "Die Auferstehung der Toten. Eine akademische Vorlesung über 1 Kor. 15." Munich: Kaiser, 1924.

———. "The Doctrinal Task of the Reformed Churches." In *The Word of God and the Word of Man: Lectures 1916–1924.* Translated by D. Horton. London: Hodder and Stoughton, 1928.

———. *The Epistle to the Romans.* Translated by E. C. Hoskyns. 2nd ed. New York: Oxford University Press, 1933.

———. *Ethics.* Translated by Geoffrey W. Bromiley. New York: Seabury, 1981.

———. *The Göttingen Dogmatics: Instruction in the Christian Religion, Vol. I.* Translated by Geoffrey Bromiley. Grand Rapids: Eerdmans, 1991.

———. *The Holy Spirit and the Christian Life: The Theological Basis of Ethics.* Translated by R. Birch Hoyle. Louisville: Westminster John Knox, 1993.

———. *How I Changed My Mind.* Richmond: John Knox, 1966.

———. *Karl Barth-Eduard Thurneysen Briefwechsel.* Bd. 1, *1913–1921.* Gesamtausgabe V., *Briefe.* Zurich: Theologischer Verlag, 1973.

———. *Karl Barth-Eduard Thurneysen Briefwechsel.* Bd. 2, *1921–1930.* Gesamtausgabe V., *Briefe.* Zurich: Theologischer Verlag, 1974.

———. *Karl Barth-Emil Brunner, Briefwechsel 1916–1966.* Edited by Eberhard Busch. Zurich: Theologischer Verlag, 2000.

———. *The Knowledge of God and the Service of God According to the Teaching of The Reformation: Recalling the Scottish Confession of 1560.* The Gifford Lectures delivered in the University of Aberdeen in 1937 and 1938. London: Hodder and Stoughton, 1938.

———. "The Problem of Ethics Today." In *The Word of God and the Word of Man: Lectures 1916-1924.* Translated by D. Horton. London. Hodder and Stoughton, 1928.

———. *The Resurrection of the Dead.* Translated by H. J. Stenning. New York: Revell, 1933.

———. "Rechtfertigung und Heiligung." In *Gesamtausgabe, III: Vorträge und Kleinere Arbeiten, 1925-1930.* Zurich: Theologischer Verlag, 1994.

———. *Der Römerbrief.* Edited by H. Schmidt. In *Gesamtausgabe. Abt. 2: Akademische Werke 1919,* edited by Hinrich Stoevesandt. Zurich: Theologischer Verlag, 1985.

———. *Offene Breife, 1909-1935.* Zurich: Theologischer Verlag, 2001.

———. "The Word of God and the Task of the Ministry." In *The Word of God and the Word of Man: Lectures 1916-1924.* Translated by D. Horton London. Hodder and Stoughton, 1928.

———. *Theology and Church: Shorter Writings 1920-1928.* Translated by Louise Pettibone Smith. New York: Harper & Row, 1962.

———. *The Theology of John Calvin.* Translated by Geoffrey Bromiley. Grand Rapids: Eerdmans, 1995.

———. *The Theology of the Reformed Confessions.* Translated and annotated by Darrell Guder and Judith Guder. London: Westminster John Knox, 2002.

———. *The Theology of Schleiermacher: Lectures at Gottingen, Winter Semester of 1923/24.* Translated by Geoffrey Bromiley. Edinburgh: T. & T. Clark, 1982.

———. *Unterricht in der Christlichen Religion II, Die Lehre von Gott/Die Lehre vom Menschen 1924/1925. Gesamtausgabe, Abt. II, Akademische Werke.* Zurich: Theologischer Verlag, 1990.

———. *Unterricht in der Christlichen Religion III, Die Lehre von der Versöhnung/Die Lehre von der Erlösung 1925/1926, Gesamtausgabe, Abt. II, Akademische Werke 38* Zurich: Theologischer Verlag, 2003.

Barth, Karl, and Eduard Thurneysen. *Revolutionary Theology in the Making: Barth-Thurneysen Correspondence, 1914-1925.* London: Epworth, 1964.

Barth, Karl, and Rudolph Bultmann. *Lettters: 1922-1966.* Edited by Bernd Jaspert. Translated by and edited by Geoffrey W. Bromiley Grand Rapids: Eerdmans, 1971.

Berkouwer, G. C. *Faith and Sanctification.* Grand Rapids: Eerdmans, 1952.

———. *The Triumph of Grace in the Theology of Karl Barth.* Grand Rapids: Eerdmans, 1956.

Biggar, Nigel. *The Hastening that Waits: Karl Barth's Ethics.* Oxford: Clarendon, 1993.

Bultmann, Rudolf. *Faith and Understanding.* London: SCM, 1969.

Busch, Eberhard. *Karl Barth and the Pietists: The Young Karl Barth's Critique of Pietism and Its Response.* Translated by Daniel Bloesch. Downers Grove: InterVarsity, 2004.

———. *Karl Barth: His Life from Letters and Autobiographical Texts.* Translated by John Bowden. Eugene: Wipf and Stock, 2005.

Camfield, F. W., ed. *Reformation Old and New: A Tribute to Karl Barth.* London: Lutterworth, 1947.

Chung, Sung Wook. *Admiration and Challenge: Karl Barth's Theological Relationship with John Calvin*. New York: Peter Lang, 2002.
Clough, David. *Ethics in Crisis: Interpreting Barth's Ethics*. Aldershot, UK: Ashgate, 2005.
Cullberg, J. *Das Problem der Ethik in der dialektischen Theologie. I. Karl Barth*. Uppsala: Lundesquist, 1938.
Dalferth, Ingolf U. "Karl Barth's Eschatological Realism." In *Karl Barth: Centenary Essays*, edited by S. W. Sykes. New York: Cambridge University Press, 1989.
Dawson, Dale R. *The Resurrection in Karl Barth*. Burlington, VT: Ashgate, 2007.
Duke, James O., and Robert F. Streetman, eds. *Barth and Schleiermacher: Beyond the Impasse?* Philadelphia: Fortress, 1988.
Evans, Donald. *The Logic of Self-Involvement*. London: SCM, 1963.
Fergusson, David. "Barth's Resurrection of the Dead: Further Reflections." *Scottish Journal of Theology* 56 (2003) 65–72.
Fisher, Simon. *Revelatory Positivism? Barth's Earliest Theology and the Marburg School*. Oxford: Oxford University Press, 1988.
Freudenberg, Matthias. *Karl Barth und die reformierte Theologie: Die Auseinandersetzung mit Calvin, Zwingli und den reformierten Bekenntnisschriften während seiner Göttinger Lehrtätigkeit*. Neukirchen-Vluyn: Neukirchener Verlag, 1997.
Geense, A. *Auferstehung und Offenbarung. Über den Ort der Frage nach der Auferstehung Jesu Christi in der heutigen deutschen evangelische Theologie*. Göttingen: Vandenhoeck & Ruprecht, 1971.
Green, Clifford. *Karl Barth: Theologian of Freedom*. London: Collins, 1989.
Grieb, Katherine A. "Last Things First: Karl Barth's Theological Exegesis of I Corinthians in *The Resurrection of the Dead*." *Scottish Journal of Theology* 56 (2003) 49–64.
Hart, John W. *Karl Barth vs. Emil Brunner: The Formation and Dissolution of a Theological Alliance, 1916–1936*. Issues in Systematic Theology 6. New York: P. Lang, 2001.
Hartwell, Herbert. *The Theology of Karl Barth*. Philadelphia: Westminster, 1964.
Hauerwas, Stanley. *Character and the Christian Life: A Study in Theological Ethics*. 2nd ed. Notre Dame: University of Notre Dame Press, 1994.
Heppe, Heinrich. *Reformed Dogmatics Set Out and Illustrated from the Sources*. Foreword by Karl Barth. Translated by G. T. Thomson. London: Allen & Unwin, 1950.
Hoekema, Anthony. "Karl Barth's Doctrine of Sanctification." Inaugural Address at Calvin Seminary Chapel, Grand Rapids, Michigan, 1965.
Hoyle, R. Birch. *The Teaching of Karl Barth: An Exposition*. New York: Scribner's, 1930.
Hunsinger, George. "A Tale of Two Simultaneities: Justification and Sanctification in Calvin and Barth," *Zeitschrift für Dialektische Theologie* 3 (2002) 316–37.
———. *How to Read Karl Barth: The Shape of His Theology*. New York: Oxford University Press, 1991.
Husbands, Mark Anthony. "Barth's Ethics of Prayer: A Study in Moral Ontology and Action." PhD diss., University of St. Michael's College, Canada, 2005.
Jüngle, Eberhard. *Karl Barth, A Theological Legacy*. Translated by Garrett E. Paul. Philadelphia: Westminster, 1986.
Küng, Hans. *Justification: The Doctrine of Karl Barth and a Catholic Reflection*. Translated by T. Collins et al. Philadelphia: Westminster, 1981.

Lombard, J. C. "Die Leer van die Heiligmaking by Karl Barth." PhD diss., Free University of Amsterdam, 1957.
McConnachie, John. *The Barthian Theology and the Man of Today.* Freeport: Books for Libraries Press, 1933. Reprint, 1972.
Maeng, Y. G. "The Command of God: A Study of Karl Barth's Theological Ethics." PhD diss., Emory University, 1974.
Mangina, Joseph L. *Karl Barth on the Christian Life: The Practical Knowledge of God.* Issues in Systematic Theology 8. New York: P. Lang, 2001.
Matheny, P. D. *Dogmatics and Ethics: The Theological Realism and Ethics of Karl Barth's Church Dogmatics.* New York: P. Lang, 1990.
McKim, D. *How Karl Barth Changed My Mind.* Grand Rapids: Eerdmans, 1986.
McCormack, Bruce L. "Afterword." *Zeitschrift für Dialektishe Theologie* 3 (2002) 364–78.
———. *Karl Barth's Critically Realistic Dialectical Theology: Its Genesis and Development, 1909–1936.* New York: Oxford University Press, 1995.
McDowell, John C. "Karl Barth's Having No-Thing to Hope For." *Journal for Christian Theological Research* 11 (2006) 1–49.
Metzger, Paul, Luis. *The Word of Christ and the World of Culture: Sacred and Secular through the Theology of Karl Barth.* Grand Rapids: Eerdmans, 2003.
Migliore, Daniel L. "Participatio Christi: The Central Theme of Barth's Doctrine of Sanctification." *Zeitschrift für Dialektishe Theologie* 3 (2002): 286–307.
———. "The Problem of the Historical Jesus in Karl Barth's Theology." PhD diss., Princeton University, 1964.
Mueller, David L. *Karl Barth.* Makers of the Modern Theological Mind. Waco: Word, 1972.
Muller, Richard A. *After Calvin: Studies in the Development of a Theological Tradition.* New York: Oxford University Press, 2003.
Neder, Adam, "'A Differentiated Fellowship of Action': Participation in Karl Barth's 'Church Dogmatics.'" PhD diss., Princeton Theological Seminary, 2005.
Neven, Gerrit W. "'Just a Little': The Christian Life in the Context of Reconciliation." *Zeitschrift für Dialektische Theologie* 3 (2002) 353–63.
Nimmo, Paul T. *Being in Action: The Theological Shape of Barth's Ethical Vision.* New York: T. & T. Clark, 2007.
———. "The Orders of Creation in the Theological Ethics of Karl Barth," *Scottish Journal of Theology* 60 (2007) 24–35.
Otterness, O. G. "The Doctrine of Sanctification in the Theology of Karl Barth." PhD diss., University of Chicago, 1969.
Rhee, Jung Suck. *Secularization and Sanctification: A Study of Karl Barth's Doctrine of Sanctification and Its Contextual Application to the Korean Church.* Amsterdam: Free University Press, 1995.
Robinson, M., ed. *The Beginnings of Dialectical Theology.* Richmond: John Knox, 1968.
Schmidt, Heinrich. *Doctrinal Theology of the Evangelical Lutheran Church.* Translated by Charles A. Hay and Henry E. Jacobs. Minneapolis: Augsburg, 1961.
Sonderegger, Katherine. "Sanctification as Impartation in the Doctrine of Karl Barth." *Zeitschrift für Dialektische Theologie* 18 (2002) 308–15.
Spencer, Archibald James. *Clearing a Space for Human Action: Ethical Ontology in the Theology of Karl Barth.* Issues in Systematic Theology. New York: Peter Lang, 2003.

———. "Clearing a Space for Human Action: Towards an Ethical Ontology in the Early Theology of Karl Barth." PhD diss., Wycliffe College, 1999.

Stubbs, David. "Sanctification as Participation in Christ: Working through the Pauline and Kantian Legacies in Karl Barth's Theology of Sanctification." PhD diss., Duke University, 2001.

Thielicke, Helmut. *Theological Ethics, Vol. 1: Foundations*. Grand Rapids: Eerdmans, 1979.

Torrance, Thomas F. *Karl Barth: An Introduction to His Early Theology, 1910–1931*. London: SCM, 1962.

Tribble, H. W. "The Doctrine of Sanctification in the Theology of Karl Barth." PhD diss., University of Edinburgh, 1937.

Webster, John. *Barth*. London: Continuum, 2000.

———. *Barth's Earlier Theology*. New York: T. & T. Clark, 2005.

———. *Barth's Ethics of Reconciliation*. Cambridge: Cambridge University Press, 1995.

———. *Barth's Moral Theology: Human Action in Barth's Thought*. Edinburgh: T. & T. Clark, 1998.

———, ed. *The Cambridge Companion to Karl Barth*. Cambridge: Cambridge University Press, 2000.

———. "The Christian in Revolt: Some Reflections on *The Christian Life*." In *Reckoning with Barth: Essays in Commemoration of the Centenary of Karl Barth's Birth*, edited by Nigel Biggar. Oxford: A. R. Mowbray, 1988.

———. *Holiness*. Grand Rapids: Eerdmans, 2003.

Werpehowski, William. "Command and History in the Ethics of Karl Barth." *Journal of Religious Ethics* 9 (1981) 298–317.

Willis, Robert E. *The Ethics of Karl Barth*. Leiden: Brill, 1971.

Ziegler, Philip. "Doing Conscience Over: The Reformulation of the Doctrine of Conscience in Karl Barth and Paul Lehmann." *Toronto Journal of Theology* 14 (1998) 213–38.

www.ingramcontent.com/pod-product-compliance
Lightning Source LLC
Chambersburg PA
CBHW050348230426
43663CB00010B/2041